THE NATIONAL TRUST

BOOK OF
FISH COOKERY

Other books by Sara Paston-Williams

The National Trust Book of Christmas & Festive Day Recipes

The National Trust Book of Traditional Puddings

The National Trust Book of the Country Kitchen Store Cupboard

Sainsbury's Guide to Poultry & Game

The National Trust Book of Pies

THE NATIONAL TRUST

BOOK OF
FISH COOKERY

Sara Paston-Williams

THE NATIONAL TRUST

ISBN 0–7078–0093–5

Copyright © Sara Paston-Williams 1988

First published in Great Britain in 1988
by the National Trust,
36 Queen Anne's Gate,
London SW1H 9AS

Designed by James Shurmer

Drawings by Eric Thomas

Phototypeset in Monotype Lasercomp
Baskerville Series 169 by
Southern Positives and Negatives
(SPAN), Lingfield, Surrey

Printed in England by The Bath Press, Avon

'F stands for fish, a most cheering sight.
Let them be caught by day or by night.
And to those who take them with net or with line,
God bless their toil, send them plenty of prime.'

William Hoyle, *The Fisherman's Alphabet*

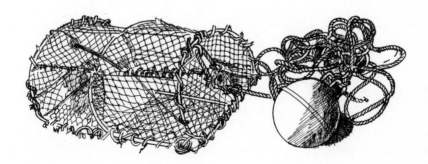

CONTENTS

INTRODUCTION

'Fish .... The brain is nourished by it, the nerves are quietened, the mind grows stronger, the temper less irritable and the whole being healthier and happier when fish is substituted for butcher's meat.'

Dr Mortimer Granville, 1881

Obviously a great fan of fish eating, Dr Granville, the noted Victorian public nutritionist, would no doubt approve of the fact that fish is enjoying renewed popularity as a result of the trend towards healthy eating. Fish has always been good for you, but never has it been more fashionable.

Fishing as an industry first developed in England between the 12th and 15th centuries. Fishing boats began to make long voyages to hunt for cod in the North Sea, and to import salted and pickled herring from Flanders and wind-dried cod, haddock, pollock and saithe from Iceland. In the Middle Ages fish was a very important item of diet because almost half the days of the year were prescribed as days of abstinence by the Church, and Lent was strictly observed as a period of fasting. On such days, fish only would be eaten.

With the Dissolution of the Monasteries and the Reformation, such fast days no longer formed part of the Church calendar, though the authorities did, rather ineffectually, try to enforce compulsory 'fysshe days'. By the end of the 17th century, the great fish market at Billingsgate was establishing itself. Fish had been traditionally sold in the streets of the City of London, but in 1699 the Thameside site at Billingsgate was declared a 'free and open market'. With improvements in transport, first road and then rail, the market for fish grew, so that in 1786, 500 horse-drawn van-loads of fish were sent to Billingsgate from Devon's main port of Brixham alone. In the 1860s and 1870s the development of the steam trawler and the use of ice for preservation enabled the rich grounds of the North Sea to be thoroughly tapped: the arrival of the fast deep-sea trawler extended the area of operation as far as Iceland and the White Sea.

The Cod War with Iceland in the early 1970s changed all this almost overnight: the British deep-sea trawling industry went into decline, dramatically pushing up the imports and price of fish. High street fishmongers began to fade away, good, fresh wet fish became a luxury and difficult to find, fish came to mean for many, frozen fish fingers and cod-in-the-bag. Other problems crowded in on the beleaguered industry:

EEC regulations, pollution, over-fishing and factory ships and disputed territories.

Despite all this most sea fish eaten in Britain today is still of the type landed at home ports, though not necessarily by British ships. With the increased interest in fish over the past few years, it is ironic that supplies can be difficult, and will get more difficult unless stricter conservation takes place.

But not all is gloom and doom. Most fish are hunted, but in recent years there has been a large increase in fish farming, particularly of salmon and trout. Shellfish – such as oysters and mussels – are also farmed. We are also eating a greater variety of fish and showing more daring in sampling the exotic and unusual: swordfish, tuna, shark, turbot, brill and monkfish rarely seen 5 years ago, are commonly found on menus of fashionable restaurants. Dogfish, once thrown back, is now an important money maker: even squid and chips is countenanced!

Britain today relies on the sea for much, much more than cod and plaice, whelks and winkles. It is the source of oil, natural gas, sand, gravel, salt, silt and fertiliser. The coast is a tremendous attraction for holidaymakers, who not only want to swim, sail and build sandcastles, but to enjoy coastal walks, watch birds and fish in the estuaries and off the coast. The tranquillity and beauty of Britain's coastlands are under threat.

The National Trust has long been aware of this problem. In 1895, the year of the Trust's foundation, it was given its first countryside property, a piece of coast at Dinas Oleu in Gwynedd, near Barmouth. Ever since, the Trust has been vigilant in its efforts to save stretches of coast in England, Wales and Northern Ireland to preserve for posterity. In 1965 the Trust realised that the threats were on the increase, and Enterprise Neptune was set up specially to try to save the coast from unsuitable development. A survey made at the time suggested that nearly three-quarters of the 3,000-mile shoreline had been damaged beyond retrieval, most of it in the previous 50 years.

Some 1,000 miles of coast were considered by that survey to be worth preserving. At the time the Trust owned or protected only about 165 miles, consisting of important landmarks and outstanding beauty spots, such as the Farne Islands in Northumberland, Blakeney Point in Norfolk, and the Giant's Causeway on the Antrim coast of Northern Ireland, as well as major nature reserves like Brownsea Island in Poole Harbour in Dorset.

Enterprise Neptune was publicly launched on 11 May 1965 by H.R.H. the Duke of Edinburgh, who enthusiastically agreed to be the campaign's patron. Its aims were to raise funds to purchase, endow, improve or buy covenants over desirable coastal properties as and when they came on the market. In 1985 the campaign was relaunched, and as

I write this book the National Trust is in the process of acquiring its five-hundredth mile of coastline. Now Enterprise Neptune is over halfway to its target, but the campaign must continue until the last mile of unspoiled coast is saved.

To all those people who helped me compile this collection of traditional fish recipes in so many different ways, a big 'thank you'. I hope you enjoy the book as much as I have enjoyed researching and writing it. A special thank you to Berenice for typing the manuscript so superbly, without complaint.

Sara Paston-Williams
April 1988

WEST COUNTRY

Portloe, Cornwall

Trade and fishing are long-established traditions of this part of the country, which is, after all, a peninsula. As far back as pre-Christian times the Phoenicians are said to have traded along the coast for tin. Boats went out to fish as well as to trade; from deep sea and offshore, to inshore and up-river, the West Country fishermen have responded to season, tide, weather, opportunity, instinct and the need for a catch.

Fishing in Dorset has always been centred on Weymouth for red mullet and Lyme Regis for scallops. Local salmon and trout are smoked at Bridport and crabs are plentiful all along the coast.

Devon is also famous for its excellent fish. Brixham, 'Mother of the Deep Sea Fisheries', is mentioned as a fishing port in the Domesday Book and for centuries supplied fish to Bristol, Bath, Plymouth and Exeter and especially to the religious houses. A dried fish industry developed, with exports to the Continent, and by 1500 pilchard curing was also established. Today, with a varied fleet of motor vessels, a new fish market and deep water jetties, Brixham remains Devon's largest fishing port and a flourishing centre for fish trading, landing mackerel, plaice, dabs, herrings, sprats, whiting, conger, soles, John Dories, squid, turbot, scallops, lobsters and crabs.

There are smaller fishing ports all along the south coast of Devon landing good quality sea fish while north Devon rivers produce good salmon which is served on local menus under the river names: Torridge, Exe, and Taw.

Until the mid 19th century, the West Country, particularly Cornwall, was remote and inaccessible. The standard of living in Cornwall was among the lowest in the country, with fish representing an unusually important staple in the diet. In the small ports of Mevagissey, Polperro, Port Isaac, Porthleven, Marazion, Padstow and scores of others, families relied for their fortunes on the skill and perseverance of the fishermen. Long hours, wild weather and treacherous seas were accepted as occupational hazards for 'no dole, no fish, no money'. Perhaps this enforced fish-eating is now responsible for the Cornishman's lack of interest in fish on his table: a shame, because there is an excellent supply of fish and shellfish of all kinds from the many fishing villages that cluster along the rocky Cornish coast. The history of Cornish fishing is distinctive for the overwhelming importance of one type of fish – the pilchard – which was caught by seine netting, a method originally unique to Cornwall and parts of Devon.

Dart Sea Bass with Rhubarb and Champagne Sauce (serves 4)

Bass is not commonly sold in fishmongers and if you do find this beautiful fish for sale, it will often cost more than salmon. Sea bass is the prime quarry of the shore angler and is in season from June to March. The fish is slim and elegant with silver and dark grey markings. The scales must be removed before cooking. Depending on its size, bass can be cooked in various ways but as the flesh can be a little on the soft side, baking, frying, grilling or barbecuing are the most successful.

For this recipe, young bass about the size of a mackerel are best. River or sea trout and mackerel can be substituted if you prefer. The fish may be used whole or filleted.

4 young sea bass, scaled and filleted	Butter for frying
Seasoned flour	Sprigs of fresh fennel to decorate

For the rhubarb and champagne sauce

8oz (225g) rhubarb, chopped	2 egg yolks
$\frac{1}{4}$pt (150ml) chicken stock	4 tablespoons (4 × 15ml) double cream
$\frac{1}{3}$pt (200ml) pink champagne	

Place the rhubarb in a small saucepan with the stock. Cover and simmer until the rhubarb is soft and the stock has almost evaporated. Blend in a

13

liquidiser or food processor to a smooth purée. Put into the top of a double saucepan or into a basin standing over a saucepan of simmering water. Add the champagne, egg yolks and double cream. Whisk over a gentle heat until the sauce thickens slightly and is quite foamy. Keep the sauce warm while you cook the fish. Dust the bass with seasoned flour. Melt some butter in a frying-pan and fry the fish for a few minutes until cooked. Remove to a warm dish and decorate with a few sprigs of fennel. Serve with the warm rhubarb and champagne sauce.

Grilled Barbican Sea Bass with Rosemary *(serves 2)*

A small restaurant on the Barbican Quay at Plymouth, Platters, specialises in all kinds of seafood including locally caught sea bass in a rosemary sauce, a delicious combination. Bass is caught in Wembury Bay and Yealm Estuary, 5 miles east of Plymouth. The National Trust owns land on both banks of this beautiful estuary following a special appeal, and the cliffs between Wembury Beach and the estuary.

Fresh mint or sage leaves may be used instead of rosemary.

2 approx. 12oz (250g) sea bass	Sea salt and freshly milled black pepper
24 tiny sprigs of fresh rosemary	
2oz (50g) butter	$\frac{1}{4}$pt (150ml) fish stock (see p.209)

Skin and fillet the fish, removing as many small bones as possible. With the point of a small knife, make 6 small incisions in the flesh of each fillet at regular intervals, cutting right through to the skin at an angle. Place a sprig of rosemary into each incision, then arrange the fish on a buttered grill tray. Season well and brush with melted butter. Cook under a hot grill, basting with the butter and juices for 4–5 minutes. Remove to a serving dish, reserving the cooking juices, and keep warm. Boil the fish stock in a small saucepan and add the cooking juices. Reduce slightly on a high heat, then strain over the fish.

Barbecued Mount's Bay Bass with Fennel *(serves 1)*

Sea bass is commonly caught in Mount's Bay and is one of the fish served regularly at the Trust's Sail Loft Restaurant on St Michael's Mount.

Bass is the ideal fish for a barbecue on the beach. Here it is cooked on a bed of fresh fennel, which can be found growing wild by the sea in many parts of the West Country. The fish can be grilled in exactly the same way. Do not worry if the fennel scorches, this will release its fragrance.

Mackerel, trout and John Dory can be cooked in the same way and other herbs may be substituted.

1 young bass, cleaned and scaled	A squeeze of lemon juice
Sea salt and freshly milled pepper	Fresh fennel
Olive oil	

Season the fish well and brush with olive oil. Sprinkle with lemon juice. Make a bed of fennel on top of the grilling rack and place the fish on top. Cook for about 7 minutes on each side or until cooked. Serve immediately with crusty wholemeal bread.

Brill with Crab Sauce   (serves 4–6)

Brill is a flat fish, smaller than turbot; in the 19th century, it was regarded as a poor man's fish. Today, it is expensive and one of the money makers for West Country fishermen.

Brill is in season all year round, but at its poorest from April to June after spawning. It can grow to 2 feet (60cm), but it is most often seen much smaller than this. The larger brill are sold in steaks like turbot, or filleted. The smaller fish can be cooked whole; steamed, grilled, fried, poached or baked.

1 large or 2 medium brill, filleted	Meat from 1 crab, brown and white mixed
Approx. ½pt (300ml) milk	
2 bayleaves	3 tablespoons (3 × 15ml) double cream
1 slice of lemon	
Sea salt and freshly milled pepper	2 tablespoons (2 × 15ml) fresh parsley, finely chopped
1oz (25g) butter	

Poach the brill very gently in the milk with the bayleaves, lemon slice, seasoning and butter for about 8 minutes. Drain and reserve the poaching liquor, discarding the bayleaves and lemon. Keep the fish warm on a serving dish.

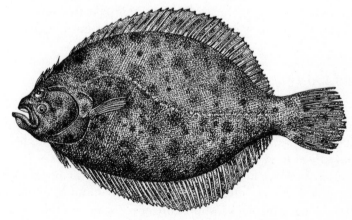

Brill

Mix the crab meat, cream and parsley together in a basin. Add enough reserved poaching liquor to make a thick sauce and pour into a saucepan. Heat gently without allowing the sauce to boil. Adjust the seasoning if necessary and pour over the waiting fish. Serve immediately.

Brill Stuffed with Scallops and Mushrooms in Cream (serves 4–6)

1 large brill	1oz (25g) butter

For the stuffing

2oz (50g) butter	4oz (125g) button mushrooms, sliced
1 tablespoon (15ml) onion, finely chopped	Beurre manié to thicken (see p.207)
4 large scallops, chopped	A squeeze of lemon juice
8fl oz (250ml) single cream	1 dessertspoon (10ml) fresh parsley, finely chopped
Sea salt and freshly milled pepper	

To prepare the brill for stuffing, leave on the head and tail, place the brill on a board, dark skin up and run a sharp knife down the backbone. Gently lift away the fillet on either side of the bone, then bend the fish back until the backbone snaps in several places. Remove these sections of bone and any attached bones with kitchen scissors, leaving a pouch-like cavity which can be stuffed easily. Melt $1\frac{1}{2}$oz (40g) of butter in a small frying-pan. Fry the onion for a few minutes. Add the chopped scallops, followed by the cream. Season well. Cover the pan and leave to cook very gently for 2–3 minutes. Melt the remaining butter in a small saucepan and fry the mushrooms very lightly. Add the mushrooms and their cooking juices to the scallops. Thicken the sauce with a little beurre manié, adding more cream if necessary. Stuff the fish and place in a buttered ovenproof dish. Dot with butter and bake in a moderate oven (350°F, 180°C, gas mark 4) for 30–40 minutes, or until tender.

Baked Conger Eel in Cider with Apples (serves 6)

Conger eel has always been popular in the South West particularly with Cornish miners. Pies of the fish used to be served on Accounting Day at the mines. The middle cut would be roasted, but the tail end, because of its boniness was used for pies, fish cakes, soups and stocks.

All eels are very rich in protein and have a fine flavour; conger is no exception. It is in season from March to October and sometimes grows up to 8 feet long. The black inshore conger is not so valuable; in the past, fishermen tried to disguise a black conger as the more valuable white by putting it into a sack of straw!

2½lb (1.2kg) conger eel, skinned

Seasoned flour

2oz (50g) butter

1 medium onion, chopped

1pt (600ml) dry cider

Sea salt and freshly milled black pepper

1lb (450g) Cox's apples, thickly sliced

2 tablespoons (2 × 15ml) Cornish clotted cream

1 tablespoon (15ml) fresh parsley, chopped

Cut the eel into steaks about 1in (2.5cm) thick and roll in seasoned flour. Melt the butter in a large frying-pan and cook the onion until golden. Remove the onion to a baking tin and brown the eel pieces in the remaining fat. Remove the eel and place on top of the onion, reserving any fat in the frying-pan. Pour over three-quarters of the cider and season. Bake in a fairly hot oven (400°F, 200°C, gas mark 6) for 20–30 minutes until the eel is tender, basting the fish with the liquid.

Fry the apple slices in the remaining butter for a few minutes until they are just crisp at the edges. Use more butter if necessary. Remove the fish from the oven and arrange on a serving platter. Arrange the apple slices around the fish and pour the cooking juices and cider into a small saucepan. Add the remaining cider and boil rapidly to reduce to about ½pt (300ml) liquid. Stir in the cream until the sauce is smooth. Pour over the waiting fish and serve garnished with parsley.

Conger Eel, Megrim and Prawn Soup (serves 8)

Conger eel with its firm flesh and good flavour is a perfect fish for soup. Megrim or West Coast sole is a fish commonly caught off the coast of Devon and Cornwall. It is sometimes served fried in fish and chip shops in Cornwall and has quite a good flavour.

1lb (450g) fish bones and trimmings

1lb (450g) conger eel in 2 steaks

1 large megrim, filleted and skinned

6oz (175g) prawns, cooked

1 medium onion, quartered

4 celery sticks, chopped

1 carrot, chopped

1 bouquet garni

2½pts (1.5 litres) water

Sea salt and freshly milled pepper

2 tablespoons (2 × 15ml) olive oil

1 medium onion, finely chopped

2 large cloves garlic, crushed

1 large leek, thinly sliced

Pinch of saffron

1 tablespoon (15ml) tarragon wine vinegar

1 red pepper, diced

2 tablespoons (2 × 15ml) fresh parsley, finely chopped

Place the fish bones and trimmings with bones and skin from the filleted megrim in a large saucepan. Add the onion, one chopped stalk of celery, carrot, bouquet garni and water. Season and bring slowly to the boil. Simmer for about 25 minutes, then strain through a sieve, pushing through some of the vegetable debris. Reserve this fish stock.

Heat the oil in a large saucepan and cook the onion and garlic until transparent. Add the leek and three chopped celery sticks and cook for another 2–3 minutes. Add the megrim, eel and saffron and pour on the stock. Bring to the boil, then simmer gently for 15–20 minutes until the eel is just cooked. Remove the eel with a draining spoon and put on one side. Add the wine vinegar and red pepper to the saucepan and boil rapidly for 5–10 minutes to reduce the liquid slightly. Stir from time to time to break up the megrim fillets.

Remove the skin and bones from the cooked eel and cut the flesh into small pieces. Lower the heat under the soup and adjust the seasoning if necessary. Add the small pieces of eel and stir in the prawns. Cook for a few seconds, then serve in individual soup bowls garnished with parsley.

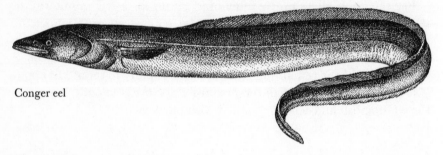

Conger eel

Hobbler's Choice   (serves 4)

This seafood dish is served at the Sail Loft Restaurant on St Michael's Mount. It takes its name from the island ferrymen who are known as 'hobblers'. The base is usually conger eel, traditionally very popular in Cornwall for pies when mixed with parsley and hard-boiled eggs and topped with shortcrust pastry. It would be served with Cornish clotted cream.

$1\frac{1}{2}$–$1\frac{3}{4}$lb (675–800g) mixed cooked fish and shellfish (conger eel, pollock, mussels, smoked mackerel and crab)

$\frac{3}{4}$pt (450ml) velouté sauce, made with cooking liquor from the fish (see p.214)

1 tablespoon (15ml) fresh parsley, chopped

A pinch of basil

2 spring onions, chopped

2oz (50g) Cheddar cheese, grated

Sea salt and freshly milled black pepper

4 tablespoons (4 × 15ml) breadcrumbs

Melted butter

Skin, bone and flake all the fish and mix with the shellfish. Fold into the sauce and add the parsley, basil, spring onions and cheese. Season to taste. Pour into a buttered ovenproof dish.

Mix the breadcrumbs with a seasoning of salt and black pepper and sprinkle over the fish. Dribble a little melted butter over the breadcrumb topping and cook in a moderate oven (350°F, 180°C, gas mark 4) until crisp and golden brown.

Roasted and Stuffed Conger Eel   (serves 6)

In the old days in Cornwall, the middle cut of conger was usually roasted whole in dripping and cider and served with red cabbage or samphire pickle. Here is a modern version.

2½lb (1.2kg) middle-cut conger, skinned

1 small onion

4oz (125g) butter

¼pt (150ml) dry cider

A little flour

For the stuffing

4oz (125g) fresh breadcrumbs

2oz (50g) shredded suet

2oz (50g) bacon, chopped finely

3 teaspoons (3 × 5ml) fresh parsley, chopped

½ teaspoon (2.5ml) mixed herbs

Grated rind of ½ lemon

Sea salt and pepper

1 small egg, beaten

Remove the bones from the fish and wash and dry it well, inside and out. Cut the onion in half and rub all over the inside of the fish. Mix all the ingredients for the stuffing together and stuff the eel. Sew it up or tie it securely with fine string or thread. Melt the butter in a baking dish and put in the fish. Pour the cider over and baste well. Roast in a moderate oven (350°F, 180°C, gas mark 4) for 1 hour, basting from time to time with the pan juices and dredging with flour. Serve the fish with a tomato or caper sauce (see p.215).

Tiddy Eel   (serves 6)

'Tiddy' is the Cornish name for potato, which is still the main vegetable grown in many parts of the county. This particular recipe for a substantial stew uses conger eel and originates from the Sennen Cove area. It would have been made formerly from salted conger soaked in milk and water before being cooked. In Cornwall, until the end of the last century, 'conger-doust' – conger eel, split and dried without salting – was exported in quantity to Catholic countries, largely for soup-making on fast days.

2lb (900g) conger eel, skinned and boned	2 tablespoons (2 × 15ml) fresh parsley, chopped
1 medium onion, sliced	1pt (600ml) milk
2lb (900g) potatoes, sliced	1pt (600ml) fish stock (see p.209)
Sea salt and freshly milled pepper	Lemon juice

Cut the eel into finger-sized strips, place in a saucepan with the onion, cover with the potato slices and season well. Sprinkle over half the parsley and pour on the milk. Lastly, add enough fish stock to cover. Season with lemon juice. Bring slowly to the boil, then cover the pan and simmer very gently for about 20 minutes, or until the eel is just tender. Serve garnished with the remaining parsley.

Padstow Spider Crab Terrine   (serves 4)

This terrine is one of the dishes served in the popular quayside restaurant at Padstow run by Rick and Jill Stein for the past ten years.

Spider crabs, so called because of their spider-like legs, are caught all round the coast of Cornwall, but disappear immediately to the Continent, generally to Spain and France. The fishermen tell me that they can't sell them to the home market, which is a shame because they have very sweet flesh. They are rather fiddly to clean as they do not have the big main claws of the common edible crab, although the meat is mainly on the legs. The best buy is the female when she is carrying eggs under her tail flaps. Any crab can be used in this recipe.

1 1lb (450g) spider crab	4fl oz (120ml) double cream
1oz (25g) butter	1 egg, separated
1oz (25g) onion, chopped	1 level teaspoon powdered gelatine
1oz (25g) carrot, chopped	Sea salt
1oz (25g) celery, chopped	A pinch of cayenne pepper
2oz (50g) tomato, chopped	1 teaspoon (5ml) lemon juice
2 tablespoons (2 × 15ml) dry white wine	Sunflower oil to oil terrine
12fl oz (360ml) water	

Remove all the meat from the crab, reserving all the shell. Break up the body shell into 2 or 3 pieces. Melt the butter in a pan and cook the onion, carrot and celery until just beginning to colour. Add the shell, tomato and wine. Stir over a high heat for 2–3 minutes, then pour over the water. Bring to the boil and simmer for 40 minutes. Strain through a sieve into another saucepan. Boil rapidly to reduce to 2 tablespoons (2 × 15ml) and allow to cool.

Bring half the cream to the boil, then take it off the heat. Whisk the egg yolk with the reduced shellfish liquor and add the hot cream. Stir continuously with a wooden spoon over moderate heat until it starts to thicken. Take off the heat, stir in the gelatine and cool the pan by setting it in a bowl of ice and water. When it is quite cool, add the crab meat. Season if necessary with salt and cayenne pepper and sharpen with lemon juice. As the mixture gets colder, it will begin to set. Whip the rest of the cream until it is thick and soft, but not stiff, and fold into the crab mixture before it sets too hard. Lastly, whisk the egg white to soft peaks and fold in. Pour the mixture into a lightly oiled $\frac{1}{2}$ pint (300ml) terrine mould. Leave to chill at least 3 hours in the fridge, before turning out on to a serving plate. Serve the terrine in slices cut with a knife dipped into very hot water.

Cornish Crab Pasties (serves 4–6)

Fish pasties have been made by generations of West Country fishermen's wives, usually from herrings, small mackerel or pilchards. Sometimes they were crescent-shaped, but if they had to fit into a dinner tin to be carried to work, they would often be made from a square of pastry, with the head and tail of the fish poking out of each end. In Victorian times, huge pilchard pasties were always sold in Truro market, kept hot in a tin oven over a small fire. The pasties were made in a long strip, with about 36 fish lying side by side across the pastry with their heads and tails protruding. The stall-holder would cut off the number of fish required.

Crab meat was not often put into pasties, but special crab and lobster pies were served to shareholders in the Cornish tin mines on Accounting Day. The main room of the mine's counting house was cleared and a feast was prepared by the wives of the clerks and officials. Starry-gazey and conger-eel pies were served alongside the shellfish pies, and joints of beef and mutton.

Crab pasties tend to be rich, so make them smaller than normal pasties. They make delicious picnic food.

1lb (450g) shortcrust pastry	Freshly milled pepper
8oz (225g) brown and white crab meat, mixed	1 tablespoon (15ml) fresh parsley, chopped
A squeeze of lemon juice	A little milk to glaze
A pinch of ground mace	

Roll out the prepared pastry $\frac{1}{4}$in (5mm) thick and cut into 4in (10cm) diameter circles. Add the lemon juice to the crab meat. Season with mace and pepper and stir in the parsley. Divide the crab mixture amongst the pastry circles. Fold over the pastry and crimp the edges together. Make a small slit in the top of each pasty and brush with a little milk to glaze. Transfer to a baking sheet and bake in a hot oven (425°F, 220°C, gas mark 7) for 20 minutes, or until golden brown and crisp. Serve hot or cold.

Dorset Crab Pie   *(serves 4–6)*

The National Trust's Golden Cap Estate, which lies 3 miles south west of Bridport, is a prime example of the success of Enterprise Neptune. The estate has been built up since 1961 and the Trust's aim is to manage it so that visitors can enjoy unspoiled views from the hilltops, the fine coastal and inland walks, the beaches and the quiet charm of the secluded farmland and woods.

This crab pie or tart is a traditional Dorset recipe.

8oz (225g) plain flour	3 eggs
Pinch of sea salt	2 teaspoons (2 × 5ml) lemon juice
Pinch of cayenne pepper	Dash of Worcestershire sauce
2oz (50g) lard	4fl oz (100ml) double cream
2oz (50g) butter	Sea salt and freshly milled pepper
2oz (50g) Cheddar cheese, finely grated	Lemon wedges and sprigs of fresh parsley to garnish
1 egg yolk	
12oz (350g) crab meat, brown and white mixed	

Sieve the flour, salt and cayenne together into a bowl. Rub in the fats until crumbly, then mix in the cheese. Mix the pastry to a dough with the egg yolk and a little cold water. Leave to rest in a cool place for at least 30 minutes. Roll out the pastry and line a 9in (23cm) flan ring. Prick the base and bake in a fairly hot oven (400°F, 200°C, gas mark 6) for 10 minutes or until golden brown.

Flake the crab meat finely into a bowl. Beat the eggs lightly with the lemon juice and Worcestershire sauce and stir into the crab meat, followed by the cream. Season to taste. Spoon the mixture into the pastry case and bake in a fairly hot oven (375°F, 190°C, gas mark 5) for 25–30 minutes.

Serve the pie hot or cold with crusty bread and a mixed salad. Garnish with lemon wedges and parsley.

Cornish Crab Tea

The crab you boil yourself is usually far superior to one already cooked by your local fishmonger. Use seawater if possible, but add extra salt; an egg should be able to float in the brine. If you are using fresh water you will need 6oz (175g) salt to 4 pints (2 litres) water. Place the brine in a large saucepan and put the crab in, fasten on the lid and bring slowly to the boil. A crab should not be plunged into boiling water, as it will 'shoot' its large claws. Simmer for 15 minutes for the first 1lb (450g), 10 minutes for the second, third and so on. Remove from the pan and cool. When the crab is cold, remove the meat in the usual way (see p.142).

A $1\frac{1}{2}$–2lb (675–900g) crab will yield approx. 12oz (350g) meat. Serve 4–6oz (125–175g) crab meat for each person.

The Sail Loft Restaurant on St Michael's Mount serves a Cornish Crab Tea: of a pot of tea, mixed crab meat, homebaked bread and butter and a slice of cake. It is a delicious treat on a summer's afternoon.

Cornish Crab Soup   (serves 6)

Mullion Cove in Mount's Bay, with its small harbour and sturdy pier, was once a busy fishing port. Here were to be found some of the wily pilchard fishermen and later crab and lobster experts who had to contend with the wildest of weather. Today the National Trust own's the Cove, the winch-house at the head of the beach and the fishermen's store.

Crabs and lobsters are caught in pots off the rocky coast using metal or plastic-coated pots; the withy pots of yesterday have now gone. The crabs and lobsters go into store out at sea and are collected once a week by lorry, or twice if the catches have been very good.

8oz (225g) crab meat, brown and white mixed

$1\frac{1}{2}$oz (40g) butter

1 large onion, chopped

1 large carrot, chopped

2 medium tomatoes, chopped

1 sprig of fresh fennel

1 tablespoon (15ml) tomato purée

$1\frac{1}{2}$pts (900ml) fish stock (see p.209)

$\frac{3}{4}$pt (450ml) milk

4 sprigs of fresh thyme

2 bayleaves

Pinch of saffron

Small bunch of parsley

1oz (25g) flour

Sea salt and freshly milled black pepper

Pinch of grated nutmeg

2 tablespoons (2 × 15ml) dry sherry (optional)

Fresh chives, chopped to garnish

$\frac{1}{4}$pt (150ml) whipping cream

Heat $\frac{1}{2}$oz (12g) butter in a saucepan and gently sweat the onion, carrot, tomatoes and fennel for about 10 minutes until soft, but not coloured. Add the tomato purée and the fish stock. Bring to the boil and simmer gently for about 20 minutes until the vegetables are cooked. Blend or process until smooth.

Meanwhile, simmer the milk with the thyme, bayleaves, saffron and stalks from the parsley for 10–15 minutes. Strain and reserve the milk. Melt the remaining butter in another saucepan and stir in the flour. Cook for 1 minute, then gradually stir in the flavoured milk. Continue cooking until smooth and season to taste with salt, pepper and nutmeg. Stir the crab meat into the vegetable stock and add the thickened milk. Stir in the sherry. Taste and adjust seasoning as necessary. Reheat gently and add the cream. Serve garnished with chopped parsley and chives, and with croûtons if you wish.

St Michael's Mount Crab-stuffed Pancakes (serves 6)

The certain history of St Michael's Mount begins with the establishing of a chapel here by Edward the Confessor as an offshoot of the Benedictine Abbey of Mont St Michel, off the coast of Normandy and Brittany. The castle dates from the 14th century, with many subsequent additions. In the 15th century the causeway to Marazion on the mainland and the harbour were built and houses and fish cellars erected. Throughout the Middle Ages pilgrims journeyed to the Mount, but with the Dissolution of the Monasteries the ownership of the Mount transferred to secular hands. The St Aubyn family purchased it in 1659 and it was they who gave it to the National Trust in 1954: the present Lord and Lady St Levan still live in the castle.

Today, a ferry runs from Marazion to this romantic island when the tide is in, otherwise visitors can walk across the causeway. Thirty people now live permanently on the island working on the Mount, on the ferry boats, or fishing. There are only 2 or 3 full-time fishermen, but most of the men have boats and fish in their spare time.

One of the young fishermen, Stephen, makes crab and lobster pots in the traditional way using local 'withies' from Trebarthian, a marshy area at the back of Marazion. Stephen learned how to make the pots from his grandfather and the results are far more attractive than the modern pots made from old car tyres and bits of metal and plastic drainpipe. However, a withy pot will normally only last two seasons and needs to be tended every day because of damage by conger eels, large crabs and by the sea itself. The metal pots will last at least 10 years with very little maintenance, but carry on making your works of art, Stephen.

Some of the local fish and shellfish end up in the Sail Loft Restaurant on the Mount. This is one of the chef's most popular recipes.

4oz (125g) plain flour

Pinch of salt

1 egg

½pt (300ml) milk, or milk and water

Sunflower oil for frying

4oz (125g) crab meat, brown and white mixed

8oz (225g) white fish, cooked

4oz (125g) prawns, shelled

4oz (125g) mushrooms, chopped

1 tablespoon (15ml) fresh chives, chopped

1 tablespoon (15ml) fresh parsley, chopped

½pt (300ml) velouté sauce, made with fish stock and milk (see p.214)

Sea salt and cayenne pepper

2 tablespoons (2 × 15ml) double cream

2oz (50g) Cheddar cheese, grated (optional)

Sieve the flour and salt together into a basin. Make a well in the centre and add the egg. Stir, then beat in the milk gradually until thick and smooth. Leave the batter to stand in a cool place for at least 30 minutes. Heat a little oil in a small frying-pan until it begins to smoke. Add 2fl oz (60ml) of batter and cook over a high heat for about 2 minutes until the pancake is lightly browned on the bottom and set firm. Turn over and brown the other side quickly. Slide on to a plate and continue in the same way with the rest of the batter. Stack the pancakes on top of each other between sheets of greaseproof paper or foil and keep warm.

Divide the crab meat, flaked white fish, prawns and mushrooms amongst the pancakes. Sprinkle with the herbs and top with a spoonful of sauce, reserving most of it for later. Season well and roll up neatly. Place the rolled pancakes in a lightly-buttered ovenproof dish and heat through in a moderate oven (350°F, 180°C, gas mark 4) for about 20 minutes. Mix the remaining sauce with the cream and pour over the pancakes. Sprinkle with cheese and continue to bake in a slightly hotter oven (400°F, 200°C, gas mark 6) until the top is brown and bubbling. Serve immediately with a mixed salad.

Dartmouth Crab Soufflé *(serves 4–6)*

Dartmouth Harbour has offered refuge to shipping for thousands of years, and overseas trade has been the lifeblood of the port. Prosperity came in the 14th and 15th centuries with the wine trade from Bordeaux; in the 16th and 17th centuries local sailors crossed the Atlantic to Newfoundland to fish for cod and traded southwards for port and Mediterranean fruit.

Today Dartmouth is a delightful place, full of boats of all sizes. A large number of crabs and some lobsters are landed here. Crabbing is big business today: the fishermen involved have 500 pots, which they shoot all the way to the Isles of Scilly.

1oz (25g) butter

2 tablespoons (2 × 15ml) flour

½pt (300ml) milk

2 tablespoons (2 × 15ml) grated Parmesan cheese

8oz (225g) crab meat, brown and white mixed

Sea salt and cayenne pepper

2 tablespoons (2 × 15ml) single cream

3 egg yolks, well beaten

2oz (50g) stale breadcrumbs

2 tablespoons (2 × 15ml) medium sherry

4 egg whites, stiffly beaten

Melt the butter in a saucepan and stir in the flour. Cook for 1 minute, then gradually add the milk. Cook until thick and smooth, then stir in the cheese and crab meat. Season generously with salt and cayenne pepper, then stir in the cream and the egg yolks, the breadcrumbs and the sherry. Leave to cool a little. Butter 7in (17.5cm) diameter soufflé or suitable ovenproof dish. Fold in the stiffly beaten egg whites and turn into the soufflé dish. Bake in a fairly hot oven (400°F, 200°C, gas mark 6) for 25–30 minutes.

Gurnard in a Paper Envelope (serves 1)

A rather ugly fish with a large bony head and prominent spiny fins the gurnard, or 'gurnet' as it used to be called, is often plentiful in the coastal villages and markets of Devon and Cornwall, especially on the north coast. There are three types, red, grey and yellow; the red being better and rather similar to red mullet, although not as delicate. The flavour of both types is sweet but the fish is bony. Choose the larger gurnards if possible because there is more flesh. Many of the smaller fish are used as bait by West Country fishermen.

This is one of the simplest and tastiest ways of cooking gurnard and works equally well with red mullet.

1 12oz (350g) gurnard, preferably red

Sea salt and freshly milled black pepper

Sprigs of fresh thyme

Sprigs of dill or fennel

1oz (25g) butter

Wedge of lemon to garnish

Clean the fish and remove the bony dorsal fin and the rather large head, which can be used as the base for an excellent fish stock or soup later. Season the fish and stuff with thyme and dill. Dot with butter and wrap in a rectangle of greaseproof paper or foil. Bake in a fairly hot oven (375°F, 190°C, gas mark 5) for about 20 minutes. Remove from the oven, garnish with lemon and serve with a well-flavoured parsley or anchovy sauce (see p.214).

St Ives Baked and Stuffed Gurnard *(serves 4–6)*

There is a wonderful story in *Tales of the Cornish Fishermen* written by Cyril Noall about a Captain Stevens of St Ives who was in command of a sailing ship attacked by Moorish pirates. He was hurt in the attack and was fitted with a wooden arm when he returned to England. After this, the good Captain, now generally known as 'Teak Job', had to earn his living by fishing. He did not join one of the regular St Ives fishing crews, preferring to go fishing alone in the bay in a small boat, sculling the vessel with his one remaining arm. In August 1879, a large quantity of gurnards was landed at St Ives. The local market being soon glutted, these fish sold at a very low price. 'Teak Job' accordingly purchased a number of the fish, loaded them into his punt and began to scull to Portreath, 7 or 8 miles away, where he sold them at a good price. He was then 75 years old! Cornish fishermen have always been tough.

This is the best way of cooking a large gurnard weighing 2–3lb (1–1.4kg), with the head left on.

2 2½–3lb (1–1.4kg) gurnards	Grated rind of ½ lemon
1oz (25g) butter	Pinch of grated nutmeg
1 small onion, chopped	Sea salt and freshly milled black pepper
6oz (175g) mushrooms, chopped	
3oz (75g) fresh brown breadcrumbs	2 rashers streaky bacon
3 tablespoons (3 × 15ml) milk	2 sprigs fresh thyme
1 tablespoon (15ml) fresh parsley, chopped	Dry cider

Clean the fish and remove the bony dorsal fins, but leave the heads. Lengthen the body cavity of each fish by slitting the underside towards the tail.

Melt the butter and cook the onion until soft, but not coloured. Add the mushrooms and cook gently until tender. Soak the breadcrumbs in the milk. Add the parsley and lemon rind and then the onion and mushroom mixture. Season to taste with nutmeg, salt and pepper. Stuff the body cavities of the fish and place each one on a large piece of lightly-oiled foil. Top with a rasher of bacon and put a sprig of thyme in each fin cavity and sprinkle with a little cider. Wrap each fish up loosely and place on a baking tray. Bake in a fairly hot oven (375°F, 190°C, gas mark 5) for 40–50 minutes, or until cooked.

West Country Hake with Lemon Sauce (serves 4)

A great deal of good quality hake is caught off the Devon and Cornish coasts. In Cornwall most is caught off the coast at Penzance and is landed at Newlyn, the main fishing port for Mount's Bay. Newlyn grew in importance because of the pilchard and mackerel fishing: in the spring of 1838, over 120 boats were engaged in the mackerel fishery at Newlyn, nearby Mousehole and Porthleven, the other side of Mount's Bay. The fish was principally marketed by the wives of the fishermen in their scarlet cloaks and large black beaver hats, who hawked their husbands' catches through the adjoining towns and villages. The fish itself was carried in 'cowals', or specially shaped baskets supported on the women's backs by a broad band which passed around their hats.

With the opening of the Cornwall Railway in 1859 London developed as a new and important market for the Cornish fish. Newlyn became the local depot for this trade, handling the catches of the Mount's Bay fleet.

In the early 19th century, as many as 40,000 hake were landed at Newlyn and Penzance within the space of 12 hours. Hake is a delicious fish with a slightly pinky flesh, and can be bought as cutlets or fillets. Cutlets of hake are excellent grilled, barbecued, baked, fried or poached as in this recipe. A good accompaniment is a spicy or tangy sauce, such as this lemon butter sauce.

4 thick hake cutlets	Sprigs of fresh fennel and slices of
Court bouillon (see p.208)	lemon to garnish

For the lemon sauce

1oz (25g) butter	Sea salt and freshly milled black
1oz (25g) flour	pepper
$\frac{1}{2}$pt (300ml) fish cooking liquor	2 egg yolks
Grated rind and juice of 2 lemons	

Poach the hake cutlets in court bouillon for about 10 minutes. Drain and keep warm, reserving the cooking liquor. To make the sauce, melt the butter in a saucepan and stir in the flour. Cook for a few minutes, then add the cooking liquor, lemon rind and juice. Continue to cook, simmering gently for about 5 minutes. Season well. Beat the egg yolks in a small basin and add a little of the hot sauce, stirring well. Pour this egg and sauce mixture back into the saucepan and stir until the sauce thickens. Do not allow the sauce to boil or it will curdle.

Pour a little of the sauce over the hake and garnish with sprigs of fennel and twists of lemon. Serve the rest of the sauce separately.

Plymouth John Dory in Cider and Cream *(serves 4)*

Plymouth was one of the old trawler ports with fishing grounds around the Eddystone Lighthouse. Smacks went up to 40 miles out on a daily basis, for catches including hake, conger, dory, halibut, sole, turbot, red mullet, brill and skate. In the 1870s, Plymouth smacks worked in Mount's Bay, landing catches at Newlyn for the last Penzance to Paddington train at 3.50 p.m. The Great Western Railway rates were 60 shillings per ton for cod or mackerel and 45 shillings for herring. But the Plymouth fleet declined with the advent of steam trawling; only 14 sailing trawlers remained in 1922 and all had disappeared by 1939.

John Dory is known as 'Plymouth's proudest fish' and is indeed an excellent firm, fleshy white fish, though ugly to look at. It has two dark 'thumb-prints' on either side by the gills. Just as St Peter is said to have marked the haddock (see p.120), he is also attributed with the legend of landing a John Dory. The fish groaned so loudly at having been captured that the Saint picked it up between his finger and thumb and threw it back into the sea, leaving it branded for ever with the mark of the Apostle.

John Dory is in season all the year round and is usually 12–16 inches long, but can grow much larger. The body takes up less than half the length, but the head is very good for soups and stock. Steaks can be cut from the larger fish or it may be filleted. Simple cooking such as grilling, frying, poaching or baking is best, as the fish has a very fine flavour. The texture of the fish is a little like a scallop and is excellent served cold with mayonnaise.

4 thick steaks or large fillets of John Dory	1 tablespoon (15ml) parsley, chopped
3 tablespoons (3 × 15ml) seasoned flour	1 tablespoon (15ml) lemon juice
2oz (50g) butter	$\frac{1}{4}$pt (150ml) dry West Country cider or dry white wine
1 tablespoon (15ml) olive oil	Sea salt and freshly milled black pepper
1 tablespoon (15ml) fennel, chopped	
1 tablespoon (15ml) tarragon, chopped	2 tablespoons (2 × 15ml) clotted cream

Skin the fish steaks or fillets and roll in seasoned flour. Heat the butter and oil in a pan and fry the fish until brown. Add the herbs, lemon juice and cider and continue to cook for a further few minutes. Remove the fish on to a serving dish and keep warm. Adjust the seasoning of the sauce if necessary, then add the cream. Cook for another minute until the sauce is smooth, then pour over the waiting fish. Serve with buttered potatoes and a green vegetable.

Cider Baked John Dory   (serves 4)

1 large or 2 medium John Dory, cleaned

Sprig or sprigs of fresh fennel

½oz (12g) butter

Sea salt and freshly milled black pepper

1 large lemon, sliced

½pt (300ml) dry West Country cider or dry white wine

Tuck the fennel into the body cavity of the fish. Place in a buttered ovenproof dish and season well. Arrange the lemon down the centre of the fish and pour on the cider. Cover loosely with kitchen foil and bake in a moderate oven (350°F, 180°C, gas mark 4) for 30–40 minutes.

Brixham John Dory and Scallops with Watercress Sauce   (serves 4)

2 2–2½ (900g–1kg) John Dory, filleted

2 tablespoons (2 × 15ml) dry white wine

Warm fish stock (see p.209)

1 bouquet garni

1 shallot, sliced

6 black peppercorns

8 scallops, cleaned

For the watercress sauce

1 bunch watercress

2 egg yolks

1 tablespoon (15ml) cold water

1 tablespoon (15ml) white wine

Sea salt and freshly milled pepper

Lemon juice

Place the John Dory in a pan and pour over the wine and enough warm fish stock just to cover the fish. Add the bouquet garni, shallot and peppercorns. Bring slowly to the boil and poach very gently for 2 minutes. Slice the white part of the scallops in half, reserving the corals on one side. Add the white scallop to the pan and poach for a further minute, then add the corals and continue poaching for about 30 seconds. Remove the fish on to a warm serving platter and keep warm. Strain the poaching liquor and reduce to 2 tablespoons (2 × 15ml).

To make the sauce, remove all the leaves from the watercress and blanch quickly in boiling water. Drain and refresh in cold water. Dry and chop finely. Beat the egg yolks with the water and wine in a basin until pale and frothy. Still beating, add the reduced cooking liquor, followed by the watercress. Place the basin over a pan of simmering water and whisk the sauce gently until it has thickened and is slightly foamy. Adjust the seasoning as necessary and add lemon juice to taste. Pour over the waiting fish and serve immediately with new potatoes tossed in butter and parsley.

Cold Port Isaac Lobster

(serves 2)

Port Isaac was once an important herring fishing centre: its fish were either salted here, packed in barrels and exported to Italy, or they were smoked in the kipper houses that still stand on the quayside. Today these houses are used for cooking, selling and dressing crabs, crawfish and lobsters. The quality of the dressed shellfish is excellent, with no additives.

The National Trust has only one house in this quaint Cornish fishing village and it must be the smallest. Five-sided, three-storeyed, with one room on each floor, the Birdcage stands halfway up the lane which climbs the east side of the valley. Every house is at a different level from its neighbours, for the slopes are steep and the valley bottom narrow. It is one of my favourite places to visit on a winter's afternoon.

Buying Live Lobsters

First, make sure that the lobster is lively. Its tail should spring back into place when uncurled. Avoid drowsy, listless specimens which will have been out of the water for too long.

Check that the two main claws are present and that the lobster feels heavy when you pick it up. All shellfish should either be in a tank of water or at least kept and sold in moist, cool conditions.

The best size for a lobster, when the flesh is sweet and tender is $1-1\frac{1}{2}$lb (450–675g) which they reach in 9 to 12 years. Much larger lobsters should be cheaper per lb.

Like crabs, lobsters go into hiding to shed their armour. They are at their poorest in June when they have shot their roe: so connoisseurs like to eat them in early spring and late autumn.

Identifying Hen and Cock Lobsters

In both lobsters and crawfish, the tail of the hen is broader and there is slightly more shell around her tail to protect her eggs (coral or berries). It is not against the law to sell berried lobster, which is a great shame as stocks of lobster are dwindling rapidly.

Cooking a Lobster or Crawfish

Live lobsters are coloured a blotched greeny blue, sometimes almost black, for they vary their camouflage according to their environment.

Cook the lobster in boiling water for 10 minutes to the lb. While still warm, twist off the main claws and crack them. Twist or cut off the little legs to use for stock.

Using a sharp knife cut the body in half from the head to the end of the tail. Discard the sac between the eyes which is a kind of stomach and contains gravel, and the dead men's or devil's fingers, the feathery gills,

31

which are inedible. Remove the black intestinal line which runs down the tail.

Serving a Cold Lobster

Serve the lobster shells and claws on a bed of ice with salad, brown bread and butter and mayonnaise (see p.210). Alternatively, all the meat can be taken out of the shell, sliced up and served on a bed of salad with mayonnaise.

Cadgwith Lobster Tart   *(serves 4)*

Cadgwith is another tiny fishing village on the Lizard peninsula with thatched cottages clustering around a shingle beach scattered with colourful crab and lobster boats. The Cadgwith fishermen are a superstitious lot; they never fish on a Friday, especially Good Friday, and none of their boats is ever painted green. They always turn their boats out to sea clockwise, never take pasties on board (because of the wind inside!) nor whistle on board in case it conjures up the wind.

On a small coastal strip north of Cadgwith, cared for by the Trust, stands a huer's hut, a reminder of the times when a 'huer' was appointed to watch for pilchard shoals (p.46).

This lobster tart can be made with lobster, crawfish, or crab. It is excellent served hot or cold.

6oz (175g) shortcrust pastry	1 egg yolk
8oz (225g) lobster or crawfish, cooked	7½fl oz (225ml) double cream
2 eggs	1oz (25g) Parmesan cheese, grated
	Sea salt and cayenne pepper

Roll out the prepared pastry thinly and use it to line an 8in (20cm) flan ring, standing on a greased baking sheet. Prick the bottom of the pastry well. Flake the lobster or crawfish meat and pile it into the flan case. Beat the eggs, egg yolk and cream together, then beat in the cheese. Season well and pour the custard into the flan. Bake in a fairly hot oven (375°F, 190°C, gas mark 5) for 30–40 minutes or until well risen and golden brown. Serve hot or cold.

Boscastle Lobster Mousse   *(serves 4)*

From the end of the 18th century Boscastle grew in importance as the only harbour on the long length of coast from Clovelly in north Devon to Padstow in north Cornwall. The railway did not reach this part of Cornwall until 1893, so all heavy goods had to be carried by sea: coal, timber and manufactured goods were imported, with return cargoes of slate, china clay and manganese ore from a mine in the Valency Valley, which runs down to Boscastle Harbour. More than a dozen ketches and schooners traded regularly through the little port in the 19th century.

The tortuous harbour entrance, with the island of Meachard as an extra hazard, meant it was never safe for sailing vessels to enter Boscastle unassisted. They were towed or 'hobbled' in by 'hobbler' boats manned by 8 oarsmen. Hauling goods up Boscastle's steep hills needed strong teams of horses, many of them kept at the Palace Stables, now the youth hostel, and there was constant work for the blacksmith in the forge, now the National Trust's shop and information centre.

The National Trust began to acquire land at Boscastle in 1955. It soon came apparent that the loss of the breakwater, blown up by a drifting sea mine in 1941, was causing damage to the quay and it would have to be replaced. In the winter of 1962, which turned out to be exceptionally cold and stormy, the Trust's building gang from Cotehele began the job, following it up with the repair of the quays and slipways at the head of the harbour.

The trading role of the harbour had declined almost to nothing by the 1950s and with the breakwater in ruins, few fishermen would risk mooring their boats inside the jetty. Once the breakwater was rebuilt fishing revived, since Boscastle is the nearest harbour to the rich shellfishing grounds off Lundy. Now, there is a regular, if hazardous, fishery and a Fishermen's Association runs the harbour in co-operation with the National Trust.

Crab or crawfish can be used instead of lobster to make this creamy mousse.

1 1½–2lb (675–900g) lobster, cooked, or 8oz (225g) shellfish meat

3 tablespoons (3 × 5ml) powdered gelatine

3 tablespoons (3 × 15ml) water

½pt (300ml) whipping cream

2 tablespoons (2 × 15ml) mayonnaise (see p.210)

Juice of 1 lemon

Freshly milled black pepper

2 egg whites

Strips of lemon peel to garnish

Remove all the meat from the lobster (see p.31). Beat or process the meat until smooth. Mix the gelatine with the water in a small basin and dissolve over a saucepan of boiling water. Stir into the lobster meat. Whisk the cream and fold into the lobster with the mayonnaise, lemon juice and a seasoning of pepper. Whisk the egg whites until stiff and fold into the mousse. Pour into a wetted mould or 7in (17.5cm) diameter soufflé dish and refrigerate until firm. Unmould if you want, and garnish with lemon peel.

Penberth Baked and Stuffed Mackerel in Cider
(serves 6)

Although mackerel are sold and eaten all over Britain, they are mainly fished in the South West. During the winter months, they migrate to their spawning grounds south of Ireland and west of the English Channel. Once they have spawned they start to feed voraciously and between April and June West Country fishermen catch them with drift nets. The great centre of this fishery has always been Newlyn near Penzance in Cornwall, where it has been known for as much as half the total English catch to be landed.

In June and July the fish move inshore in small shoals and feed on small fish rather than plankton. This is when the small boats go out with hooks and lines and 'feather' for mackerel, which lasts until September, when the fish begin to disperse for their winter rest in the deeper water. This seasonal activity means that mackerel are at their best between April and September.

The fishermen of Penberth Cove, near Land's End, go out in their small boats to catch mackerel in the summer. Penberth is perhaps Cornwall's most delightful little fishing cove, a lively, working place typical of the small fishing communities once common in Cornwall, with mackerel and shellfish boats tightly moored against the waves that sweep up the slipways. The headland and cove with much of the valley behind were transferred to the National Trust in 1957. The Trust's policy is to let the scattered granite cottages to working families with business in the valley: daffodils and violets are grown for market in many of the sheltered valley gardens.

Small fresh mackerel are best simply grilled or barbecued, while the large ones can be filled with a stuffing and baked.

4 large mackerel, cleaned	$\frac{1}{2}$pt (300ml) local dry cider
2 teaspoons (2 × 5ml) fresh horseradish root, grated	$\frac{1}{2}$oz (12g) butter
1 teaspoon (5ml) onion, grated	Sea salt and freshly milled black pepper
4oz (125g) cream cheese	4 bayleaves

Pound the horseradish and onion with the cream cheese and mix in 2 tablespoons (2 × 15ml) cider until smooth. Spread this mixture inside the body cavity of each fish and arrange in a buttered ovenproof dish. Season with salt and pepper, place a bayleaf on each fish and pour over the remaining cider. Cover the dish with a lid or kitchen foil and bake in a fairly hot oven (375°F, 190°C, gas mark 5) for 25–30 minutes. Serve immediately with crusty wholemeal bread.

Barbecued Mackerel with Gooseberry Sauce (serves 1)

There are many traditional Cornish recipes for serving mackerel with gooseberry sauce, a combination that dates back to the time of the Norman Conquest, but it is good served with any sharp-tasting fruit sauce such as apple or rhubarb and champagne (see p.13) which counteracts the richness of the fish.

Mackerel is excellent for beach barbecues and until recently was so plentiful that all summer visitors to Cornwall and Devon could rely on catching a carrier bag full on one short fishing trip. Wild fennel grows in profusion around many West Country beaches and has more bite than the leaves of the cultivated Florentine fennel.

1 medium mackerel, cleaned	2 or 3 sprigs of fresh fennel leaves
Olive oil	Sea salt and freshly milled pepper

For the gooseberry sauce

8oz (225g) green gooseberries	Pinch of ground nutmeg
1 tablespoon (15ml) cold water	Sugar to taste
$\frac{1}{2}$oz (12g) butter	

Make 2 or 3 diagonal cuts across both sides of the fish. Brush with olive oil and place fresh fennel in the body cavity. Season well. Place over a hot barbecue, open fire, or under a hot grill and cook for about 5 minutes on each side.

To make the sauce, poach the gooseberries in a little cold water until very tender. Sieve the fruit and mix with the butter. Add the nutmeg and sugar to taste. Serve either hot or cold.

Mackerel Baked in Tea (serves 6)

'Ent [empty] the tea-pot' is a commonly heard directive in Cornwall, where large quantities of tea are drunk at most meals. There is a strong tradition of Methodism in Cornwall and the Methodists were, and many still are, zealous teetotallers. Once a year, old and young paraded the town of St Ives, with huge silk banners declaring 'Strong drink is raging' etc! Traditional tea treats were held by local Methodist chapels in most Cornish towns and villages.

Tea was also drunk at 'croust', 'crib' or 'the drinkings', a snack eaten away from home by farm-workers, clay-workers, quarrymen and miners. In some places of work it was possible to brew tea; in others a bottle of cold tea was the alternative, very refreshing for the miners who worked in appallingly hot, wet conditions. In the china clay areas of mid-Cornwall, 'kettle boys' were employed to get kettles boiling for tea and pasties warmed by the time the men came in for dinner.

This traditional Cornish recipe uses up any leftover cold tea. Serve as a dish for a summer lunch or supper. Herrings, sprats and pilchards can be cooked in the same way.

6 mackerel, cleaned	$\frac{1}{4}$pt (150ml) white vinegar
6 bayleaves	$\frac{1}{4}$pt (150ml) cold tea
1 tablespoon (15ml) brown sugar	Fresh parsley, finely chopped, to garnish
12 whole black peppercorns	

Place the fish, with the heads removed, in an ovenproof dish with a bayleaf inside each fish. Sprinkle with the sugar and peppercorns and pour over the vinegar and cold tea mixed together. Cover with a lid or foil and bake in a moderate oven (350°F, 180°C, gas mark 4) for 40 minutes. Carefully lift out the fish, remove the bayleaves and arrange on a serving dish. Strain over the cooking liquor. Leave to cool and then chill for several hours before serving garnished with parsley.

Serve with warm crusty wholemeal bread, a cold potato salad or a hot jacket potato.

Soused Mackerel from Mousehole (serves 6)

Mackerel taken in the spring were mostly consumed fresh; those caught in the autumn, which were better quality, were salted in great numbers by the Cornish for winter use. In the spring of 1838, over 120 boats were engaged in the mackerel fishery at Newlyn, Mousehole and Porthleven. With the opening of the Cornwall Railway a new and important market was developed for the spring mackerel. By 1884, the number of mackerel drivers (boats) had increased to nearly 400, employing 2,700 men. Newlyn became the local depot for this trade and the great fleet of drivers had permanent moorings off the shore before the harbour was built. Each vessel kept a 4-oared boat at these moorings to land the catches. The Mousehole mackerel drivers, on the other hand, liked 3-oared jolly boats to bring their fish ashore. Each of these was in the charge of a boy, 10–14 years old, who was known as a 'yawler'. While the season lasted, he was the absolute slave of the lugger who employed him.

The first 'up-country' trawlers began to frequent the western waters as far back as 1843 but the disastrous effects of trawl fishing were not fully appreciated until much later. However, once the railways had come to Cornwall there was a vast increase in the number of visiting trawlers which trawled over the best mackerel driving grounds, day and night from February to April, frequently fouling and cutting the nets of the local drifters. The trawlers were followed by large steam drifters, and the fate of the famous Mount's Bay fleet of sailing drivers was sealed.

The old name of Porth Enys – island port – is still in use in Mousehole, with its harbour mouth blocked in winter by the huge timber beams or 'baulks' to keep out the sea. Centuries ago it was one of the busiest harbours in the bay. Today the harbour is almost empty of working boats, but the village has retained its character.

Herrings can be substituted for the mackerel if you wish.

6 mackerel, cleaned	10 peppercorns
Sea salt and freshly milled pepper	3 bayleaves
$\frac{1}{2}$pt (300ml) dry cider	Sprig of fresh thyme
6 whole cloves	1 medium onion, sliced
Blade of mace	

Cut the heads and tails off the fish and bone them. Season well and roll up skin-side outwards. Arrange closely together in an ovenproof dish. Pour over the cider and sprinkle with the cloves, mace and peppercorns. Tuck in the bayleaves and thyme and scatter the fish with slices of onion.

Cover the fish with foil and bake in a cool oven (300°F, 150°C, gas mark 2) for about 1$\frac{1}{2}$ hours. Lift the fish carefully on to a serving dish, removing all the flavouring ingredients. Strain the cooking liquor over the fish and leave to marinate and cool for several hours before serving with crusty wholemeal bread and local draught cider.

Cornish Smoked Mackerel

I consider the best Cornish smoked mackerel is now produced by The Cornish Smoked Fish Company at Charlestown near St Austell. The company was set up in 1971 by Martin Pumphrey on the quayside of the small harbour. At first he concentrated on smoking mackerel, which was then plentiful off the Cornish coast. As the mackerel supply dwindled, so the company has gradually diversified and now smokes salmon, trout, cod's roe, sprats and kippers.

The mackerel is smoked on the bone rather than being filleted before smoking. The flavour is excellent, very rich, moist, a great treat and not too expensive!

Salcombe Smokies

These are hot smoked mackerel fillets produced by Salcombe Smokers at Kingsbridge in South Devon, a long-established firm recently taken over by a new owner, Mr Barron. He is currently researching into additives and colourings used for smoked fish in this country and feels that there is an increasing demand for natural uncoloured products. Salmon, prawns, whiting, pollock, roe, and haddock as well as the famous mackerel fillets are smoked on the premises and Mr Barron has reduced by up to 50 per cent the permitted colouring added to the normal run. The smoked fish is supplied wholesale to various retail outlets and a mail order service operates from Clarksons of Devon, at Ottery St Mary.

Monkfish and Scallop Pie   (serves 4)

Monkfish or angler fish is a deep-water fish caught off the coasts of Devon and Cornwall. Only the tail of the angler fish, which has a central bone, but no others, is eaten. The flesh has an excellent flavour and a similar texture to scallops, which makes this a very successful combination.

8 scallops, cleaned	6oz (175g) button mushrooms, sliced
8oz (225g) monkfish	Pinch of saffron
1pt (600ml) milk	1lb (450g) mashed potato
3oz (75g) butter	2oz (50g) cheese, grated
2oz (50g) flour	
Sea salt and freshly milled black pepper	

Cut the scallops and monkfish into chunks, leaving the corals whole. Poach very gently in the milk for about 5 minutes. Strain, reserving the milk.

Melt 2oz (50g) butter in a saucepan and stir in the flour. Cook for a minute, then gradually add the reserved milk. Bring to the boil stirring well, and cook for a few minutes until the sauce is thick and smooth. Add the mushrooms and saffron and cook for another 2 minutes. Stir in the scallops and monkfish and season well. Pour into a lightly buttered ovenproof dish and top with mashed potato. Dot with the remaining butter and sprinkle with grated cheese. Bake in a fairly hot oven (400°F, 200°C, gas mark 6) for about 30 minutes, or until golden on top.

Porthleven Monkfish Kebabs with a Fennel Dressing

(serves 6)

Porthleven is another Mount's Bay port, which grew up as a result of the Cornish pilchard and mackerel fishing in the 19th century. It is an attractive place with an active fishing industry.

Other firm-fleshed fish, such as cod, halibut, grey mullet, mackerel, salmon, turbot or shark, can also be cooked in this way. A mixture of fish is an excellent idea for a barbecue.

6 6oz (175g) fillets of monkfish

For the marinade

2fl oz (60ml) olive oil

Juice of $\frac{1}{4}$ lemon

1 teaspoon (5ml) fennel, chopped

Pinch of sea salt and freshly milled black pepper

For the fennel dressing

3fl oz (90ml) olive oil

1 tablespoon (15ml) white wine vinegar

$\frac{1}{2}$ teaspoon (2.5ml) sea salt

Freshly milled black pepper

1 teaspoon (15ml) fennel, chopped

1 large shallot, finely chopped

Cut the fish into cubes. At least one hour before cooking, put all the marinade ingredients – the olive oil, lemon juice, fennel and seasoning – into a shallow dish and add the fish. Turn over in the marinade 2 or 3 times during the hour. Thread the fish on to skewers and grill or barbecue for a few minutes on each side, brushing from time to time with the marinade, until only just done.

Mix all the ingredients for the fennel dressing together in a jam jar. Shake vigorously, adding any remaining marinade and pour over the fish. Serve immediately with hot crusty wholemeal bread and a salad.

Monkfish

Monkfish in a Tomato and Pepper Sauce   (serves 4)

1 teaspoon (5ml) sunflower oil

1 large onion, chopped

1 clove garlic, crushed

6oz (175g) mushrooms, sliced

1 small red pepper, deseeded and sliced

1 small green pepper, deseeded and sliced

2 small courgettes, sliced

Pinch of tarragon

1 tablespoon (15ml) fresh parsley, chopped

6oz (175g) tin tomatoes, chopped

1lb (450g) monkfish, boned and cubed

Sea salt and freshly milled black pepper

8 black olives and watercress to garnish

Heat the oil in a heavy saucepan and gently fry the onion and garlic until soft but not coloured. Add the mushrooms, peppers and courgettes and continue cooking until soft. Add the herbs and tomatoes, cover and simmer for 2 minutes. Continue cooking uncovered for a further 5 minutes until the liquid has reduced a little. Stir in the cubes of monkfish and simmer for about 5 minutes until the fish is cooked. Season to taste with salt and pepper. Serve hot or cold garnished with black olives and watercress. Accompany with savoury rice or crusty bread.

Monkfish and Mushrooms in Pastry   (serves 4)

The idea for this delicious recipe came from a friend who used to cook at the Riverside Restaurant in Helford. I hope she will approve of my adaptation.

12oz (350g) monkfish

8oz (225g) flat mushrooms

1oz (25g) butter

1 small onion, finely chopped

1 tablespoon (15ml) fresh herbs, finely chopped (thyme, or marjoram and parsley, mixed)

Grated rind of $\frac{1}{2}$ a lemon

Squeeze of lemon juice

Sea salt and freshly milled black pepper

Approx. 1lb (450g) flaky pastry

Beaten egg to glaze

Bone the monkfish and divide into 4 pieces. Chop the mushrooms very finely. Melt the butter in a saucepan and soften the onion. Add the mushrooms and cook until most of the moisture has disappeared. Add the herbs and lemon rind and season to taste with salt, pepper and lemon juice. Leave to cool.

Divide the pastry into 4 pieces and roll out to make 4 squares. Place a piece of monkfish on each square of pastry and top with some of the mushroom mixture. Fold over the pastry to make a triangle, or make a parcel if your prefer. Place on a greased baking tray and glaze with beaten egg. Bake in a fairly hot oven (400°F, 200°C, gas mark 6) for about 25 minutes, or until golden brown and crisp. Serve with a creamy sauce such as hollandaise (see p.209).

Weymouth Red Mullet cooked in Paper   *(serves 1)*

In the 19th century, the Dorset port of Weymouth was renowned for its mullet, both red and grey. In fact, red mullet is the finer and belongs to quite another family: it is known as the 'woodcock of the sea', because like the woodcock, its liver is considered a delicacy and is usually left inside the fish after cleaning. The Duke of Portland and his aristocratic friends used to travel from London to Weymouth especially to eat red mullet. The medium-sized fish were available for 3d or 4d each, but His Grace was known to pay 2 guineas for red mullet weighing 1½lbs.

A famous method of cooking red mullet is in buttered greaseproof paper or foil, because the flesh is liable to break up when cooked and served. In this way all the flavour of the fish is preserved.

1 large red mullet	1 mushroom, chopped
1 teaspoon (5ml) onion, grated	A knob of butter
1 teaspoon (5ml) fresh parsley, chopped	A squeeze of lemon juice
1 teaspoon (5ml) wild fennel, chopped	Sea salt and cayenne pepper
	A lemon slice to garnish

Clean the fish through the gills retaining the liver, if you wish. Scale it and place it on an oval of buttered greaseproof paper or foil. Sprinkle over the onion, parsley, fennel and mushroom. Top with a knob of butter and the lemon juice. Season well with salt and a very little cayenne pepper. Wrap the fish in the paper, securing it well, and slide on to a baking dish. Bake in a moderate oven (350°F, 180°C, gas mark 4) for about 20 minutes. Serve the fish in its paper garnished with a slice of lemon. Accompany with a good rich parsley sauce (see p.216), or a little melted butter flavoured with a dash of anchovy essence and a good squeeze of lemon juice.

Red mullet

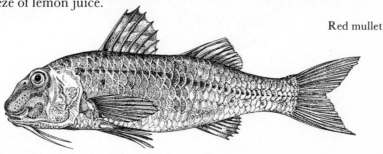

Mullet, Monkfish and Saffron Stew   *(serves 8)*

3 2lb (900g) grey mullet

1lb (450g) monkfish

1pt (600ml) prawns

3 onions, roughly chopped

1 medium carrot, chopped

1 celery stick

2 tablespoons (2 × 15ml) olive oil

2 green peppers, chopped

14oz (400g) tin of tomatoes

2 cloves garlic, crushed

1 tablespoon (15ml) tomato purée

Pinch of saffron

Strip of orange peel

$\frac{1}{4}$pt (150ml) dry vermouth

Sprig of fresh thyme

2 bayleaves

Sea salt and freshly milled black pepper

Dash of Tabasco sauce

2 tablespoons (2 × 15ml) fresh parsley, chopped

Clean the mullet, reserving their heads and tails, and peel the prawns, reserving the peelings. Put the peelings and mullet heads and tails in a large saucepan with one onion, the carrot and the celery. Add water to cover and bring slowly to the boil. Simmer for about 20 minutes, then strain the stock.

Heat the olive oil in a large pan and cook the 2 remaining onions, until soft, but not coloured. Add the green peppers and cook for a few minutes, then add the tomatoes. Slice each mullet into 3 or 4 pieces and place on top of the vegetables. Chop up the monkfish and add this, followed by the prepared stock, garlic, tomato purée and saffron. Lastly, add the orange peel, vermouth and herbs. Simmer gently for about 20 minutes before adding the prawns. Heat gently, then season to taste with salt, pepper and Tabasco sauce. Serve immediately in soup bowls garnished with parsley and with plenty of crusty wholemeal bread.

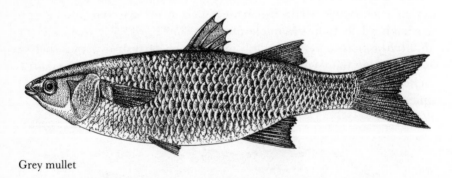

Grey mullet

Taw Mussels in Cider and Cream (serves 4)

Taw mussels are famous in the West Country, and this is a local way of cooking them. They are landed at Barnstable together with prawns, plaice and sole from Bideford Bay. Clams may be used instead of mussels in this recipe.

4pts (2 litres) fresh mussels

½pt (300ml) dry Devonshire cider

Squeeze of lemon juice

1 bayleaf

1 whole clove

1 medium carrot, chopped

1 celery stick, chopped

1 small onion, chopped

1 egg yolk

3 tablespoons (3 × 15ml) double cream

1 tablespoon (15ml) fresh parsley, chopped

Wash and scrub the mussels and pull off the beards. Put the cider into a saucepan with the lemon juice, bayleaf, clove, carrot, celery and onion. Simmer gently until soft, then strain, reserving the liquor. Put the mussels in a large pan with the reserved liquor, cover and cook over a high heat for 3–4 minutes, shaking the pan from time to time, until the mussels are open. Remove from the pan and discard any remaining beards and the top shells. Transfer to a serving dish and keep warm.

Simmer the stock for a few minutes, then cool a little. Beat the egg yolk and cream together, then stir into the stock. Reheat gently until the liquor has thickened, but do not allow to boil. Pour over the waiting mussels and sprinkle with parsley. Serve with crusty wholemeal bread and plenty of local cider.

Baked Poole Oysters with Cream and Parmesan (serves 1)

Poole Harbour in Dorset is one of the largest and most sheltered natural harbours in the world, with all the characteristics necessary for good oyster production. Not surprisingly, oysters have been cultivated commercially for food here since pre-Christian times. The first major commercial users of the harbour were the Romans who regarded the oyster as almost a staple food.

Archaeological evidence suggests that oysters remained a major source of food locally right through the Middle Ages, although to what extent they were farmed commercially is unknown. By the 17th century, great quantities of Poole oysters were being pickled and transported to London, Holland, Spain, Italy and as far afield as the West Indies. In the early 19th century the oyster beds were all but wiped out, but after several unsuccessful attempts at reviving the industry, eventually the 'Poole Oyster Fishery Company' was established. The Company now leases 100 acres of seabed and employs 2 vessels full-time in the demanding process of cleaning, stocking and dredging.

At the entrance to Poole Harbour is Brownsea Island, 500 acres of heath and woodland owned by the National Trust, though part of the island is run as a nature reserve by the Dorset Naturalists' Trust. For a small island Brownsea presents an astonishingly wide range of habitat – seashore, salt marsh, heathland, coniferous and deciduous woodland, freshwater lakes and a brackish lagoon – and this is reflected in the richness and diversity of the bird and animal life. One of the largest heronries in the country is in a mature Scots pine wood within the nature reserve, and the red squirrel, extinct elsewhere in Southern England, survives on Brownsea, free from competition with the grey squirrel. There is also a small resident population of sika deer.

2–4 large oysters	1–2 teaspoons (1–2 × 5ml) double cream
Tabasco sauce	
2–4 drops of lemon juice	Parmesan cheese, freshly grated (if possible)
Sea salt and freshly milled black pepper	

Open the oysters (see p.198) retaining the liquor. Arrange each one on the deep half of its shell. Season with Tabasco sauce, lemon juice, salt and pepper. Mix the oyster liquor with the cream and spoon over the oysters. Dredge lightly with cheese and place in an ovenproof dish or baking tray. Bake in a hot oven (425°F, 220°C, gas mark 7) for a few minutes only until just bubbling and a light golden brown on top. Eat immediately with brown bread.

Grilled Porth Navas Oysters   (serves 1)

Porth Navas, near Falmouth in Cornwall, is the source of the world-famous Helford River oysters, said to be the sweetest in the world. No one really knows how long they have been taking oysters from the Helford River but the beds are old and well tried and were probably there in Roman days. Len Hodges, the helpful manager of the Duchy of Cornwall Oyster Farm, is the fourth generation of his family to run the fishery. Certainly conditions are ideal, for in bad winters, when Colchester and Whitstable beds have been wiped out, the Helford beds have survived well enough to be able to supply those striken areas with young oysters for fattening.

At Porth Navas you can have oysters opened for you to eat picnic style, but take along your own bread and butter and something to drink. Clams can be used in this recipe.

2–4 large oysters

Freshly milled black pepper

A knob of butter

2 teaspoons (2 × 5ml) breadcrumbs

Fresh chives, or shallots, finely chopped

Fresh parsley, finely chopped

Lemon wedges to garnish

Open the oysters, retaining their liquor (see p.198). Arrange each one on the deep half of its shell with the liquor. Sprinkle with black pepper. Melt the butter in a small pan and fry the breadcrumbs until crisp and golden brown. Sprinkle over the oysters and top with chopped chives or shallot and parsley. Cook under a hot grill for a few minutes. Garnish with lemon wedges and serve with brown bread and butter.

Trelissick Oysters with Orange　　　*(serves 2)*

Oyster beds in the River Fal, like those in the Helford, have been cultivated since Roman times. The beds just below Trelissick, a National Trust estate tucked away up the estuary of the Fal, are still worked using flat-bottomed motor boats. Trelissick is a great Cornish garden, although most of the large estate is farmland and woods with superb views of the tidal estuary and the sea in the distance.

This is another very simple way of cooking fresh oysters from Cornwall. Clams or scallops can be cooked in the same way.

4 large oysters

2 teaspoons (2 × 5ml) orange rind, grated

Juice of $\frac{1}{2}$ an orange

1 tablespoon (15ml) lemon juice

2oz (50g) brown breadcrumbs

2 tablespoons (2 × 15ml) fresh chives, finely chopped

Sea salt and freshly milled black pepper

2 standard eggs, beaten

Strips of orange rind to garnish

Open the oysters (see p.198) and remove from their shells, reserving their liquor and the deep half of the shell. Slice the shellfish and poach

Oyster

them very gently for 2 minutes in the orange and lemon juice and oyster liquor. Reserve 1 tablespoon (15ml) of breadcrumbs, but add the remainder to the oysters with the orange rind and chives. Season with salt and pepper. Add the beaten eggs and stir over a gentle heat until the eggs are cooked. Divide the mixture amongst the reserved shells and sprinkle over the remaining breadcrumbs. Cook under a very hot grill for a few minutes until the crumbs are crisp. Garnish with orange rind and serve immediately.

The Fair-maids of Cornwall

The pilchard – in its young form, the sardine – is a sub-tropical member of the herring family whose range extends to the shores of the West Country in the late summer and autumn. It is a much more delicate fish than the herring and travels badly. In the past, if exported it had to be preserved by salting, smoking, and in more modern times, by canning. Even nowadays, it is still unusual to find fresh pilchards for sale in shops any distance from the coast where they are caught.

Ever since the Middle Ages there has been a prolific pilchard fishery in Cornwall with vast numbers caught during their late summer visits to the waters off St Ives and other ports on the north and south coasts; the old name for pilchards used in the 16th century was 'pylcher' or 'pilchar'. Although the pilchard industry has always been precarious, dependent on the unpredictable movement of the shoals, by Elizabeth I's reign it already provided a significant part of England's export trade and was protected by numerous laws. Predominantly an inshore occupation in these early days, it was also the training ground for the seamen who, under Drake and Hawkins, harrassed Spain and contributed to the defeat of the Armada of 1588.

At this time, much of the curing of pilchards was done by smoking, which earned them the name 'fumedos', Spanish for 'smoked'. Vast numbers were exported to Spain, but an order of 1591 decreed that 'no more fumedos were to be made so that the Queen's enimays might not be supplied with provisions'. Nonetheless, the name, corrupted to 'fair-maids' by the Cornish, continued to be applied to salted barrelled pilchards.

By the 19th century, the pilchard fishery was a vital and profitable trade in the West Country. The shoals appeared without warning and only briefly; they could also disappear for some years, as happened in the 1920s. It was the job of the 'huer', who kept watch from a high vantage point on the cliffs, to scan the surface of the water for the characteristic reddish stain that marked the shoal of pilchards. He directed the waiting boats towards the shoal with a blast on his trumpet and semaphore signals made by furiously waving a 'bush' – wooden hoops covered with white linen – in each of his hands. Once the men in the first boat saw the signal from the cliffs, the cry of 'hewa, hewa' – Cornish 'hesvan' for a shoal of fish – went up, while the boat moved quickly to surround the shoal with a seine net, more than a quarter of a mile long and about 70 feet wide, weighing almost 3 tons with its floats and sinkers. A smaller boat, 'the lurker', guarded the gap to prevent the fish from escaping and finally, a third boat, 'the voyler', went inside the circle and drew the pilchards together so that the whole net and its contents could be towed into shallow water, where it acted as a keep-net for the live fish until they were removed for curing by men called 'blowsers'. The fish were scooped from the seine with 'tuck nets' and transferred by means of small tuck baskets to the 'dipper boats' which ferried them ashore. Sometimes, because of bad weather, it would take a week to transfer the millions of trapped fish. They were then hurried, still fresh, through the streets to curing cellars or 'pilchard palaces' where they were salted and packed into barrels. Although most of the pilchards ended up like this, the fishermen were able to claim some of the catch as part of their wages. A good catch meant 'meat, money and light, all in one night' – pilchard oil, known as 'train', was formerly used in lamps.

Cornwall was a poor area and the people needed the food for the winter when there was little work and less money. A Cornish cottager would lay in about 1,000 fish for the winter, the housewife curing her own supply in a 'buzza' – a large earthenware pot. The price of salt was always a problem for industry and individual – 7lbs was needed for every 100 fish. During the Napoleonic Wars, the tax on salt was increased and until its removal in 1825, salt was part of the stock-in-trade of Cornish smuggling.

The extension of the Great Western Railway into Cornwall in 1859 opened up new markets, requiring a regular supply of fish, and led to a concentration of the industry on St Ives, which in 1869 had 286 seine nets. Heavy in-shore fishing led to a decline in catches and to counteract this, larger lug-rigged boats began working well out into the Atlantic. Their faster yacht-like hulls allowed rapid journeys home with the catch and the pilchard fishery's first steam lugger *Patmos* was built in the 1870s. Despite these innovations pilchard fishing declined due to the joint influences of demand and long-term changes in the migratory movements of the fish. The seine net fishery collapsed in the 1870s, precipitating a government enquiry; the strain on what was left was shown in 1896. In that year an invasion by over 100 East Coast drifters and trawlers, who fished in rough weather and even on Sundays, so incensed the devout Methodist Cornish, that fighting broke out in Penzance and Newlyn. At the turn of the century there was a brief resurgence, with 6 million pilchards caught on one day in 1904. Then quite suddenly, just before World War I, pilchards began to disappear from the Cornish coast. Nobody is sure why this happened, but it put an end to the pilchard fishery. The fish still appear unpredictably and in small numbers, sometimes in the North Sea, sometimes in the English Channel. You can occasionally buy them in ports like Brixham in Devon and Polperro in Cornwall if the fishermen have been lucky. Otherwise, the only pilchards most of us come across are caught off the coast of South Africa and tinned with tomato sauce.

Cornish Scrowlers *(serves 4)*

A Cornish 'scrowler' was a fresh pilchard, which was cleaned and split open, rubbed all over with a mixture of salt, sugar and black pepper, then left overnight. The next day the fish was 'scrowled' on a gridiron over a clear fire. A favourite drink to accompany scrowlers or fair-maids was 'mahogany', a powerful mixture of black treacle and gin.

Herrings or mackerel may be used instead.

4 fresh pilchards, cleaned	Freshly milled black pepper
Sea salt	Soft brown sugar (optional)

Split the fish open and rub all over with equal quantities of salt, pepper and sugar. Leave overnight in a cool place. The next day grill or barbecue the fish quickly on both sides. Serve immediately.

Starry-gazey Pie *(serves 6)*

This traditional Cornish dish, originally made of pilchards, was common in the coastal areas of west Cornwall. It is still made each year in Mousehole on 23 December or Tom Bowcock's Eve. Legend has it that Tom Bowcock, a local fisherman, saved the community from hunger by his daring fishing exploits 200 years ago. After weeks of bad weather, when no one could put to sea, he is said to have ventured out alone in a desperate search for fish and to have returned to shore with 'seven sorts of fish'. These were put into a starry-gazey pie.

The pilchards are baked whole under the pastry so that no oil from the fish is lost and it drains back into the body as the pie cooks, but the heads poke up through the pastry to 'gaze at the stars'. The fish are arranged on the pastry base like spokes on a wheel with the heads pointing outwards on the rim of the dish. Under the blanket of pastry there might be a spoonful of mustard, herbs, onion, breadcrumbs, hard-boiled eggs, pieces of fat bacon, pulp from the cider press, or pickled rock samphire. In richer versions of the pie, savoury egg custard was also included. Later, in Victorian times, a starry-gazey pie was often baked with the fish heads clustered through a hole in the centre with parsley in their mouths, while the tails of the fish decorated the outer rim. The tops of starry-gazey pies should be brushed over with a little saffroned milk.

As the pilchards became scarcer, mackerel or herrings were used to make a starry-gazey pie.

6 fresh pilchards, cleaned

6 tablespoons (6 × 15ml) white breadcrumbs

4 tablespoons (4 × 15ml) milk

2 tablespoons (2 × 15ml) fresh parsley, chopped

1 medium onion, chopped

Grated rind of 1 lemon

Sea salt and freshly milled pepper

10oz (275g) shortcrust pastry

2 hard-boiled eggs, chopped

3 rashers back bacon, chopped

$\frac{1}{4}$pt (150ml) dry farmhouse cider

Few strands of saffron

6 small sprigs of fresh parsley

Scale and fillet the fish, but leave on the heads. Soak the breadcrumbs in 3 tablespoons (3 × 15ml) milk and leave to swell a little. Then add the parsley, half the onion, the lemon rind and the seasoning. Stuff the fish with the mixture and fold them up to look like whole fish. Line a round greased pie-dish or plate with half the prepared pastry rolling it out very thinly. Arrange the stuffed fish on the pastry with the heads on the edge of the dish. Scatter the remaining onion, hard-boiled egg and bacon around the fish and season well. Pour over the cider. Roll out the remaining pastry to make a lid for the pie, leaving the heads of the fish exposed. Press the pastry down well between each head sealing with a little milk or water. Decorate as you wish and then brush well with milk which has had a few strands of saffron soaking in it, or with beaten egg. Bake in a fairly hot oven (400°F, 200°C, gas mark 6) for about 15 minutes, then reduce the heat to 350°F (180°C, gas mark 4) and continue to cook for another 30–35 minutes. Serve the pie hot with a small sprig of parsley in the mouth of each fish.

Clotted cream may be spooned into the pie after baking if you wish.

Port Gaverne Dippy (serves 6)

Port Isaac and its subsidiary harbours of Port Gaverne and Portquin had the largest pilchard fishery on the north coast of Cornwall, apart from St Ives. The National Trust owns the beach, foreshore and two fish cellars at Port Gaverne, where the pilchards were once cured. The oldest, Rashleigh Cellars, lie nearest to the sea; Union Cellars were built in 1801, the year of the Union of Great Britain and Ireland. A smoking house was built on to these cellars in the 1920s when there was a short-lived revival in fishing.

Pilchard cellars were rectangular around an open courtyard with three sides surrounded by lean-to roofs. The fishermen's seine nets, ropes, baskets and other tackle were stored in the roof spaces, while the floors were carefully graded to carry the oil from the fish into tanks below ground. The pilchards were unloaded from the boats into horse-drawn carts which delivered them to a heap in the middle of the courtyard. The women 'bulkers' worked at great speed to stack the fish in layers between French salt along the cellar wall with their heads pointing outwards. The pile went on increasing until it was as high as the women could conveniently reach; usually about 5 feet. There the fish remained for a month, much of the oil running out into the tanks. They were then packed in straight-sided barrels and further pressed by means of wooden levers inserted into purpose-built slots in the walls, with a heavy sea-washed boulder on its free end. As the fish were forced down into the barrels so the rest of the oil was expressed. All round the coast one finds these slots in old walls close to the sea, sometimes cut into the living rock. Local coopers made the special barrels. Nothing from the curing presses was wasted: the oil drained from the fish went to the leather tanners; the skimmings from the water in which the fish were washed was bought by soap boilers; and any broken or damaged fish were sold off for manure. At the end of the pilchard season, 'cellar feasts' or suppers were often held for the women who had worked so hard in the pilchard cellars.

In 1873 Portquin had 100 inhabitants, but 20 years later it was deserted and remained so for a long period. It seems that the pilchards failed to arrive for several seasons and the nearby Doyden antimony mine, which provided employment for the men out of the pilchard season, closed down. The Trust now has four holiday cottages in the village.

In the old days pilchards were simmered in thin cream with chunks of potatoes to provide a complete meal in one pot. The thin cream was known as 'dippy'. Herrings or mackerel may be used instead.

6 fresh pilchards, cleaned	$\frac{1}{4}$pt (150ml) thin cream
1$\frac{1}{2}$lb (675g) potatoes, peeled and diced	1 tablespoon (15ml) fresh parsley, chopped for garnish
Sea salt and freshly milled black pepper	

Scale the fish and cut off heads and tails. Wash and dry well. Place the fish in a saucepan with diced potato. Season well and pour over the cream. Cover the pan and simmer very gently for 15–20 minutes or until the potatoes are tender. Serve immediately garnished with parsley.

Pilchard Hot-pot *(serves 6)*

For some years before the end of the pilchard seine fishery a great change had taken place in the method of dealing with the fish. Owing to the invention of curing in tanks, the process of laying the pilchards in bulk was entirely dispensed with and as a result many hundreds of men, women and children were robbed of their former means of support. The new process is said to have been introduced first at Mevagissey and it is certainly a curious fact that shortly afterwards the vast shoals of pilchards disappeared from the Cornish coast. Many of the old fishermen regarded this as a direct judgement of Heaven on the infamous invention of curing in tanks!

The old fish-curing tanks can still be seen at Polperro on the south coast of Cornwall, where the fish were salted before being packed in barrels and sent to Italy. There is not much fishing done in Polperro today, but 60 years ago it was the main livelihood. As well as pilchards, conger, ling, pollock and whiting were caught on lines. These were sold by auction at the fish market – the first boats back usually getting the best price – and packed in boxes with ice and taken by horse and cart to Looe Station to catch the train to Billingsgate. The boats that were late back missed the train so had to sell their catch at whatever price they could get for it.

The National Trust owns cliffs on either side of the picturesque harbour of Polperro, and the old fishermen's net loft standing at the entrance to the harbour, which has been renovated recently to house a display of the history of fishing in Polperro.

This recipe for pilchards is a modern version of dippy.

6 8oz (225g) fresh pilchards	Sea salt and freshly milled pepper
4oz (125g) butter	1lb (450g) potatoes, partly cooked
2oz (50g) flour	2oz (50g) Cheddar cheese, grated
1 teaspoon (5ml) tomato purée	1 tablespoon (15ml) fresh parsley, chopped
2pts (1.2 litres) milk	

Clean and scale the fish. Split them open and remove the bones. Arrange them in a buttered ovenproof dish. Melt 2oz (50g) butter in a saucepan and stir in the flour and tomato purée. Cook for 1 minute, then gradually add the milk. Cook until smooth and thick, then season to taste. Pour over the fish and top with sliced par-boiled potatoes. Dot with the remaining butter and sprinkle with cheese. Bake in a moderate oven (350°F, 180°C, gas mark 4) for 20–30 minutes or until the fish is cooked. Cook under a hot grill until brown just before serving. Serve garnished with parsley.

Branscombe Mouth Plaice

(serves 6)

The National Trust looks after 4 miles of coast from Branscombe Mouth to Dunscombe Cliff, south of Salcombe Regis, in east Devon, part of the land designated by the Countryside Commission as the East Devon Heritage Coast. The South Devon Coast Path is routed along the cliffs.

The row of characteristic 19th-century coastguard cottages which have been converted for holiday use at Branscombe West Cliff, and the Watch House at Weston Mouth, are reminders of the lively smuggling trade once carried on in east Devon. Fishermen still operate from Branscombe Mouth catching plaice, dabs, skate, whiting, sprats and mackerel. The plaice can be replaced by lemon sole or megrim.

12 plaice, filleted	$\frac{1}{4}$pt (150ml) mayonnaise (see p.210)
Juice of $\frac{1}{2}$ a lemon	Small tin anchovy fillets
3 oranges	Small red pepper, sliced in rings
Sea salt and freshly milled black pepper	Fresh parsley, chopped
1$\frac{1}{2}$oz (40g) butter	2 tablespoons (2 × 15ml) French dressing

Sprinkle the fish with the lemon juice and the juice of half an orange. Season with salt and pepper. Grate the rind from 1 orange finely and scatter over the fish. Roll up the fillets and secure with a cocktail stick. Arrange them in a buttered ovenproof dish. Squeeze the juice of the remaining half orange over the fish and dot with small pieces of butter. Cover with foil and bake in a moderate oven (350°F, 180°C, gas mark 4) for 20 minutes, or until just tender. Remove from the oven and let cool.

Lift the cold fillets carefully on to a shallow serving dish and remove the cocktail sticks. Add the juice and grated rind of half an orange, drop by drop, to the mayonnaise and coat the fillets with it. Decorate with anchovy fillets and rings of red pepper. Sprinkle with parsley.

Peel the remaining oranges and slice thinly. Dip them in the French dressing and serve as a garnish to the fish. Serve with a tomato salad.

Devonshire Salmon in Cider

(serves 4–6)

West Country salmon is really delicious and of excellent quality. Rivers such as the Lyn, Taw, Torridge, Camel, Fowey, Tamar, Tavy, Dart, Teign and Exe, draining from Dartmoor, Exmoor and Bodmin Moor, used to be very well stocked but, like everywhere, the 'bars of silver', as south Devonians fondly called salmon, are becoming much scarcer. These same rivers, with the exception of the Exe, also offer fine sea trout fishing particularly in July, August and September.

This recipe is the traditional way of cooking salmon in Devon. The fish is baked in local cider with herbs and the liquor enriched with Devonshire scalded or clotted cream. Sea trout may be cooked in the same way.

2lb (900g) salmon	1 tablespoon (15ml) fresh fennel, chopped
1oz (25g) butter	
Sea salt and freshly milled black pepper	4oz (125g) clotted cream
	1 tablespoon (15ml) fresh parsley, chopped
Approx. ½pt (300ml) dry West Country cider	

Well butter an ovenproof dish which will just fit the piece of salmon. Season the fish well. Pour enough cider to come half-way up the salmon. Add the herbs and cover with kitchen foil or a lid. Bake in a moderate oven (350°F, 180°C, gas mark 4) for 20 minutes. Remove the fish and discard any skin and bones. Keep warm on a serving dish. Pour the cooking liquor into a saucepan and boil rapidly to reduce by half. Pour this reduced stock over the waiting fish and spoon over the cream. Put back in the oven for a further 15 minutes. Sprinkle with parsley and serve with buttered new potatoes and a green vegetable or salad.

Tamar Salmon Baked with Cream and Cucumber (*serves 4*)

The River Tamar forms the geographical and political boundary between Devon and Cornwall. Just beyond Calstock, the river takes one of its innumerable sharp turns and passes under a densely wooded cliff. Hidden in the oaks and chestnuts at the top, over 200 feet up, stands Cotehele House; one of the most interesting and romantic late medieval houses in the country, now owned by the National Trust. A little further downstream are the warehouses and abandoned lime-kilns of Cotehele Quay, a busy place in the mid 19th century. The water would have been crowded with a variety of sailing boats, schooners, ketches and barges, paddle steamers and many other small craft.

Today, all is peaceful on the quay, with no activity on the river apart from the occasional pleasure boat, or the salmon fishers working their nets. Over the last few years the salmon have been much scarcer and fishing is very strictly regulated.

4 salmon steaks (about 6oz (175g) each)	½pt (300ml) double cream
	½ cucumber
Salt and freshly milled black pepper	Pinch of dill
2oz (50g) butter	Segments of lemon and dill or fennel to garnish
1 small bayleaf	

Season the salmon steaks well with salt and freshly ground black pepper. Butter an ovenproof dish generously and arrange the fish in it. Add the bayleaf and pour the cream over the fish. Bake in a moderately hot oven (375°F, 190°C, gas mark 5) for 20–25 minutes or until the fish is cooked. Remove the salmon from the oven and keep warm. Cut the unpeeled cucumber into matchstick strips and place in a saucepan with the dill. Cook gently for a minute in its own juices and season to taste. Serve immediately with the salmon and some new potatoes in parsley butter. Decorate with segments of lemon and fronds of dill or fennel.

Spiced Salmon from Antony House   (serves 4)

Where the little River Lynher suddenly turns east and joins the Tamar the church and village of Antony cling to the slope of the hill close to its shore. Some 2 miles downstream is Antony House, a fine classical building erected in 1721 on the site of a much older house. Sir Richard Carew, who wrote *The Survey of Cornwall* published in 1602, was born in the old house in 1555.

This recipe is adapted from a volume belonging to the Carew family entitled *E. Trelawney, Chelsea Accounts 1720*. At one end of the book are household accounts; at the other an assortment of recipes, mainly domestic and medicinal, including instructions 'To pickle Salmon'. In the original recipe, the salmon was 'Boiled very deliberately for little more than a quarter of an hour according to ye thickness of ye fish', then 'pickled over ye fire with lemon peel and wine vinegar'. Spices were added when the salmon was cold.

1½lb (675g) salmon	1 onion, sliced
3 whole cloves	2–3 strips of lemon peel
Pinch of ground cinnamon	Sea salt and freshly milled pepper
1 dessertspoon (10ml) black peppercorns	Mixture of $\frac{2}{3}$ white wine vinegar to $\frac{1}{3}$ water

'Cut the salmon into such pieces as you like best.' Place in a shallow pan with the cloves, cinnamon and peppercorns and cover with the wine vinegar and water mixture. Bring to the boil, then poach very gently for about 10 minutes. Leave to cool in the liquor overnight. The next day remove the skin and bones from the fish and serve cold with wholemeal bread and a cucumber and tomato salad.

Chilled Smoked Trout and Salmon Soup (serves 4)

Bridport has long been an important centre for the fishing industry in Dorset, specialising particularly in red mullet, crabs and salmon. There is an excellent smokery producing good quality local smoked salmon and trout which can be used to make this delicious soup.

10oz (275g) locally smoked salmon

$\frac{3}{4}$pt (450ml) fish stock (see p.209)

$\frac{3}{4}$pt (450ml) single cream

1 smoked trout

Juice of $\frac{1}{2}$ a lemon

Freshly milled white pepper

Fresh chives, chopped, to garnish

Blend or process the smoked salmon and fish stock to a fine purée. Rub the purée through a fine sieve, then stir in the cream. Skin, bone and flake the smoked trout and add to the soup. Season with lemon juice and pepper to taste. Chill well before serving sprinkled with chopped chives.

Baked Scallops (serves 2–4)

This traditional West Country way of cooking scallops enhances their delicate flavour. If the shellfish are very fresh, elaborate sauces are not necessary and often mask the flavour.

8 scallops, cleaned

Sea salt and freshly milled black pepper

A squeeze of lemon juice

4oz (125g) butter

4 tablespoons (4 × 15ml) double cream

4 tablespoons (4 × 15ml) fresh brown breadcrumbs

1 tablespoon (15ml) fresh parsley, chopped

Chop the white flesh of the scallops roughly, leaving the orange corals whole. Scrub the rounded part of 4 scallop shells, or use small ovenproof dishes. Divide the fish amongst the shells. Season well with salt, pepper and lemon juice. Dot with half the butter and spoon over the cream. Sprinkle the breadcrumbs evenly between the shells and top with the remaining butter. Cook in the centre of a moderate oven (375°F, 190°C, gas mark 5) for about 8–10 minutes, or until the scallops are cooked and the top is crisp, bubbling and golden brown. Sprinkle with parsley and serve with crisp brown bread and plenty of dry cider.

Scallops in Apple and Cider Sauce
(serves 4)

2lb (900g) medium or small scallops, cleaned

¼pt (150ml) dry West Country cider

2oz (50g) butter

1½ tablespoons (22.5ml) flour

1pt (600ml) milk

¼pt (150ml) apple purée

Sea salt and freshly milled black pepper

1 tablespoon (15ml) fresh parsley, chopped

Put the scallops in a saucepan with the cider. Poach very gently for 2–3 minutes until just tender. Melt the butter in a second saucepan and stir in the flour. Cook for a minute, then gradually add the milk. Continue cooking until the sauce is thick and smooth. Add the scallops and cider together with the apple purée. Season to taste and pour into a buttered shallow ovenproof dish. Bake in a hot oven (425°F, 220°C, gas mark 6) for about 10 minutes, or brown quickly under a hot grill. Sprinkle with parsley and serve with rice and a green vegetable or salad.

Scallop and Potato Soup
(serves 6–8)

Clams or other shellfish may be used instead of scallops.

12 scallops, cleaned

1pt (600ml) milk

A sprig of fresh thyme

2oz (50g) butter

1 small onion, chopped

2 cloves garlic, crushed

3 medium leeks, sliced

2lb (900g) potatoes, diced

1¾pt (1 litre) fish stock (see p.209)

Sea salt and freshly milled pepper

Pinch of grated nutmeg

Fresh chives and fresh basil, chopped to garnish

Slice the scallops and poach them in the milk with the thyme for 3–4 minutes. Remove them and reserve on one side. Melt the butter in a large saucepan and sweat the onion, garlic and leek for about 5 minutes. Add the potatoes and sweat again for a few minutes. Add the stock and the flavoured milk, including the thyme. Bring to the boil, then simmer for about 45 minutes. Remove the thyme and blend or process the soup. Season to taste with salt, pepper and nutmeg. Add the scallops and serve sprinkled with herbs.

Grilled Torbay Sole with Scalded Cream   (serves 4)

Torbay sole, a speciality of the Tor Bay area in South Devon is the same species as the 'witch' caught off the coast of North Yorkshire. It is not the true Dover sole, but has a similar blunted shape, is a beautiful pinkish purple, and is excellent to eat.

Scalded, clawted, clouted or clotted cream is one of the best known foods of the South West; the Cornish variety being slightly thicker. Before the days of cream separators, the cream was heated or scalded in the dairies of small farms to destroy the bacteria that would otherwise turn it sour. In the past, clotted cream has been added to many West Country dishes both sweet and savoury and was always very popular with fish.

Any sole can be used for this delicious creamy dish.

2 Torbay sole, filleted	1 tablespoon (15ml) fresh parsley, finely chopped
Sea salt and freshly milled black pepper	2 teaspoons (2 × 5ml) fresh chives, chopped
Juice of $\frac{1}{2}$ a lemon	1oz (25g) melted butter
4oz (125g) clotted cream	

Season the inside flesh of each fillet with salt, pepper and lemon juice. Mix the clotted cream with the parsley and chives and spread over two of the fillets. Put the matching fillets on top to make two sandwiches and brush the skin of each with melted butter. Line the grill pan with kitchen foil and place the fish on top. Cook under a hot grill for a few minutes on each side. Serve immediately.

Fillets of Torbay Sole Baked in Cider   (serves 4)

The Sidmouth Landscape Appeal, run jointly by the National Trust and the Sid Vale Association, has recently been set up to protect the area around Sidmouth. The appeal has acquired over 200 acres of land of outstanding natural beauty with spectacular cliffs including nearly 100 acres on Salcombe Hill and several acres on Peak Hill, both hills offering marvellous coastal panoramic views. It will form part of the East Devon Heritage Coast, along with the 4 miles of coast between Branscombe and Salcombe Regis.

Torbay sole is one of the fish landed at Sidmouth.

4 Torbay sole fillets	$\frac{1}{2}$pt (300ml) cider
Sea salt and freshly milled black pepper	Beurre manié to thicken (see p.207)
	Fresh chives, finely chopped

Season the sole fillets well and arrange in a buttered ovenproof dish. Pour over the cider, cover and bake in a moderate oven (350°F, 180°C, gas mark 4) for 25–30 minutes. Strain the cooking liquor into a saucepan and keep the fish warm. Thicken the liquor with beurre manié. Add the chives and adjust the seasoning if necessary, pour over the fish and glaze slightly under a hot grill just before serving.

West Country Fish Stew   (serves 8–10)

Any firm-fleshed fish which will retain its shape in cooking will be good in this fish stew. Here, I suggest the best fish from the West Country including some shellfish, but use what is available from your fishmonger. The only thing to remember is not to overcook the fish. The vegetables can also be varied.

Approx. 4lb (1.8kg) assorted fish (conger eel, red mullet, turbot, John Dory, monkfish, black bream, gurnard, prawns, lobster, mussels, scallops, clams)	2 celery sticks, diced
	2 leeks, white part only, diced
	4 beef tomatoes, skinned, seeded and chopped
2lb (900g) fish bones and trimmings	Bouquet garni
4pts (2 litres) water for the stock	$\frac{1}{4}$pt (150ml) dry white wine
Olive oil	1 tablespoon (15ml) lemon juice
1 large onion, chopped	Good pinch of saffron
4 cloves garlic, crushed (optional)	Sea salt and freshly milled pepper
1 head of fennel, chopped	Cayenne pepper
2 large potatoes, diced	Fresh parsley, chopped, to garnish
2 medium carrots, diced	

Clean and fillet all the fish and shellfish reserving the heads, skin and bones. Place the reserved bones etc. in a large saucepan with the other fish trimmings and cover with the water. Simmer gently to make a fish stock.

Cut all the fish into pieces about 1in (2.5cm) thick, or into convenient sized pieces for eating with a spoon. Melt a little oil in a very large heavy-based pan and gently fry the onion, garlic and fennel until soft, but not coloured. Add all the other vegetables except the tomatoes and continue to cook until soft and slightly golden but not brown. Add the tomatoes, the bouquet garni, the wine and the strained fish stock, followed by the lemon juice and saffron. Bring to the boil and simmer stirring occasionally, for about 10 minutes. Strain through a sieve into a clean pan, forcing the liquid from the vegetable pulp into the pan with the back of a wooden spoon to give the soup extra body. Season with salt and pepper and bring back to simmering point. Check the seasoning again and add a pinch of cayenne. Now add the pieces of fish to the simmering soup, starting with the fish with the firmest flesh such as conger eel, monkfish or turbot. Leave for 1–2 minutes, then add the mullet, bream and John Dory, etc. Cook for another minute, then remove from the heat and add the mussels, prawns, lobster and scallops. The fish should be just cooked through, not overcooked.

Using a perforated spoon, transfer the chunks of fish and shellfish into individual hot bowls. Pour the soup over and garnish with parsley. Serve immediately with warm crusty bread or croûtons.

Freshly made saffron bread, with its shiny crust and saffron flavouring, is especially well-suited to serving with fish soups and stews like this one. Serve it still slightly warm from the oven.

Stir-fried Squid *(serves 4)*

There are quite good landings of squid on the coasts of Devon and Cornwall. Squid is tender, unlike octopus, delicious to eat and very easy to cook. Some are tiny, the body part about 3in (7.5cm) long, excellent for quick frying as in this recipe. Others are more substantial, the body part over 6in (15cm) long, good for stuffing and stewing.

To prepare squid for cooking

You can often buy ready-prepared squid fresh or frozen, but if you buy it straight from the boat, this is how you prepare it. Pull the head gently away from the body pouch and discard the soft innards that come out with it. Discard the insides of the pouch, and the transparent 'pen'. Peel off the purplish-red veil of skin which covers the pouch and wash very thoroughly inside and out. Cut it into rings including the two edible triangular fins. Cut the tentacles into $\frac{3}{4}$in (20mm) slices and put them with the rings. Discard the head and the ink sac. The squid is now ready to cook. This recipe is based on one given to me by the Sea Fish Authority.

1lb (450g) squid, prepared	$\frac{1}{2}$ red pepper, chopped
2 tablespoons (2 × 15ml) sunflower oil	4oz (125g) beansprouts
2 cloves garlic, crushed	$\frac{1}{4}$pt (150ml) fish stock (see p.209)
$\frac{1}{2}$ fresh chilli, sliced	1 tablespoon (15ml) soya sauce
1 bunch of spring onions, chopped	1 teaspoon (15ml) cornflour
2 celery sticks	2oz (50g) roasted peanuts
2 medium carrots, chopped	Sea salt and freshly milled black pepper
$\frac{1}{2}$ green pepper, chopped	

Heat the oil in a large frying-pan or wok. Fry the garlic and chilli for 1 minute. Add the sliced squid and continue cooking for a further 2 minutes. Stir in the onions, celery, carrots, green and red peppers and beansprouts. Fry for a further 2 minutes, then pour in the stock and the soya sauce mixed with the cornflour. Cook over a high heat, stirring until the sauce thickens. Add the peanuts, season and serve.

Stuffed Squid (serves 6)

For this recipe you need squid with bodies at least 6in (15cm) long; smaller ones are too fragile.

6 large squid	3oz (75g) brown breadcrumbs
4 tablespoons (4 × 15ml) olive oil	2oz (50g) fresh parsley, chopped
1 large onion, chopped	2oz (50g) blanched almonds, chopped
3 cloves garlic, finely chopped	Sea salt and freshly milled pepper
3 rashers smoked bacon	
2 tablespoons (2 × 15ml) dry white wine	

For the sauce

1 14oz (400g) tin of tomatoes	2 tablespoons (2 × 15ml) fresh parsley, chopped
1 tablespoon (15ml) tomatoe purée	Sea salt, sugar and freshly milled pepper
$\frac{1}{4}$pt (150ml) dry white or red wine	
1 medium onion, chopped	

Prepare the squid as before, but leave the body pouch whole. Chop the tentacles to put in the stuffing. Heat the oil in a frying-pan and gently fry the onion, garlic, bacon and tentacles until lightly coloured. Moisten the breadcrumbs with the wine – any surplus liquid should be drained off.

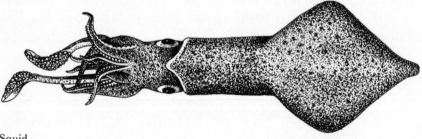

Squid

WHY NOT BECOME A MEMBER OF THE NATIONAL TRUST NOW ?

Members are entitled to free admission to all National Trust properties-200 houses, gardens, nature reserves and many car parks. Ask at the shop for details of membership, including the new reduced rate FAMILY MEMBERSHIP or write for details to:-

CORNWALL INFORMATION OFFICE,
LANHYDROCK PARK,
BODMIN, CORNWALL PL30 4DE

If you join here before leaving, your admission charge will be refunded.

THE NATIONAL TRUST

Cotehele

Cornwall

Transfer the fried mixture into a bowl and add the moistened bread-crumbs, parsley and almonds. Season well. Stuff the squid about two-thirds full to allow for expansion, and sew it up with a trussing needle and fine string or thread. Place the stuffed squid in an ovenproof dish with a lid and mix the sauce ingredients together. Season with salt, sugar and pepper. Pour over the squid and cover tightly with a lid. Bake in a moderate oven (350°F, 180°C, gas mark 4) for 40–60 minutes depending on the size of your squid. Serve hot or cold.

Wild Browns Baked in Cider   (serves 4)

Wild brown trout can be found in many moorland streams and rivers on Exmoor, Dartmoor and Bodmin Moor. The flavour of a freshly caught wild brown trout is unbeatable and the fish should be cooked very simply, either fried, grilled or baked as in this recipe.

4 fresh trout, cleaned	Sea salt and cayenne pepper
2oz (50g) butter	¼pt (150ml) dry Devonshire cider or white wine
1 teaspoon (5ml) fennel, chopped	
1 teaspoon (5ml) fresh parsley, chopped	Squeeze of lemon juice
	Beurre manié to thicken (see p.207)

Mix half the butter with the herbs and place a small lump in the body cavity of each fish. Place the trout in a buttered ovenproof dish and season well. Pour the cider and lemon juice over the fish. Cover loosely with foil and bake in a moderate oven (350°F, 180°C, gas mark 4) for 20 minutes. Remove from the oven and baste with the juices. Dot with the remaining butter, then put back in the oven without the foil. Continue to cook for a further 10 minutes until cooked. Remove the fish to a serving dish and keep warm. Thicken the cooking liquor with beurre manié and pour over the trout.

West Dart Stuffed Trout   (serves 4)

The Duchy of Cornwall fishery in the Dartmoor National Park offers many miles of inexpensive fishing for salmon, sea trout and trout. One of the most popular stretches is the West Dart near Hexworthy. The National Trust owns 2 areas of woods, mainly oak, on the west bank of the Dart at Holne Woods and Hembury, both affording very fine views of this lovely stretch of the river.

4 fresh trout, cleaned

8oz (225g) fresh salmon, cooked

1 heaped tablespoon (15ml) fresh
parsley, chopped

$\frac{1}{2}$oz (12g) butter

4 rashers green streaky bacon

4 sprigs of fresh thyme

$\frac{1}{4}$pt (150ml) dry white wine

Sea salt and cayenne pepper

Mix the salmon and parsley together and stuff the body cavity of each trout with the mixture. Place in a buttered ovenproof dish with a slice of bacon wrapped round each fish. Top with a sprig of thyme and pour the wine over the trout. Season with salt and cayenne pepper. Cover loosely with kitchen foil and bake in a fairly hot oven (400°F, 200°C, gas mark 6) for about 30–40 minutes.

Grilled Respryn Sea Trout with Mint (serves 4)

The magnificent River Fowey rises on Bodmin Moor and flows out into the sea at the town of Fowey on the south coast of Cornwall. Both sea trout and river trout are caught in the Fowey as well as salmon.

The most delicious salmon trout I have ever tasted was caught for us by the late Bill Stephens, who was butler at Lanhydrock House near Bodmin. When the National Trust took over the running of the estate, Bill stayed on to help until his retirement. He used to like to do a bit of fishing for relaxation and Respryn Bridge near Lanhydrock was his favourite spot. The bridge spans the River Fowey and its name shows that there was a ford here – 'res' is Cornish for ford – and a chapel dedicated to St Martin stood beside it by the 12th century.

A favourite way with salmon trout when the Robartes family lived at Lanhydrock was to eat it cold with mayonnaise coloured a pale green by the addition of a little, very fine spinach purée.

Tarragon, sage, rosemary or basil can be used to flavour the trout instead of mint in the following recipe.

4 14–16oz (400–450g) fresh trout,
cleaned

1 tablespoon (15ml) fresh mint,
finely chopped

Grated rind and juice of 2 lemons

Sea salt and freshly milled black
pepper

Melted butter or oil

Dry the fish with kitchen paper, then make 2 or 3 diagonal cuts across the body on each side down to the backbone. Season inside and out with mint, lemon rind, salt and pepper. Put the trout in a shallow dish and pour over the lemon juice. Leave in a cool place for 1–2 hours.

Remove the fish from the marinade, brush with melted butter or oil and cook under a hot grill for about 5 minutes on each side, or barbecue. Serve immediately.

Scalloped Lyn Sea Trout   *(serves 4)*

The rivers that offer good salmon fishing, with the exception of the Exe, also offer fine sea trout fishing. One of these is the East Lyn, where sea trout fishing takes place at the Watersmeet and Glenthorne Fisheries. Fishing tickets for both trout and salmon are obtainable locally. The National Trust owns over a thousand acres east of Lynmouth, which includes the steep wooded valleys of the East Lyn as far upstream as Rockford Bridge, and the Hoar Oak Water as far as Combe Park above Hillsford Bridge. At Watersmeet, where the Trust has an information centre, the two rivers unite and flow swiftly to the sea at Lynmouth beneath Lyn and Myrtleberry Cleaves.

This recipe uses cooked sea trout, but river trout or salmon may be used instead. The dish can either be served as a starter in scallop shells or individual ovenproof dishes, or for a main course in one large dish.

8oz (225g) sea trout, cooked	Sea salt and freshly milled black pepper
8oz (225g) Florentine fennel, trimmed	1½oz (40g) flour
2oz (50g) butter	½pt (300ml) milk
8oz (225g) green streaky bacon, chopped	¼pt (150ml) fish stock (see p.209)
A squeeze of lemon juice	1 level teaspoon (5ml) Dijon mustard
	Brown breadcrumbs, fried in butter

Skin and bone the fish and break it up into large chunks. Chop the trimmed fennel into small pieces and melt ½oz (12g) butter in a small saucepan. Cook the fennel gently in the butter for about 10 minutes, shaking the pan from time to time. Add the chopped bacon, increase the heat and cook for a few minutes, stirring frequently. When the bacon is cooked, season with lemon juice and plenty of pepper. Leave to cool before mixing with the fish. Melt the remaining butter in a saucepan and stir in the flour. Cook for a minute, then gradually stir in the milk and stock. Continue cooking until the sauce is thick and smooth. Season with mustard, a little salt and plenty of pepper. Gently fold in the fish and fennel mixture and divide amongst buttered scallop shells or put into one large ovenproof dish. Cover loosely with foil and bake in a hot oven (425°F, 220°C, gas mark 7) for 20–25 minutes or until thoroughly heated through. Remove the foil and sprinkle generously with fried breadcrumbs. Serve immediately with a green vegetable or green salad, if the dish is a main course.

Casserole of Fowey Sea Trout (serves 2)

The demand for sea trout has increased so dramatically over the last few years that sea-farming has become a viable operation in order to meet the demand. One such farm was set up several years ago at the mouth of the Fowey in Cornwall and produces excellent fish which have become a local speciality. The Fowey sea-farmed trout are steelhead trout, which is the native sea-going trout of the Pacific shores of America. The trout starts its life in the farm's own hatcheries and is then transferred into the sea, where it thrives on natural foods.

This unusual way of serving the trout in a casserole with cider was recommended to me by the fish farm.

1 2lb (900g) sea trout, filleted	1 oz (25g) flour
2oz (50g) butter	2pts (1.2 litres) local dry cider
8oz (225g) onions, chopped	Sea salt and freshly milled pepper

Melt the butter in a fireproof casserole and fry the onions until golden. Dip the trout fillets in flour and add to the casserole. Brown lightly. Stir in any remaining flour and cook for 1 minute. Gradually stir in the cider and cook until smooth. Season with salt and pepper. Cover with a lid and cook in a moderate oven (350°F, 180°C, gas mark 4) for 1 hour. Serve immediately.

Terrine of River and Smoked Trout (serves 6–8)

This recipe was given to me by the British Trout Association; it is a combination of fresh river trout and smoked trout, both of which are readily available in the West Country and of excellent quality.

2 1½lb (675g) fresh trout	Freshly ground black pepper
2 8–10oz (225–275g) smoked trout	2–3 tablespoons (2–3 × 15ml) fresh parsley, chopped
2oz (50g) white bread	
2½fl oz (65ml) dry sherry	Grated rind and juice of ½ a lemon
2 large eggs, separated	12oz (350g) fresh spinach
¼pt (150ml) double cream	

Fillet and skin the fresh trout and cut into pieces. Flake the smoked trout. Soak the bread in the sherry for a few minutes then place in a blender or processor with the flesh of the fresh trout. Add the egg yolks, cream and pepper and process until smooth. Check the seasoning and add the beaten egg whites. Process again until the mixture is very thick. Mix the flaked smoked trout with the chopped parsley, lemon rind and lemon juice. Blanch the spinach leaves in boiling water for 1 minute, drain, refresh in cold water, drain again and pat dry with absorbent kitchen paper making sure that they are really dry. Remove any large veins and coarse stalks from the spinach and use three-quarters to line the base and sides of an oiled 2lb (900g) loaf-tin letting the leaves overlap the edges of the tin by a few inches. Spread half the fresh trout mixture into the tin and top with the smoked trout mixture smoothing it to make an even layer. Spread with a final layer of fresh trout mixture. Fold over the overlapping spinach leaves and cover the terrine with the remaining leaves. Cover with a double layer of kitchen foil and prick a few holes in it. Stand the loaf-tin in a roasting tin half-filled with water and bake in a moderate oven (350°F, 180°C, gas mark 4) for about 1 hour or until the terrine is just firm to the touch. Remove from the oven and leave to cool and set for 30 minutes if you are serving the terrine warm. Carefully turn out of the tin and serve with hot brown toast or French bread. This terrine can also be served cold.

Poached Turbot with Mussel Sauce (serves 4)

This great flat fish is in season all the year round, but at its poorest for eating from April to August, after spawning. It is unusual and a huge treat to see a large turbot these days, but in the past, especially in Victorian times when the turbot was renowned in cookery, it was a common sight. Enormous diamond-shaped copper fish kettles once used exclusively for poaching turbot can be seen in the kitchens of many great houses. Most large fish today go to the catering trade.

The fish can be poached whole or in fillets or steaks, and can be grilled, fried and baked in foil. Most recipes for sole are suitable if using fillets.

The classic English recipe for turbot is poached and served with lobster sauce, but as the price of both turbot and lobster is very high, I suggest serving the fish with a mussel sauce for a change.

1½–2lb (675–900g) turbot fillets	3 tablespoons (3 × 15ml) dry white wine
Approx. ½pt (300ml) milk	1pt (600ml) fish velouté (see p.214)
1 bayleaf	Juice of ½ a lemon
1 slice lemon	1 tablespoon (15ml) soured cream
Sea salt and freshly milled pepper	Fresh parsley, chopped, to garnish
2pts (1.2 litres) fresh mussels, scrubbed	

Poach the fish very gently in the milk with the bayleaf, lemon slice and seasoning for about 8 minutes. Remove from the poaching liquor and keep warm on a serving dish. Use the poaching liquor to make the fish velouté. Steam the mussels open in a large pan with the wine for about 3 minutes. Remove the meat from the shells and reserve the cooking juices. Blend or process the mussels adding the cooking juices and a little velouté sauce until smooth. Stir this mussel purée into the remaining velouté and bring to simmering point. Adjust the seasoning if necessary and just before serving, stir in the lemon juice and the soured cream. Pour over the waiting fish and serve garnished with parsley.

Chicken Turbot with Saffron Sauce (serves 4–6)

The small turbot weighing 2–3lb (900g–1.3kg) are known as chicken turbot, and they make an excellent meal for 4–6 people on a special occasion. A large brill could be cooked in exactly the same way although its flavour is not as good.

1 chicken turbot, cleaned	1oz (25g) butter
Milk or milk and water to cover	Beurre manié to thicken (see p.207)
1 slice of lemon	1 tablespoon (15ml) fresh parsley, chopped
Pinch of saffron	
Sea salt and freshly milled pepper	4oz (125g) whole prawns, to garnish

Place the turbot in a large frying-pan or roasting tin, dark side downwards. Cover with milk, or with half milk and half water. Add the lemon slice and saffron. Season with salt and pepper and dot with the butter. Bring to the boil and simmer very gently for about 15 minutes until the flesh has lost its transparency and comes easily away from the bone. Remove the fish from the cooking liquor to a serving platter and keep warm.

Bring the poaching liquor to the boil, discarding the lemon slice and reduce a little. Thicken with beurre manié and check the seasoning. Pour over the waiting fish and serve immediately with chopped parsley and prawns.

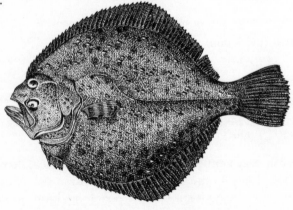

Turbot

Turbot Steaks in Watercress Sauce (serves 4)

This old Cornish recipe is typical of the way turbot was once served in the homes of the gentry.

4 turbot steaks
Cold water to cover

1 medium onion, sliced

For watercress sauce

1oz (25g) butter
1oz (25g) flour
½pt (300ml) cooking liquor
1 bunch of watercress, washed and trimmed

Sea salt and freshly milled pepper
3 tablespoons (3 × 15ml) double cream

Place the fish steaks in a frying-pan and just cover with water. Poach very gently with the onion for about 8 minutes, or until cooked. Remove the fish with a draining spoon and discard the skin and bones. Reserve the cooking liquor. Arrange the turbot on a serving platter and keep warm. Melt the butter in a small saucepan and stir in the flour. Cook for 1 minute, then gradually add ½pt (300ml) of the reserved cooking liquor. Continue cooking until the sauce is smooth and thick. Chop the watercress and add to the sauce. Season to taste and add the cream. Pour over the waiting fish and heat in a fairly hot oven (400°F, 200°C, gas mark 6) for about 10 minutes, or glaze under a hot grill for a few minutes. Serve immediately.

WALES

Caernarvon Castle, North Wales

Early man in Wales found seafood of all kinds: the long coastline and fast-flowing rivers ensured a plentiful supply of both sea and freshwater fish, while the predominantly rocky shores were a natural home for lobsters and crabs.

Early methods of catching fish have survived particularly strongly in Wales, virtually unchanged for 2,000 years. At low tide, lines of basket-work putcher weirs for catching salmon can be seen extending into the Severn Estuary from the suspension bridge. On the fast ebb tide the salmon hurtles into the putcher and gets stuck. Kype traps are much bigger than the putcher, but work on the same principle. They will catch anything from the largest salmon or conger eel to the smallest sprat. These traditional methods on the Severn may not continue much longer, however, because the fishermen cannot get local supplies of the withy needed to weave the traps. Also, if the proposed Severn Barrage is constructed, it will dramatically alter the character of the estuary; the ebb tides may become slower and the low tides may not fall enough so that the putchers and kypes simply will not work.

Caesar and Pliny wrote about the strong Welsh coracles made of animal skin stretched over a willow frame and, although their once widespread use throughout Wales has now diminished, their descendants can still be seen on three Welsh rivers – the Teifi, Tywi and Taf. The tradition of seine netting continues in the estuaries of the Teifi, Tywi, Conwy and Dee.

By the Norman Conquest herring fishing was well established in Wales as a part-time, seasonal, inshore occupation, when the herring catch was at its best and men could be spared from their agricultural activities. Some offshore fishing took place in the autumn, but probably the only port to have a properly developed herring industry in the Middle Ages was Aberystwyth on Cardigan Bay, which remained the busiest fishing harbour in Wales until the end of the 19th century. In 1724, the herring fishery at Aberystwyth was 'so exceedingly abundant that a thousand barrels have been taken in one night'.

The 16th century was the era of the great herring fishing explosion all along the Welsh coast, although Swansea and Cardiff did not develop as important fishing ports until the late 18th century, when the great herring shoals were declining. Milford Haven only realised its potential after the Great Western Railway's thousand-foot fish dock was opened there in 1888. With coal from the Welsh coalfields, Milford was able to run a large fleet of steam trawlers by the end of the century and proved of major importance during World War I; catches were sent to Billingsgate by a special daily train service. Returning to normal after 1918, Milford trawlers ranged from Bear Island in the Arctic to the Moroccan coast.

Five fish were traditionally served on Welsh tables: from the sea, mackerel and herring; from the river, trout, salmon and sewin (the Welsh name for sea trout). Cockles were a common food for coastal dwellers and are still of some importance in Carmarthen Bay. The mention of cockles still produces a faraway look in the eyes of many inhabitants of Llanelli, who eat them with tremendous enthusiasm and relish. I was told exactly where to buy them and how to serve them, so at 9 o'clock in the morning I was in Llanelli market eating my way through bags of delicious fresh cockles! Winkles and limpets were another source of free food for coastal dwellers as were razor-shells, which are still treasured in Wales, where they are baked in their shells and dressed with lemon juice and butter. Also, the oyster fishing industry of Mumbles and Port Einon on Gower flourished in the mid-19th century.

Today, most species of British fish can be caught along the Welsh coast, although the commonest are the thornback ray or skate, sea bass and flounder in summer and whiting and sand dabs in winter. An increasing quantity of dogfish is being caught off the south coast in Carmarthen Bay and off the coast of Pembrokeshire, most of which finds its way to London and the fish and chip shops. The saying is that

'Londoners will eat anything fried in batter'! Tope and spur dog, varieties of shark, are also caught in Carmarthen Bay.

Much of the coastline of Wales is now under threat from unsympathetic developers. The National Trust has identified nearly 300 miles as needing urgent protection and aims to acquire as much as possible for future generations to enjoy. A special 'Wales Coastline Appeal', which comes under the umbrella of the Trust's Enterprise Neptune Appeal, was set up to raise money to do this. It is particularly poignant that the very first piece of land acquired by the National Trust was at Dinas Oleu near Barmouth in Gwynedd 90 years ago. From this small beginning, the Trust now owns and cares for many thousands of acres of beautiful coast and countryside in Wales.

Baked Sea Bass from Porth-clais   (serves 4)

Sea or salmon bass is caught all around the Welsh coast. In season from June to March, it is at its best from June until September.

Bass is caught in St Bride's Bay in Dyfed where the National Trust owns $15\frac{1}{2}$ miles of the coast and protects a further $8\frac{1}{2}$ miles. The tiny inlet of Porth-clais, owned by the National Trust near St David's Head, was bought in 1974 with Enterprise Neptune funds. A breakwater at the entrance to Porth-clais harbour keeps out the worst of the tidal surge.

It is said that bass should be prepared for the table like salmon, but the flesh is a little softer. If very large, the fish can be filleted or cut into steaks and baked, grilled or fried, but it is usually bought whole and then baked, with or without stuffing, or steamed. Sea bass is also excellent barbecued. Most of the recipes for dealing with it are designed to enhance its flavour, using herbs, garlic, onion or fruit.

1 $2\frac{1}{2}$–3lb (1.2–1.4kg) sea bass, cleaned and scaled	2 cloves garlic, chopped
3 tablespoons (3 × 15ml) olive oil	1oz (25g) toasted almonds, chopped
White part of 1 small leek, chopped	1 tablespoon (15ml) fresh parsley, chopped

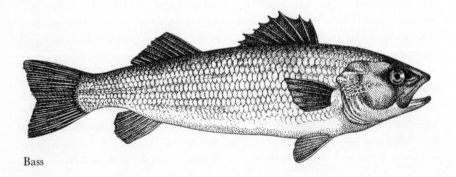

Bass

1 tablespoon (15ml) fresh tarragon, chopped	Sea salt and freshly milled black pepper
Grated rind and juice of 1 lemon	1oz (25g) brown breadcrumbs
1 wineglass dry white wine	

Place the prepared fish on an oiled baking dish. Combine the leek, garlic, almonds, parsley and tarragon and stuff the cavity of the fish with the mixture. Brush with the remaining olive oil and pour over the lemon juice and white wine. Sprinkle with the lemon rind and season well, then sprinkle over the breadcrumbs. Bake in a fairly hot oven (400°F, 200°C, gas mark 6) for 25–30 minutes, basting with the oil and juices halfway through cooking time.

Penclawdd Cockles

Cockles were popular with the Romans in Wales; excavated sites have revealed vast quantities of their shells. They have remained a common food for coastal dwellers throughout the centuries, and there is still a sizeable cockle industry at the Burry Inlet village of Penclawdd on the north coast of the Gower peninsula near Llanelli, one of the three main cockle fisheries in Britain.

Traditionally, cockling has been women's work, but as local industry declined in the area and the collieries began to close, more and more men were forced to join the women out on Llanrhidian Sands and cockling became the main occupation of the whole village of Penclawdd. The cockle beds lie 2 or 3 miles out, on the far side of Llanrhidian Marsh, criss-crossed by gullies and small streams, and with a treacherous incoming tide. The National Trust bought a thousand acres of these salt marshes in 1967 with Enterprise Neptune funds.

Cockling is hard and uncomfortable work; in winter the sands might well be covered by a layer of ice. Cockles are still gathered in the old traditional way with a hand rake or 'cran', a sickle-shaped iron scraper or 'scrap' and a riddle or sieve to regulate the size of the cockles. Those that are big enough are packed into sacks. All professional gatherers must be licensed and cockling here is governed by very strict regulations. Fifty years ago the journey across the wide sands and marshes to the cockle beds was made by donkey but as the demand for cockles increased, horses and carts began to take their place. Today, Landrovers and tractors have only recently replaced many of the horses.

The cooking of the cockles used to be done in the gatherer's own garden, but now each gatherer has a sterilising plant where the cockles are washed, boiled in buckets under high pressure steam and shelled, ready to be refrigerated. You may still find cockles sold alive in some parts of South Wales, but it is more common to see them cooked and shelled.

Penclawdd cockles are renowned for their flavour and tenderness; delicious eaten straight from the bag with pepper and vinegar, they could soon be a taste of the past. The villagers were very worried about pollution in the estuary when I was at Penclawdd last spring. The cockle beds had moved to the other side and were more difficult to get at, so no one knows what the future may hold. Even now, more and more cockles sold in Wales originate in Norfolk and are transported live to Wales.

To Cook Penclawdd Cockles *(serves 1–2)*

The way they cook cockles in this area is to fry some fresh breadcrumbs and chopped spring onions in butter in a heavy pan until the crumbs are crisp and golden. Quickly stir in some freshly-boiled cockles and season with pepper and salt. Cover the pan with a lid and shake vigorously over the heat for a few minutes until the cockles are warmed through. Serve with a generous sprinkling of chopped parsley and eat with home-made bread and yellow, salted Welsh butter. (If you want to cook your own live cockles see pp.183–184.)

Porthmadog Cockles *(serves 1–2)*

Like laverbread, cockles were sold door-to-door in the villages around the estuaries where they were gathered. Cockles already boiled and shelled were carried in a wooden pail balanced on the seller's head; the live cockles were sold from large baskets carried on the arm.

This recipe for cockles and eggs comes from the Porthmadog Cricieth area, also noted for its cockles. The rich fish and egg mixture was eaten between slices of barley bread or oatcakes as a special treat. In the past, women would walk from Penrhyndeudraeth in Snowdonia to Porthmadog to sell cockles. They would knock on doors, dancing and singing the following rhyme:

> *'Cockles and eggs, thin oat cakes,*
> *The girls of Penrhyn doing the shakes!'*

6oz (175g) cockles, cooked and shelled

Bacon fat

2 eggs, beaten

Freshly milled black pepper

Fry the cockles in a little bacon fat for a few minutes, then pour over the beaten eggs. Stir well with a wooden spoon until the egg is lightly cooked. Season with pepper. Serve immediately with crusty brown bread for lunch or supper.

Gower Cockles and Bacon

(serves 1)

Although the best site for cockles is now at Penclawdd, there is another area further west, which used to be more important. Known as the Three Rivers Inlet, where the rivers Taf, Tywi and Gwendraeth meet, the cockle beds on the windswept sands at Laugharne, Llanstephan and Ferryside still produce some cockles. The National Trust owns a small piece of land near Ferryside and Llansaint at St Ishmaels.

The combination of cockles and bacon is delicious and very popular in South Wales. Sometimes the cockles are sprinkled with oatmeal before being fried.

2 rashers fat smoked streaky bacon	Freshly milled black pepper
$\frac{1}{4}$pt (150ml) freshly boiled cockles	Slice of hot brown toast

Fry the bacon gently in a frying-pan until it has yielded plenty of fat and is brown and crisp. Remove from the pan and keep warm. Add the cockles to the pan and cook them in the bacon fat for a few minutes until they are lightly browned on the outside. Season with black pepper and serve immediately on the brown toast garnished with the bacon rashers.

Welsh Cockle Pie from South Pembrokeshire

(serves 4)

2pts (1.2 litres) live cockles	1oz (25g) butter
2 spring onions, chopped finely	1oz (25g) flour
4 rashers smoked streaky bacon, derinded	$\frac{1}{2}$pt (300ml) milk
Sea salt and freshly milled pepper	8oz (225g) shortcrust or flaky pastry

Steam the cockles in a large pan with a very little water until the shells open. Remove the meat and place it in a pie dish. Sprinkle over the chopped onions and the rashers of bacon cut into strips. Season with pepper. Melt the butter in a small saucepan and stir in the flour. Cook for a couple of minutes, then gradually add the milk, stirring all the time. Cook until the sauce is smooth and thick. Season to taste. Roll out the prepared pastry and cover the pie dish in the usual way. Bake in a hot oven (425°F, 220°C, gas mark 7) for 20–30 minutes, or until golden brown.

Cockles with a Cheese Topping   (serves 4)

Cook as above, but instead of making a pastry lid, top with 3oz (75g) grated cheese, preferably Welsh. There are a number of small farms, particularly in Pembrokeshire, producing excellent cheese which can be bought from really good cheese shops all over the country. Some of the Welsh farmhouse cheeses to look out for are Llanboidy, Llangloffan and Ty'n Grug. Excellent Welsh goat's and sheep's cheese is also made.

Devilled Crab from Martin's Haven   (serves 4)

Lobster and crab fishing in Wales has always been essentially a livelihood and the catch was not commonly for local consumption, apart from hotels and restaurants. The Welsh fishermen traditionally prefer to eat crab, which are caught in many places off the predominantly rocky shores of West and North Wales. One such part of the west coast is the Marloes peninsula, situated 12 miles south-west of Haverfordwest and acquired in 1981 by the National Trust, largely with money from Enterprise Neptune. The peninsula consists of about 4 miles of spectacular coast, plus 2 islands, Midland Isle and Gateholm. Marloes Sands, to the east of the islands, is a glorious remote stretch of beach, backed by superb rock and cliff scenery with offshore views of the nature reserves of Skomer and Skokholm Islands.

At the western extremity of the Marloes peninsula is the attractive rocky cove of Martin's Haven, which is the starting place for boat trips to Skomer Island, across the treacherous currents of Jack Sound. The tiny cove with its shingle beach has long been used by local people for fishing and lobster potting.

1lb (450g) crab meat, brown and white mixed	1 tablespoon (1 × 15ml) onion, finely chopped
2 tablespoons (2 × 15ml) stale breadcrumbs	½ green pepper, very finely chopped

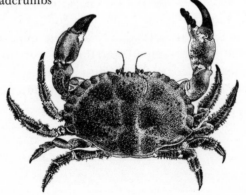

Edible crab

1 dessertspoon (10ml) fresh parsley, chopped

1 rounded teaspoon (5ml) made mustard

1 teaspoon (5ml) horseradish sauce

Pinch of cayenne pepper

Sea salt and freshly milled black pepper

$\frac{1}{4}$pt (150ml) double cream

Few drops of Tabasco sauce

Mix the crab meat with the breadcrumbs. Add the onion, green pepper, parsley, mustard and horseradish sauce. Season to taste with salt, cayenne and black pepper. Moisten with the cream and lastly add a few drops of Tabasco sauce, but do not make the mixture too hot. Pile into a shallow buttered ovenproof dish and bake in a moderate oven (350°F, 180°C, gas mark 4) for about 30 minutes, or until well browned. Serve with hot brown toast, or a rice pilaf and a green salad.

Fishguard Herrings for Supper *(serves 4)*

The humble herring has been extremely important to the people living all along the west coast of Wales. Places like Fishguard and Aberporth in South Wales, Aberystwyth and Aberdyfi in West Wales and Nefyn and Aberdaron in North Wales were once noted for their herring catches. In the 17th century salt for the herrings was produced by boiling freshwater-brine with seawater in the North Wales river mouths, but even though salt was in reasonably good supply, the tax upon it proved a burden on the herring industry for nearly 200 years.

Fishguard derives its name from the Norse 'Fiskrgardr', but the town's Welsh name is 'Abergwaun' and when fresh herrings were sold in the streets, the sellers would cry 'Sgadan [herrings] Abergwaun' as they trundled barrowloads of gleaming herrings up the steep hill from the quay of the little grey town. Fishguard also had a red herring industry at one time; the old salting and smoking house down on the quay in Lower Town is now the Yacht Club. Herrings are again being caught and brought in, together with large quantities of dogfish and hake.

This recipe for herrings, with its Scandinavian combination of fish and apples, is taken from Bobby Freeman's fascinating book of Welsh food, *First Catch Your Peacock*. Bobby runs the Welsh Cookery Centre at Llangoedmor, near Cardigan.

4 medium herrings, cleaned

1 rounded teaspoon (5ml) made mustard

Salt and freshly milled pepper

1$\frac{1}{2}$oz (40g) butter

2lb (900g) potatoes, peeled and sliced

1 large onion, sliced

1 large cooking apple, sliced

1 teaspoon (5ml) fresh sage, chopped

3 tablespoons (3 × 15ml) tarragon vinegar

$\frac{1}{4}$pt (150ml) water

$\frac{1}{4}$pt (150ml) dry cider

Fillet the fish and spread the inside flesh with mustard. Season well with salt and pepper and roll up. Lightly butter an ovenproof dish with ½oz (12g) butter and line it with some of the potato slices. Add the sliced onion and the sliced apple and place the rolled fillets on top. Sprinkle with chopped sage, vinegar and more seasoning. Cover with the remaining slices of potato. Add a mixture of cider and boiling water – do not even half fill the dish or it becomes too watery. Dot with the remaining butter, cover with a lid or foil and bake in a moderate oven (350°F, 180°C, gas mark 4) for 45 minutes. Remove the lid and allow the top to brown for a further 30 minutes.

This is good served hot with a green salad or green vegetable.

Roast Penbryn Herrings with Brown Mustard Sauce (serves 6)

From the Middle Ages until the last century, Penbryn Beach, on the west coast of Wales, was the scene of considerable maritime and commercial activity. In 1777 a ship called the *Blessing* was built here for the purpose of Irish Sea trading. Huge quantities of salted or smoked herring were exported, mainly to Ireland.

Most households inland and on the coast would buy about 500 fresh herrings, usually in November when the fish were at their best, and salt them for the winter. A layer of salt was put in the bottom of a barrel, followed by a layer of unwashed herrings. These layers were continued until the barrel was full, then the top was placed on the barrel and the fish were stored in a dark, cool place for at least 2 months. When required for use, the herrings were washed repeatedly in a tub of fresh water and then left overnight in more water. Next day, they were hung up by a skewer through their eyes in the chimney nook to dry.

The most acceptable way of cooking salted herrings in the counties of South and West Wales, was to roast them individually in front of an open fire by means of a long toasting fork or a pair of fire tongs. In some districts of Cardiganshire and Carmarthenshire, they were roasted in rather a unique way; the fish were placed across the horizontal bars of a special iron grilling frame known as an 'alch', suspended over an open peat fire. The herrings were allowed to cook slowly by direct heat until well cooked and were then eaten with 'bwdran' or thin flummery and potatoes in their jackets for mid-day dinner or for supper. This was a very popular dish during the winter months.

Mustard has been served as an accompaniment to herrings for centuries. This recipe is from *Lloyd George's Favourite Dishes*, a recipe book compiled by Cricieth Women's Institute and published in the 1920s.

6 medium-sized fresh herrings, cleaned	Sea salt
1oz (25g) butter	Sprigs of fresh parsley

For the brown mustard sauce

1½oz (40g) butter	1 teaspoon (5ml) vinegar
1½oz (40g) flour	1 teaspoon (5ml) made mustard
1pt (600ml) fish stock	Pinch of cayenne pepper
Juice of 1 lemon	Sea salt

Scale the fish and cut off their heads. Wipe with a clean cloth and make 3 incisions diagonally across the fish, cutting down to the backbone but not through it. Grill quickly under a very hot grill with a very little butter until brown on each side. Dust lightly with salt, garnish with parsley and serve with brown mustard sauce and brown crusty bread.

To prepare the sauce, melt the butter in a saucepan and stir in the flour. Cook until golden brown, then gradually add the stock. Cook until the sauce is smooth and thick. Bring to the boil and add the lemon juice, vinegar and mustard. Season with cayenne pepper and salt. Strain and serve.

Lleyn Sweet Pickled Herrings *(serves 6)*

The Lleyn peninsula, where Caernarvonshire extends its arm towards Ireland, is said by many of its inhabitants to be a magic place, and there is certainly the same strange Celtic atmosphere found in Anglesey, the St David's area of Wales, Ireland and Cornwall. Many of its people use Welsh as a first language. I have many childhood memories of happy holidays spent at Porth Neigwl or Hell's Mouth and it was wonderful to return there and find it largely unchanged.

The National Trust owns about 4 miles of coastline at the tip of the Lleyn, beginning just to the south of Porth Oer, often called the Whistling Sands, and 2 tiny islands just off the coast – Dinas Bach and Dinas Fach. On the south coast of the Lleyn the National Trust owns over 400 acres of coastal land on the Plas-yn-Rhiw Estate. The estate is centred on a small manor house, medieval with Tudor and Georgian additions, in an idyllic position overlooking Porth Neigwl.

Many coastal places on the Lleyn peninsula were noted for their herring catches until the beginning of the 20th century, when the herring began to disappear with the coming of the large trawlers. The fish were cured in the sun on the roofs of cottages ready for the winter to avoid starvation. One such cove is Porth Gwylan, a mile east of Tudweiliog on the north-facing coast of the Lleyn, which was bought by the National Trust in 1982 partly with Enterprise Neptune funds. The Trust owns the harbour of Porth Gwylan as well as several acres of low cliffs and clifftop. Rusting capstans at Porth Gwylan tell of beach-launched fishing craft in the past, but no one puts to sea from there now.

This Welsh recipe for pickled herrings, which comes from the Lleyn, is similar to many others from all over the country, but a little black treacle is added before baking. Black treacle used to be the main sweetening agent in Welsh cookery, as it was in Scotland and the North of England, because it was cheaper than refined sugar. Treacle was sold by the jugful in Welsh grocers' stores.

6 fresh herrings, cleaned	Sea salt
1pt (600ml) cider vinegar	1 medium onion, sliced
$\frac{1}{4}$pt (150ml) cold water	1 teaspoon (5ml) black treacle
1 teaspoon (5ml) pickling spice	1 teaspoon (5ml) cornflour

Cut off the heads and tails of the fish and split them open. Arrange the fish in an ovenproof dish and cover with the vinegar and water. Add the spice, salt and onion. Dissolve the black treacle in a little warm water and pour it over the herrings followed by the cornflour also dissolved in a little water. Bake in a slow oven (300°F, 150°C, gas mark 2) for about 4 hours or until the small bones have 'melted' away. Serve cold with toast or oatcakes or jacket potatoes for a more substantial meal.

Welsh Laver Bread

The edible seaweed, laver, is found on the beaches of South and West Wales. Local people gather and process their own as they have done for centuries. Alexis Soyer, the French chef of the Reform Club in London, was delighted when he discovered this unusual food in the middle of the last century. He made it a smart society dish for a while, but it is only the Welsh who have retained a liking for it into modern times.

The real centre of the laver trade is Penclawdd near Llanelli, the last village of north Gower before the peninsula joins the mainland. Gathering it for large-scale processing can be frustrating, because laver may grow on a beach one year and not the next, and can get smothered by sand in heavy seas. It cannot be collected during stormy weather either, so its supply is somewhat erratic. Picking laver is hard and uncomfortable and working in the processing plant on the Loughor Estuary at Penclawdd, run by the Roberts brothers, is also hard as the seaweed has to be washed and washed again at least three times before boiling. In the past it was a well-organised trade; there were large drying houses built along the shore where the weed was cured so that it would keep well. Today the returns are small, despite the luxury prices often charged in speciality shops. Local supplies are not enough, so dried laver still comes down from Scotland, as it has since 1880.

Once fresh laver has been rinsed many times and steeped for hours in water, it is boiled for about 5 hours, the excess water is drained off and the pulp is stirred in a saucepan, traditionally with a wooden spoon or a silver fork. If you are cooking laver yourself at home, it can be cooked for 40 minutes in a pressure cooker. This brownish-black purée is sold in Wales as laverbread.

Cellophane-wrapped packets of laverbread mixed with oatmeal can be bought in the markets of South and South-west Wales, especially Swansea, and lately in supermarkets and some speciality food shops. It can be purchased by mail order fresh or tinned from Drangway Laverbread in Swansea; their tinned laver is sold by Harrods and Fortnum and Mason. Fresh laverbread can also be sent by Datapost by John Sullivan, a Welshman from Abergavenny who is an excellent supplier of fine fish, vegetables and groceries. Until recently laverbread was also sold from door to door locally around Swansea and Llanelli by women carrying the little paper-wrapped shilling packages of laver in huge wicker baskets.

Laverbread goes particularly well with salmon, white fish, lobster, scallops, oysters and prawns. Season it with lemon juice and serve hot or cold. It is also excellent heated and spread on fried bread or toast with a rasher of crisp bacon or put into soups.

Laverbread Cakes (*serves 4–6*)

This is the most usual way to serve laverbread in Wales.

1lb (450g) fresh or tinned laverbread   6 rashers smoked back bacon
4oz (175g) fine oatmeal

Mix the laverbread and the oatmeal together and form into little cakes about 2in (5cm) across and ¾in (2cm) thick. Flatten and shape them with a palette knife. Fry the bacon rashers and keep warm. Slide the laver cakes into the hot bacon fat and fry fairly quickly for 2–3 minutes on each side, shaping and patting the cakes with a palette knife as they fry. Lift out carefully and serve immediately with the bacon rashers.

Laver Sauce

This is the traditional Welsh accompaniment for mutton and lamb grazed on sea-shore pastures. It is also excellent with salt duck, a traditional Welsh dish. To make the sauce, laverbread is mixed with

Seville orange or lemon juice, butter and some mutton or chicken stock. By substituting cream or milk for the stock, this sauce is delicious with salmon and sewin (sea trout) or with shellfish and lobster.

2 cupfuls fresh or tinned laverbread $\frac{1}{2}$pt (300ml) double cream or milk
$\frac{1}{2}$oz (12g) butter Juice of 1 Seville orange
$\frac{1}{2}$oz (12g) flour

Melt the butter in a saucepan and stir in the flour. Cook for a couple of minutes, then gradually add the cream or milk and orange juice. When the sauce is smooth and creamy, beat in the laver.

Variation: For real devotees of laverbread, omit the flour and cream and make a purée of laverbread with a knob of butter and Seville orange juice, or sweet orange juice sharpened with lemon juice.

Laver Salad

This way of serving laver probably dates back to medieval times. It makes an unusual starter and one that Bobby Freeman popularised in her restaurant. This recipe comes from *First Catch Your Peacock*. 'Dress some prepared laver with a little olive oil and lemon juice or wine vinegar and a grind or two of black pepper. Serve with fingers of dry toast.'

Baked Stuffed Mackerel from Mwnt (serves 1)

Mackerel is caught all around the Welsh coast from late June until early September, although it has not been as plentiful the last few years because of overfishing by large trawlers. Mackerel should be eaten very fresh – straight from the sea in fact – or its flavour will not be as good. The fish should be firm, stiff and brilliantly coloured with bright eyes. Once its colour and eyes have dulled, mackerel is not worth buying.

Before World War II, mackerel was very plentiful indeed in Cardigan Bay. One of the places where the fish was landed was at Mwnt, about 4 miles north of Cardigan, which is now part of the Heritage Coastline. It is an area of outstanding natural beauty with short clifftop walks, a small hill and a sandy beach. The National Trust owns nearly 100 acres of land here, part of it purchased in 1971 with Enterprise Neptune funds.

The traditional Welsh ways of cooking mackerel are to fry, grill or bake it. In this recipe the mackerel can either be left whole or boned and stuffed. Use fresh fennel or parsley in the stuffing.

1 very fresh mackerel, cleaned

½oz (12g) butter

1 teaspoon (5ml) grated onion

2 tablespoons (2 × 15ml) fresh breadcrumbs

1 teaspoon (5ml) fresh herbs, finely chopped

A little grated lemon rind

Sea salt and freshly milled pepper

Cut the head and tail off the mackerel and wash and dry it well. Melt half the butter in a small saucepan and soften the onion. Stir in the crumbs, herbs and lemon rind and season well. Pack this mixture into the cavity of the fish, season the outside flesh well and dot with the remaining butter. Wrap securely in kitchen foil and place in a baking dish or tin. Bake in a fairly hot oven (400°F, 200°C, gas mark 6) for 20–30 minutes. When the mackerel is cooked, unwrap the foil and place the fish on a hot serving dish with any cooking juices. Serve with a jacket potato and hot beetroot.

Mackerel Fillets the Porthmadog Way (serves 6)

In the area around Porthmadog on the Traeth Bach Estuary in North Wales, mackerel were often cooked in olive oil. From early times, until the end of the last century, Porthmadog was an important port, trading largely with the Mediterranean. Consequently, olive oil was readily available in and around the port.

3 large fresh mackerel, filleted

Seasoned flour

3 tablespoons (3 × 15ml) olive oil

1 medium onion, finely chopped

2oz (50g) mushrooms, finely chopped

1 clove garlic, crushed

Sea salt and freshly milled pepper

1 teaspoon (5ml) fresh parsley, chopped

1 teaspoon (5ml) fresh thyme, chopped

2 teaspoons (2 × 5ml) vinegar

Dry the mackerel fillets well and dip them in seasoned flour. Heat 2 tablespoons (2 × 15ml) olive oil in a frying-pan until really hot and fry the fish until golden brown on both sides. Arrange on a warm serving dish. Add the remaining oil to the cleaned pan and soften the onion in it. Add the mushrooms and garlic and cook very slowly for about 5 minutes. Season the mixture well and stir in the herbs and vinegar. Arrange a spoonful of this mixture down the centre of each fillet and serve immediately with new potatoes and sliced tomatoes fried in butter.

Steamed Teifi Salmon

(serves 2)

Gerald the Welshman, writing towards the end of the 12th century, noted that 'The noble river Teivi flows here, and abounds with the finest salmon, more than any other river in Wales . . .'

The great feature of salmon fishing in these parts has for centuries been the use of coracles and nets. The coracle is a light manoeuverable craft once seen on almost every Welsh river. The fishermen go out in pairs to fish for salmon from coracles. Each has his own craft, steering it with a paddle in one hand and holding one end of a drag net in the other. Once a fish is caught, the net is lifted out of the water, the two coracles draw together and the salmon is taken out. The design of the coracles and the nets varies from river to river depending on the conditions – the speed of current, depth of water and so on.

This recipe is from Cenarth, the village at the great salmon leap on the River Teifi. It is an excellent way of cooking salmon and can be served hot with parsley or fennel sauce or cold with bread and butter. A double saucepan or proper steamer can of course be used instead of the following more primitive, but nevertheless effective, method.

2 thick salmon steaks	A few fennel leaves
Sea salt and freshly milled pepper	Parsley sauce to serve (see p.216)
1oz (25g) butter	

Place the salmon steaks on a buttered enamel plate. Season them well and top with a large knob of butter and a few fennel leaves. Cover with another plate or a saucepan lid and place over a pan of boiling water. Steam the fish for about 15 minutes depending on the thickness of the steaks, but make sure that they are not overcooked. Serve hot with parsley sauce or leave to get cold and serve with mayonnaise and bread and butter.

Salmon Cooked in Milk

(serves 4)

In Welsh cottage kitchens they poached salmon or sewin, Welsh sea trout, in milk to counteract its dryness.

2lb (900g) fresh salmon	$\frac{1}{2}$ bayleaf
Sea salt	Milk to cover

Salt the salmon well and place it in a pan which just fits it. Add the $\frac{1}{2}$ bayleaf and pour over enough milk to cover the fish. Bring slowly to the boil. Simmer very gently for 5 minutes then remove from the heat and leave the salmon in the milk for a further 10 minutes. Test to see if the fish is cooked – the inside should just be losing its transparent look. If it is, remove the fish and keep warm. Use some of the fish cooking liquor to make fennel or parsley sauce (see pp.215 and 216). The remaining liquor can be used to make a fish soup.

Cut the salmon into 4 thick slices and serve warm with jacket potatoes and the sauce of your choice. The fish can also be served cold with fresh cream.

Breconshire Salmon and Onions *(serves 1)*

The National Trust owns some 8,000 acres of the mountain range of Brecon Beacons. When I visited the area in March there was a sprinkling of snow on the tops of the mountains and they looked spectacular against a brilliant blue sky.

This recipe was a traditional way of cooking salmon from the River Usk. It is based on one taken from S. Minwell Tibbot's book, *Welsh Fare* produced for the Welsh Folk Museum at St Fagans' near Cardiff.

1 thick salmon steak	1 small onion, sliced
Bacon fat	Fresh parsley, finely chopped

Place the fish in lukewarm salted water and bring slowly to simmering point. Remove from the water and drain well. Remove all the skin and the bones. Flake the flesh. Heat some bacon fat in a frying-pan and fry the onion gently. Add the flaked salmon and fry for a further few minutes until the onion is cooked. Garnish with chopped parsley and serve with crusty brown home-baked bread and Welsh butter.

Hot Poached Sewin with Fennel Sauce *(serves 4–6)*

Wales is famous for its salmon or sea trout known locally as sewin, although nobody seems to know why, as the Welsh word is 'gwyniedyn'. In the past, the name 'Welsh Salmon' was also applied to it. Their flavour lies somewhere between salmon and trout; they are in fact the sea-going version of the wild brown trout and their taste is superb.

Sewin is in season between February and August and comes in all sizes from the babies of less than 1lb (450g) in weight, known as 'shiglin', to about 3lb (1.4kg) known as 'twlpin' found in late July and August, to fully grown fish, which can equal a salmon in size, known as 'gwencin', which are found in May and June and again in September. The large sewin tend to have less flavour and the flesh may have turned a pale fawny pink instead of a good clear pink, which means the fish has been in the river too long, although Welsh anglers claim that Welsh rivers are incomparably the best for large sewin.

Salmon fishing in Wales is on the decrease due to lack of fish and polluted water. Mrs Duncan Fitzwilliams who runs the Cenarth Fishing Museum in West Wales, tells me that rod and line fishermen virtually only catch sewin today. The traditional way of fishing for sewin on Welsh rivers was in coracles, but there are very few left. In E. Donovan's *Descriptive Excursions through South Wales and Monmouthshire, 1805*, there is an interesting account of Swansea market: 'Half a dozen families seated upon the panniers of their ponies . . . rode hastily down the market place with a supply of sewen . . . conveyed from Pontardulais, about ten miles to the westward . . . abounding with fish during the summer, being caught in the coracle fisheries by peasantry.'

Sewin used to be so plentiful in the past that it was not considered a luxury food by the English gentry living in Wales. Therefore, there are genuine Welsh traditions for its cookery. In south Pembrokeshire, they used to add chopped, blanched fennel leaves to a white sauce to serve with sewin, salmon or mackerel, as in this recipe. The older way was just to mix the blanched feathery leaves of fennel, which grows wild in parts of Pembrokeshire, with melted butter and pour it over the fish.

1 salmon trout weighing 2–3lb (900–1.4kg)	Court bouillon to cover (see p.208)

For the fennel sauce

2 tablespoons (2 × 15ml) fennel leaves	$\frac{1}{4}$pt (150ml) milk or cream
1oz (25g) butter	$\frac{1}{4}$pt (150ml) cooking liquor
1oz (25g) flour	Sea salt and freshly milled pepper

Clean the fish, leaving the head and tail intact. Place it in a large pan or fish kettle with enough lukewarm court-bouillon to cover. Bring slowly to simmering point, cover with a lid and let the fish simmer for 5 minutes. Turn off the heat and leave for 10–15 minutes.

Meanwhile make the sauce. Wash the fennel leaves thoroughly, put them in boiling water and simmer for a couple of minutes until tender. Cool, strain and chop the leaves finely. Melt the butter in a small saucepan and stir in the flour. Cook for 1–2 minutes, then gradually add the milk or cream and some of the fish cooking liquor. Cook until the sauce is thick and smooth, then stir in the fennel and season to taste.

Remove the fish from the cooking liquor and place on a warm serving dish. Serve with new potatoes and a green vegetable.

This dish is also very good served cold. Leave the fish to get completely cold in its cooking liquor.

Bobby Freeman's Cucumber and Lettuce Sauce for Sewin

This sauce is from Bobby Freeman's *First Catch Your Peacock* and is good with hot poached or baked sewin or salmon.

1oz (25g) butter	Good pinch of tarragon
1 small cucumber, diced	Beurre manié to thicken
1 onion, finely chopped	$\frac{1}{4}$pt (150ml) single cream
1 small lettuce, finely shredded	Sea salt and freshly milled pepper
$\frac{1}{2}$pt (300ml) chicken stock	

Melt the butter in a saucepan and soften the cucumber and onion in it. Add the shredded lettuce, followed by the stock and the tarragon. Simmer for about 20 minutes until the vegetables are soft. Liquidise in a blender or push through a sieve. Return to the saucepan and bring to the boil. Thicken the sauce with a little beurre manié and add the cream. Season to taste and reheat, but do not boil or the sauce will curdle.

Baked Teifi Sewin Stuffed with Thyme and Parsley

(serves 8–10)

The most popular way of serving sewin or salmon in the past was to cut it into steaks and fry these in plenty of bacon fat or salty Welsh butter to counteract their dryness. No sauce was served with the fish, just more butter on the hot flesh to bring out the flavour. Locally baked brown rough-textured bread was eaten with it. In the Cenarth area near Newcastle Emlyn in West Wales boiled new potatoes and broad beans were traditionally served with fried sewin.

This recipe for stuffing and baking belongs to the Cenarth area and is an excellent way of cooking large sewin which might lack flavour. The fish is enhanced by the herb stuffing.

1 large salmon trout weighing 4–5lb (1.8–2.3kg)	2oz (50g) fresh white breadcrumbs
$\frac{1}{2}$ onion, finely chopped	Grated rind of $\frac{1}{2}$ a lemon
1 hard-boiled egg, chopped	Sea salt and freshly milled pepper
3 tablespoons (3 × 15ml) fresh parsley, finely chopped	Milk to mix
1 teaspoon (5ml) dried thyme	2oz (50g) butter

Clean the fish in the usual way, leaving the head and tail intact. Dry well with kitchen paper. Mix the onion, egg, parsley, thyme, breadcrumbs and lemon rind together in a bowl. Season well and add enough milk to bind together. Stuff the cavity of the fish. Butter a large sheet of kitchen foil and lay the salmon trout on it. Dot with the rest of the butter and wrap up firmly. Lay the parcel on a baking-tray and bake in a moderate oven for about 1 hour. Open the parcel and insert a skewer to see if the fish is cooked; if not, cook for a further 10 minutes. When cooked, unwrap the fish and lay it on a warm serving dish. Serve with pats of parsley butter and new potatoes.

Cenarth Smoked Sewin

The village of Cenarth, on the banks of the River Teifi in West Wales by the famous falls where the river shoots in a series of foaming rapids, has been associated with sewin and salmon for centuries. At one time the Cenarth area was full of small fish smokeries, for this was the only method of preserving the abundant supply of fish. Gradually the small smokeries fell into disuse and were lost, but sewin and salmon are being smoked again nearby, at one of the best smokeries in the country in Llechryd. Mr and Mrs Kelsey started the now famous Cenarth Smokery in 1974 at a time when no one else in the area was smoking the local salmon and sewin. Now, as well as smoking salmon and sewin, they are also curing and smoking bacon and hams.

Smoked sewin is thought by many, including me, to be superior in flavour to smoked salmon. Serve in exactly the same way: cut very thinly and accompanied with thin brown bread and butter, wedges of lemon and freshly milled black pepper.

New Quay Skate with Black Butter (serves 6)

Skate, thornback ray and roker have been very popular fish in Britain since the 12th century and they are caught in large numbers off the coast of South and West Wales, particularly Carmarthen and Cardigan Bays. They are in season throughout the winter months.

Like dogfish, the skate are members of the shark family, with cartilaginous bones, which are very easy to deal with, especially for children. Only the ribbed wings are sold by the fishmonger and the fish is usually gutted and winged by the fishermen out at sea, because it can be three feet in length and almost as broad.

Skate used to be one of the main fish landed in the winter in the tiny picturesque fishing village of New Quay on the west coast of Wales, but when I was there last winter, the fishermen told me they were not being caught in such large numbers. Brill and turbot were now bringing in the cash, plus lobsters and scallops.

Six miles south-west of New Quay the National Trust owns Lochtyn at Llangranog, a farm with about $1\frac{1}{2}$ miles of dramatic cliff, an island, Ynys-Lochtyn, two beaches and a hilltop, Pen-y-Badell, with splendid views of Cardigan Bay.

Skate are easy fish to cook and the sweet pink flesh peels cleanly off the soft wing bones. They are best cooked very simply; either grilled, barbecued, fried or poached and can also be eaten cold with mayonnaise. The texture of the fish is similar to white crab meat so, when cold, it goes very well with crab. Skate with black butter is the classic recipe and is particularly suitable for larger wings. Don't be put off by the slight smell of ammonia when you are cooking skate; it will disappear when the fish is cooked. Some people say that skate should not be eaten very fresh, but all the fishermen I asked told me the opposite. In the past whole skate were hung up to dry in caves in Cornwall and were never attacked by flies, presumably because of their strong smell.

3lb (1.8kg) skate	2 tablespoons (2 × 15ml) wine vinegar
Court bouillon (see p.208)	
4oz (125g) butter	3 tablespoons (3 × 15ml) capers
	Fresh parsley, finely chopped

Cut the skate wings into wedge-shaped pieces and place in a saucepan. Cover with cold court bouillon and bring to the boil. Lower the heat to keep the liquid below simmering point and continue cooking for 15 minutes. Drain the fish and keep warm on a serving dish.

Melt the butter in a frying-pan and cook until it turns a deep golden colour. Pour over the waiting fish. Add the vinegar to the frying-pan, bubble for a few seconds and then pour over the fish. Scatter with capers and parsley and serve immediately with buttered new potatoes.

Fried Skate with Caper Sauce   *(serves 6)*

Small skate wings can be turned in seasoned flour and then fried in butter for about 4 minutes each side. Larger pieces may also be fried, but they should first be cooked briefly in court bouillon as above. Serve with caper sauce (see p.215).

Fried Skate Nobs

Sometimes 'skate nobs' or the cheeks of the skate can be bought at fishmongers, although usually they are the perks of the fisherman and his family. Tossed in seasoned flour, fried in butter and served with lemon, they are delicious.

Poached Skate with Orange and Tarragon Cream Sauce

(serves 6)

3lb (1.4kg) skate wings

Court bouillon (see p.208)

For the orange and tarragon sauce

4oz (125g) unsalted butter

Sea salt and freshly milled pepper

$\frac{1}{4}$pt (150ml) double cream

1 tablespoon (15ml) fresh tarragon, finely chopped

Grated rind and juice of 1 small orange

Cut the skate wings into wedge-shaped pieces and poach in court bouillon for 15 minutes. Drain, place on a serving dish and keep warm.

Melt the butter in a medium-sized frying-pan and add the cream. Stir and cook for about 5 minutes until the sauce is thick, but do not allow the butter to burn. Add the orange rind and juice and season. Lastly stir in the tarragon. Pour a little of the sauce over the waiting fish and serve the remainder in a sauce-boat.

Welsh Trout wrapped in Bacon

(serves 4)

The Welsh have three interesting traditional ways of cooking trout, which were all developed to protect the fish while it was baking in the oven. They must, therefore, belong to the more recent period of Welsh cookery when the oven was an integral part of the fireplace and in daily use; otherwise, freshwater fish would simply have been fried in either butter or bacon fat.

Welsh rivers and streams are fast-flowing and ideal for trout, salmon and sewin. Trout was frequently served for breakfast as it was so plentiful. Quarrymen and miners used to go down to local streams on Sunday mornings and tickle enough trout for breakfast, but now many of the streams have become polluted. Welsh dry-cured bacon prepared at home would have been used in the old days for this dish. Excellent traditionally smoked bacon is again available in the markets of rural Wales.

Freshly caught trout and home-smoked bacon would make this dish superlative, but the method of cooking does improve farmed trout as long as the bacon is good quality and has been properly smoked. Avoid bacon from plastic packs because it is too wet.

4 very fresh trout	8 long thin rashers smoked streaky bacon
Sea salt and freshly milled black pepper	Fresh parsley, finely chopped

Clean the fish, leaving on the heads and tails. Season the cavities well. De-rind the bacon and stretch the rashers a little. Wind 2 rashers around each trout. Arrange the fish close together in an ovenproof dish without a lid. Season with plenty of black pepper and bake in a moderate oven (350°F, 180°C, gas mark 4) for 20 minutes. Serve immediately, sprinkled with chopped parsley.

Baked Trout with Oatmeal (*serves 4*)

This is the second traditional Welsh way of cooking fresh trout. The seasoned oatmeal is used as a covering to protect the fish.

4 fresh trout	Seasoned fine or medium oatmeal
Sea salt and freshly milled black pepper	Fresh parsley, finely chopped
Bacon fat	

Clean the fish, leaving on the head and tails. Dry thoroughly and season the cavities with salt and black pepper. Melt a little bacon fat in an ovenproof dish in the oven. Roll the trout in seasoned oatmeal and arrange them side by side in the melted fat. Cover with a lid or kitchen foil and bake in a fairly hot oven (375°F, 190°C, gas mark 5) for about 20 minutes. Remove the lid or foil and allow to brown. Serve immediately, sprinkled with chopped parsley.

Sea trout

Baked Trout with Onions (serves 4)

This is the third traditional Welsh way of cooking fresh river trout.

4 fresh trout

Sea salt and freshly milled pepper

Bacon fat

1 large onion sliced or fresh chives, chopped

Clean the fish, but do not remove the heads and tails. Season the cavities of the fish lightly. Place the trout in an ovenproof dish and dissolve a little bacon fat in a little warm water. Pour this over the fish. Place the onion slices on top of the fish, or sprinkle with chives. Cover with a lid or foil and bake in a moderately hot oven (375°F, 190°C, gas mark 5) for about 20 minutes. Remove the lid or foil and allow to brown before serving.

NORTHERN IRELAND

Carrickfergus Castle, N. Ireland

Ireland is an island with plenty of loughs and rivers, so fish and shellfish have always been in good supply, forming an essential part of the diet. However, the Irish tend to be rather conservative and although there are plenty of traditional dishes, they are rather modest about them. There are a very small number of Irish cookery books and, despite my pleas on BBC Radio Belfast for traditional Irish seafood recipes, few were forthcoming. It is also very difficult to associate dishes with one particular area of the country.

The National Trust owns some of the most beautiful coastline in Northern Ireland, stretching from the extraordinary Giant's Causeway and the North Antrim Coast round to the unspoilt beauty of Fair Head and Murlough Bay. Further south, the Trust owns two small pieces of coastline, including the village of Kearney, and manages the foreshore of Strangford Lough. Still further south, Murlough Nature Reserve at

Dundrum is managed by the National Trust. Much of this glorious coastline has been purchased with, or with the help of, Enterprise Neptune funds.

Strangford Clam and Potato Soup

For many centuries Strangford Lough was fished by the local population to provide food for themselves and for supplying the Belfast market. Apart from fish such as herring, mackerel, whiting and skate, various kinds of shellfish were marketed from the lough. The decline of the Strangford fisheries seems to have been gradual, although steady, over the years due to overfishing, competition from trawlers, pollution and disease. However, clams and oysters are now both being farmed in the lough very successfully.

The Strangford Lough Wildlife Scheme was started in 1966 by the National Trust to protect the foreshore, initially for the wildfowl, waders and other birds which were under pressure there because in the past many families around the shores of the lough have depended upon the trade of wildfowling for at least part of their livelihood. Today wildfowling on Strangford Lough is only a hobby. The Scheme now is concerned with all aspects of wildlife, including, increasingly, conservation of marine life. The potential for shellfish farming is considerable provided that there is proper management. Strong tidal currents bring microscopic floating life through the narrow channel at the entrance to the lough at Portaferry. This plankton forms food for many species including shellfish, but could easily be destroyed by increased pollution in the narrows and the lough.

18 clams

$\frac{1}{4}$pt (150ml) water

1pt (600ml) milk

$\frac{1}{2}$ leek, finely chopped

1 small carrot, finely chopped

1 celery stick, finely chopped

3 potatoes, finely diced

1 tablespoon (15ml) fresh parsley, finely chopped

$\frac{1}{2}$ teaspoon (2.5ml) fresh thyme, finely chopped

1 bayleaf

Sea salt and freshly milled pepper

Pinch of grated nutmeg

Beurre manié to thicken (see p.207)

Fresh chives, finely chopped to garnish

2 tablespoons (2 × 15ml) double cream

Scrub the clams well to remove all the sand and soak for a few hours in salt water if they have been freshly gathered. Put them in a large pan with a little water, cover with a lid and steam them open. Remove the fish, reserving the cooking liquor. Take out the clam meat from the shells and remove the beards and black parts. Chop up half the clams roughly,

92

keeping the rest whole. Strain the reserved liquor through muslin to remove any grains of sand and pour into a large saucepan with the milk. Add the leek, carrot, celery, potato, parsley, thyme and bayleaf. Season well with salt, pepper and nutmeg. Bring to the boil, then simmer gently for about 20 minutes until the vegetables are tender. Thicken with beurre manié and just before serving add the clams. Heat through very gently and check the seasoning again. Garnish with chopped chives and stir in the cream. Serve immediately with brown soda bread or wholemeal bread.

Portaferry Baked Clams   (serves 6–8)

There has been a revival in the fishing of clams over the last 30 years on the east coast of Northern Ireland: from Donaghadee to Portaferry it is now a thriving industry. Many of the clams sold at Billingsgate come from Ireland and more are exported further afield, particularly to France.

48 large clams	3oz (75g) Irish cheddar, grated
8oz (225g) herb butter (see p.217)	4 tablespoons (4 × 15ml) white or
Sea salt and freshly milled pepper	brown breadcrumbs

Scrub the clams well to remove the sand. Soak for a few hours in salt water. Put them in a large saucepan, cover and steam the shells open. Remove the clams, reserving their liquor for soup, if you wish. Take the meat out of the shells and remove the beards and black parts. Replace the clam meat in half the shells and stand the shells securely in a tin or ovenproof dish filled with sea salt. Top each with a knob of herb butter. Season well and sprinkle cheese and breadcrumbs over the clams. Cook in a fairly hot oven (375°F, 180°C, gas mark 5) for 10 minutes. Serve immediately with a glass of Guinness and plenty of crusty bread.

Dundrum Carpetshell Soup (serves 8)

'Cockles and mussels alive, alive Oh!'

Many of the cockles sold in Ireland and exported to France at an alarming rate are really members of the clam family. Their Latin name is *Venerupis decussata* and they are known locally as 'carpetshells'. They have a smooth surface with a slight ridge running vertically over the shell. Small clams, mussels, scallops or a mixture of any of these shellfish can also be used for this soup, which comes from the coastal village of Dundrum in County Down. Just south of Dundrum is Murlough Nature Reserve, which was established as Ireland's first nature reserve by the National Trust in 1967.

48 carpetshells or cockles
2oz (50g) butter
2oz (50g) flour
2pts (1 litre) cockle cooking liquor
1pt (600ml) milk

1 celery stick, finely chopped
2 tablespoons (2 × 15ml) fresh parsley, finely chopped
Salt and freshly milled pepper
$\frac{1}{4}$pt (150ml) double cream

Steam the cockles open in the usual way (see p.92) and remove the meat, reserving the cooking liquor. Melt the butter in a large saucepan and stir in the flour. Cook for a few minutes, then gradually add the strained cockle cooking liquor and the milk, stirring all the time until smooth. Add the celery and parsley and season to taste. Cook for about 10 minutes or until the celery is tender. Just before serving, add the cockles and stir in the cream. Serve immediately with crusty brown Irish soda bread or wholemeal bread.

Cockle

County Down Boiled Cockles

(allow 4oz [125g] per person)

In many places on Strangford Lough, especially in the northern half which is extremely shallow, cockles may be found lying on or just in the sand. Deeper digging sometimes reveals sand or mud-gapers and occasionally the long slim razor-shell clam. All these shellfish, as well as mussels, limpets, winkles, oysters and whelks, have played an important role in the diet of the lough-side dwellers. Large dishes of boiled cockles were put in the centre of the table and eaten with relish.

Steam the cockles open in the usual way (see p.92) and remove the meat from the shells. Place the meat in a saucepan with a little butter, pepper and salt. Heat through gently and serve very hot with brown Irish soda bread or crusty wholemeal bread and a glass of Guinness.

Kearney Cod Baked in Cream

(serves 4)

The village of Kearney and 300 acres of land including foreshore on the coast of County Down in the Little Ards, 3 miles east of Portaferry, was bought in 1965 by the National Trust with money collected during the first campaign of Enterprise Neptune. Kearney is a tiny settlement or 'clachan' with 13 houses, several of which are now available for holiday accommodation. There seems no obvious reason for its existence, but certainly a group of dwellings existed here in the 18th century: Kearney's inhabitants were primarily farm workers, possibly wreckers or smugglers in their spare time, and they must have fished to pay the rent.

4 thick cod cutlets	Single cream
1oz (25g) butter	Beurre manié to thicken (see p.207)
2 dessertspoons (2 × 10ml) onion, finely chopped	2 tablespoons (2 × 15ml) very thick cream
1 bayleaf	Fresh parsley to garnish
Sea salt and freshly milled pepper	

Melt the butter in a pan and fry the chopped onion for a few minutes. Add the fish and brown on both sides. Place the fish and onion in an ovenproof dish, add the bayleaf and season well. Pour over the cream. Cover and bake in a moderate oven (350°F, 180°C, gas mark 4) for about 10 minutes, or until the fish is cooked through. Remove the bayleaf and thicken with beurre manié. Taste and adjust the seasoning if necessary. Add the thick cream to enrich the sauce. Serve immediately garnished with parsley and accompanied with buttered new potatoes and a green vegetable or salad.

Portavogie Cod Cobbler

(serves 4)

This recipe is based on one given to me by the Irish Sea Fisheries Service, or Bord Iascaigh Mhara, who work hard to encourage the cooking and eating of fish. It uses cod from Portavogie, a village in County Down near Strangford Lough, which has a fishing fleet catching mainly cod, herring, mackerel, brill, turbot and monkfish.

1½lb (675g) cod fillet   2oz (50g) flour

1pt (600ml) milk   3½oz (100g) Irish cheddar, grated

1 bayleaf   Salt and freshly milled pepper

2oz (50g) butter

For the scone topping

8oz (225g) plain flour   3oz (75g) Irish cheddar, grated

1 teaspoon (5ml) baking powder   1 egg yolk

Pinch of salt   Milk to bind and glaze

2oz (50g) butter

Cut the cod into large pieces. Put the milk and bayleaf into a saucepan and bring to the boil. Simmer for about 10 minutes to flavour the milk, then strain and discard the bayleaf. Melt the butter in a saucepan, stir in the flour and cook for a couple of minutes. Gradually add the flavoured milk and stir in the cheese. Season well. Pour half the cheese sauce into the bottom of an ovenproof dish, then put in the fish. Cover with the remaining cheese sauce.

To make the scone topping, sieve the flour, baking powder and salt together into a mixing bowl. Rub in the butter. Stir in 2oz (50g) cheese and add the egg yolk and enough milk to make a workable dough. Roll out on a floured board to a thickness of about ½in (1cm), then cut into small rounds with a scone cutter. Place the scones on top of the fish so that they cover the surface. Glaze them with a little milk and sprinkle the remaining grated cheese over them. Bake in a hot oven (450°F, 230°C, gas mark 8) for about 25–30 minutes, or until the scones are golden brown.

Serve immediately with a green vegetable or salad.

Cutlets of Cod's Roe

(serves 4)

As in the remote islands of Scotland, the innards of fish were always eaten in Ireland. People were not in the habit of throwing away anything and since large quantities of white fish, like cod, were salted and dried for winter use, the livers, roes and heads were a by-product of the salting industry and were used in many original ways. They were eaten with great relish as a welcome variation in the diet.

Roes were usually boiled in a special muslin bag, then fried in butter. Cod's roes are a seasonal delicacy appearing in February and March and are often served as a breakfast dish in Ireland with fried or grilled bacon rashers and slices of fried potato or with mashed potato and butter. They are usually sold in pairs to keep the membrane intact.

1lb (450g) fresh cod's roe	8oz (225g) smoked bacon rashers
3oz (75g) plain flour	3 tablespoons (3 × 15ml) bacon fat
1 large egg, beaten	Lemon wedges to garnish

Simmer the cod's roe in boiling salted water for about 10 minutes. Drain and peel off the skin. Cut the cod's roe into slices about $\frac{1}{2}$in (1cm) thick and roll in flour. Dip the slices into the beaten egg, then roll in flour again. Fry or grill the bacon, then heat the resulting bacon fat until really hot. Fry the cutlets of cod's roe on both sides until golden brown.

Serve with a rasher of bacon on top of each cutlet and garnished with lemon wedges.

Cod's Roe Fritters   (serves 4–6)

A simple frying batter made of flour and water which gives a very crisp result is used in this recipe. However, you can also use a richer recipe including an egg and milk. Cod's roe fritters make an excellent lunch or supper dish served with mustard, horseradish or tomato sauce or anchovy butter (see pp.210–216).

1lb (450g) fresh cod's roe	3 teaspoons (3 × 5ml) malt vinegar
4oz (125g) plain flour	Fat for deep frying
Pinch of sea salt	Bacon rolls and lemon wedges to garnish
Approx. $\frac{1}{4}$pt (150ml) cold water	

Simmer the cod's roe in boiling water for about 10 minutes. Drain and peel off the skin. Cut into slices about $\frac{1}{2}$in (1cm) thick. Make a batter with the flour, salt, cold water and vinegar. Heat the fat until smoking hot, then dip the slices of cod's roe into the batter and drop them into the fat. Fry a few at a time until golden brown and puffy. Drain on absorbent kitchen paper and serve immediately with grilled bacon rolls, lemon wedges and a suitable sauce.

Cod's Roe Ramekins

(serves 6)

This recipe makes an unusual starter or supper dish. It can be cooked in one large ovenproof dish instead of small ramekins.

8oz (225g) cooked cod's roe

$\frac{1}{2}$oz (12g) butter

4oz (125g) breadcrumbs

2 teaspoons (2 × 5ml) fresh parsley, chopped

Salt and freshly milled black pepper

1 egg, separated

Milk

Cook the cod's roe as above, remove the skin and chop finely. Grease 6 small ramekin dishes with the butter. Put the chopped roe in a basin and stir in the breadcrumbs and parsley. Season well. Beat the egg yolk and add the milk to it. Pour this liquid over the roe and breadcrumbs and leave to stand until the crumbs are soaked. Whisk the egg white until very stiff and fold into the mixture. Almost fill the ramekins and bake in a hot oven (425°F, 220°C, gas mark 7) for 10–15 minutes or until well-risen, firm and golden brown.

Roe Cakes

(serves 4)

These make a change from traditional fish cakes.

1lb (450g) cod's roe, cooked

8oz (225g) potatoes, cooked

$\frac{1}{2}$oz (12g) butter

1 medium onion, finely chopped

Sea salt and freshly milled pepper

1oz (25g) seasoned flour

Oil for frying

Bacon rashers

Put the skinned roe in a bowl. Add the cooked potatoes and mash the two together with a potato masher. Melt the butter in a frying-pan and cook the onion until soft and transparent, but not browned. Add the onion and butter to the roe mixture. Season well. Divide the mixture into 8 pieces and shape into round cakes about $\frac{1}{2}$in (1cm) thick on a floured board. Coat in seasoned flour to prevent them sticking. Leave in a cool place for 1 hour before shallow frying in hot oil until brown and crisp on both sides. Serve very hot with fried or grilled bacon rashers.

Herring and Vegetable Soup

(serves 6)

This recipe was given to me by the Sea Fish Industry Authority. Herring soup used to be made with a red or salt herring which was grilled, then put in a soup plate or bowl. Boiling water was poured over it and 5 or 6 boiled potatoes were added, producing a complete, cheap and nutritious meal.

2pts (1 litre) fish stock (see p. 209)	1 dessertspoon (1 × 10ml) tomato purée
8oz (225g) carrots, diced	Sea salt and freshly milled pepper
8oz (225g) swede, diced	Fresh dill to garnish
1lb (450g) fresh herring fillets, chopped	

Put the stock in a large saucepan. Add the carrot and swede and cook for about 20 minutes, or until tender. Add the chopped fillets of fish and cook gently for a further 5 minutes. Allow to cool slightly. Add the tomato purée and season to taste with salt and pepper. Liquidise or blend until smooth. Leave in the fridge overnight.

Next day, reheat until the soup just begins to simmer. Serve hot with crusty bread and garnished with sprigs of dill.

Irish Potted Herrings *(serves 6)*

As in many other countries, in Ireland there has been a long tradition of pickling or 'potting' herrings to preserve them. At one time, the herring was the most common fish and many of the traditional Irish fish recipes use herring. Red herrings, salted and heavily smoked, were obtainable all the year round. These were hung up by skewers on the kitchen rafters until they were needed. They were then grilled over a turf fire or steamed on top of a potful of potatoes.

12 fresh herrings	12 black peppercorns
Dry mustard powder	1 lemon, thinly sliced
Sea salt and freshly milled pepper	$\frac{3}{4}$pt (450ml) wine vinegar
1 bayleaf	8fl oz (240ml) water
6 whole cloves	1oz (25g) butter
2 blades of mace	

Remove the heads, tails and fins from the fish. Scale and gut them and wash them well, but do not bone them. Pat the fish dry. Season the insides of the fish with mustard, salt and pepper. Lay the fish in an ovenproof dish or casserole. Place a thin slice of lemon on each fish and pour over the vinegar and water – it should almost cover them. Dot with the butter. Cover with a lid and bake in a fairly hot oven (400°F, 200°C, gas mark 6) for 25–30 minutes. Cool in the liquid, before serving with Irish soda bread and a glass of stout.

Fried Herrings and Onions (serves 4)

In Ireland, herrings were usually coated in oatmeal and fried, but this combination is very good.

8 fresh herring fillets	8oz (225g) onions, sliced
Seasoned flour	Fresh parsley, finely chopped
Butter for frying	

Coat the fish in the flour. Melt some butter in a frying-pan and fry the onions until they are golden brown. Remove them and put in the herring fillets. Add more butter as required. Fry the fish on both sides for about 4 to 5 minutes and serve immediately with the onions. Sprinkle over the parsley and eat with crusty bread.

Salt Ling with Colcannon (serves 6)

Salted and dried ling were once a staple food in Ireland. The low hedges used to be covered in the month of July with what appeared to be white kite-shaped garments, but were in fact large flattened fish being dried in the sun after salting. Ling was very cheap and a popular purchase for dinner on Friday and other fast days, always served with potatoes. Sometimes in poor cottages, where utensils and fuel were scarce, the fish was cooked in the same pot as the potatoes.

Salt ling can still be found in a few places and is very good served with the traditional Irish colcannon, a mixture of mashed potatoes, cabbage and onion sometimes fried in dripping.

Colcannon is one of the dishes which used to be served at Hallowe'en feasts. No other day was celebrated in Ireland with so many special dishes, all vegetarian of course. No matter which dish was chosen for the feast, a wedding ring, carefully wrapped in greaseproof paper, was put into it to decide the destiny during the coming year of the person finding it on their plate.

1½lb (675g) salt ling	Mixture of milk and water to cover
1 small onion, sliced	Beurre manié to thicken (see p.207)

For the colcannon

6 large potatoes, cooked and mashed	1oz (25g) butter
6 scallions or spring onions, chopped	1 tablespoon (15ml) fresh parsley, finely chopped
3½fl oz (105ml) milk	
1½ cups cabbage, cooked	Sea salt and freshly milled pepper

Cut the salt ling into 6 pieces and soak overnight in cold water. Next day, drain it and rinse again in fresh water. Drain again and put the fish in a saucepan with the onion. Cover with a mixture of half milk and half water, bring to the boil and simmer gently for 20–25 minutes, but do not overcook. Take the fish out and keep it hot while you thicken the cooking liquor with beurre manié to make a sauce for the fish.

To make the colcannon, simmer the scallions or spring onions in the milk until soft, then beat with the mashed potatoes until very fluffy. Add the cabbage, which should be finely chopped, followed by the butter and parsley. Season to taste with plenty of salt and pepper, and mix well.

Serve the fish with the sauce poured over it and accompanied with colcannon.

Dublin Lawyer *(serves 2)*

This is a famous Irish recipe for lobster and although it originates in Dublin, it is often served in Northern Ireland.

Raw lobster should be used of this dish, but most people, including me, are not keen to kill a lobster by plunging a sharp instrument into the cross on its head, or to sever its spinal cord. I follow the advice of a friend and chef and drop the lobster into a large pan of rapidly boiling water and boil for $1\frac{1}{2}$ minutes only. This means that the lobster meat is still more or less raw and gives the special flavour to this dish.

Cooked crab meat can be used instead of lobster.

2 fresh lobsters	3–4 tablespoons (3–4 × 15ml) Irish whiskey
3oz (75g) butter	
Sea salt and freshly milled pepper	$\frac{1}{4}$pt (150ml) double cream

Cut the lobster in two lengthwise. Remove all the meat from the tail, claws and head, retaining the shells. Cut the meat into chunks. Heat the butter in a frying-pan without letting it brown and add the lobster meat. Turn it in the butter for a few minutes until cooked and season well. Heat the whiskey and pour over the lobster. Set it alight and when the flames have died down add the cream to the pan juices. Gently heat through without boiling, then put the lobster mixture back into the shells. Serve immediately.

Portaferry Hot Lobster

(serves 4)

This recipe was given to me by a lady living in Portaferry, at the entrance to Strangford Lough, where lobsters are taken from the deep rocky bottom.

2 freshly boiled lobsters (see p.31)

2oz (50g) butter

4oz (125g) mushrooms, chopped

Salt and cayenne pepper

1½ wineglasses of Madeira or sweet sherry

2 egg yolks

8fl oz (240ml) double cream

Remove all the meat from the lobsters and cut it into neat pieces. Melt the butter in a frying-pan and cook the mushrooms for a few minutes. Add the lobster meat and toss it in the butter until heated through. Season well. Pour on the Madeira or sherry and bring to simmering point. Beat the egg yolks in a small basin with the cream. Pour over the lobster and reheat very gently, without boiling.

Serve as a starter in individual small dishes or the lobster shells, with plenty of thin brown bread and butter.

Mussel and Potato Stew

(serves 4)

Mussels are found all around Northern Ireland's coast and excellent pollution-free specimens come from fisheries in Strangford Lough.

This stew makes a very good lunch or supper dish. Dry cider may be used instead of white wine.

2pts (1 litre) fresh mussels

1 onion, sliced

2 carrots, sliced

1 medium leek, chopped

1 celery stick, chopped

Parsley stalks

1 bayleaf

1 teaspoon (5ml) black peppercorns

Sprig of thyme

1pt (600ml) water

½pt (300ml) dry white wine

1lb (450g) prepared potatoes

1 medium dessert apple

1½oz (40g) butter

2 cloves garlic, crushed

4 tablespoons (4 × 15ml) fresh parsley, chopped

3 egg yolks

¼pt (150ml) double cream

Sea salt and freshly milled pepper

Grated nutmeg to garnish

Put the onion, carrot, leek, celery, parsley stalks, bayleaf, peppercorns and thyme into a large saucepan. Pour on the water and wine and bring to the boil. Cover and simmer for about 30 minutes to make stock. Strain off all the vegetables and herbs, reserving the stock.

Steam the mussels open in the usual way (see p.196) and remove the meat. Reserve the liquor. Cut the potatoes into small dice and peel and dice the apple. Melt the butter in a saucepan and add the garlic, potatoes, apple, mussel liquor and $1\frac{1}{2}$pts (900ml) prepared stock. Bring to the boil, cover and simmer for about 30 minutes until the potato is tender. Add the mussels and cook gently for another 2–3 minutes. Stir in the parsley. Beat the egg yolks with the cream in a small basin. Add a few tablespoons of the soup to this and beat well. Pour back into the saucepan and stir until the stew thickens. Season to taste.

Serve immediately garnished with a little grated nutmeg and with brown or white Irish soda bread or crusty wholemeal bread.

Buttered Mussels in a Jacket Potato (serves 1–2)

Both Scotland and Ireland have traditional and ingenious recipes for cooked mussels held in portable, edible containers, which in the past acted as replacements for their shells. Hot bread rolls were used in Scotland; the crumb was taken out and the mussels packed in its place. In Ireland the container was a potato baked in its jacket and then hollowed out. The whole meal could be wrapped in a cloth and taken to work in a man's pocket.

1pt (600ml) fresh mussels	1 dessertspoon (10ml) fresh parsley,
1oz (25g) butter	finely chopped
Squeeze of lemon juice	1 large jacket potato, cooked

Scrub the mussels well under cold running water and remove the barnacles. Discard any that are broken or do not close when tapped sharply. Put the mussels in a large saucepan without water and cook over a high heat for about 3 minutes, shaking from time to time. When the shells open, strain into a colander over a bowl, reserving the liquor. Remove the meat from the shells.

Hollow out some of the potato and chop up what you have removed. Heat the butter in a small saucepan.
Toss the mussels in this, then add
the reserved liquor, lemon juice and parsley.
Heat quickly, then add the chopped potato.
Pile into the potato shell and serve
immediately.

Mussel

Hot Buttered Oysters on Toast (serves 1)

The finest oysters in Ireland are said to come from the old-established beds off County Galway, and an oyster festival is held in Galway Town each year in September to open the season. However, now there are also fisheries in Strangford Lough producing excellent oysters.

Oysters are so expensive nowadays that they are usually eaten raw with lemon juice. In Ireland they are accompanied with brown Irish soda bread and a glass of Guinness.

4–6 oysters	Lemon wedges
1oz (25g) butter	Fresh parsley, finely chopped to garnish
Slice of buttered brown toast	

Open the oysters in the normal way (see p.198), reserving their liquor. Heat half the butter in a small saucepan and toss the oysters in this for 1 minute, or until heated through. Pour the reserved fish liquor into the pan and boil up, adding the remaining butter. Pour over the buttered toast and serve with lemon wedges and garnished with chopped parsley.

Oyster and Bacon Pudding (serves 4–6)

Mussels, scallops, clams or cockles can be used instead of oysters for this savoury suet pudding, but they must be cooked very lightly first to get rid of any excess liquor, which would make the pastry too wet and heavy.

10oz (275g) self-raising flour	3 tablespoons (3 × 15ml) fresh parsley, finely chopped
$\frac{1}{2}$ level teaspoon (2.5ml) sea salt	Freshly milled black pepper
5oz (150g) shredded suet	Fresh parsley, chopped
Cold water to mix	Chives, chopped
24 large oysters	Beurre manié to thicken (see p.207)
4oz (125g) onion, finely chopped	
4 rashers smoked bacon, derinded	

Sieve the flour and salt into a mixing bowl. Stir in the suet and mix to a soft dough with cold water. Chill while you prepare the fish.

Open the oysters in the usual way (see p.198), reserving their liquor in a small saucepan. Add the oysters and heat for a few seconds to firm them up. Remove them with a draining spoon, reserving the liquor for later. Cut the oysters in two.

Roll out the prepared dough into a rectangle $\frac{1}{4}$in (5mm) thick. Scatter it with the onion, the bacon cut into strips, the parsley and the oysters. Roll up the dough and dampen the ends. Press them together well. Place on a generously buttered piece of kitchen foil large enough to allow room for the pudding to rise. Wrap up the pudding in the foil and seal well. Steam in a covered oblong dish or tin half-filled with water for 2 hours, topping up with boiling water as necessary.

Remove the pudding from the water and unwrap carefully. Save any juices from the foil and turn the pudding on to a hot serving dish.

Any cooking juices from the pudding can be added to the oyster liquor with the parsley and chives. Heat in a small saucepan, season with pepper and thicken with beurre manié. Serve separately as gravy.

Steamed and Buttered Dublin Bay Prawns (serves 4)

These are not prawns at all, but should more accurately be called Norway lobsters (*Nephrops norvegicus*). They are often misnamed 'scampi', which is a larger relative of the Norway lobster found in the Adriatic Sea. To add to the confusion, 'scampi' is also called 'lobster tails' by some producers.

Dublin Bay prawns are said to have got their name in a rather curious way. In the early 1800s, when all the fishing boats were sailing ships and there was no refrigeration, all shellfish had to be cooked and eaten fresh as soon as they were caught and landed. Most of the boats were not used primarily for Norway lobsters, but many would have been caught in the nets with other fish. These became the perks of the crew and their families. Sailing ships of all nationalities used to anchor for provisions in the waters of Lambay Deep, a sheltered spot off the coast of north Dublin near Lambay Island, before setting sail to fish their way home. Their crews, as well as local folk, were a ready market for the shellfish that the boats had caught. The womenfolk would cook and sell the freshly caught shellfish in the streets of Dublin as 'Dublin Bay Prawns'.

Most of the Dublin Bay prawns caught nowadays are cooked, shelled, frozen and exported as scampi. You almost never see them on sale whole or uncooked. The prawns are in season from April to November and like lobsters they live in cool waters, especially around the European Continental shelf. They are fished commercially in Strangford Lough. If you are lucky enough to get hold of freshly caught Dublin Bay prawns, they have a very delicate flavour and are best cooked very simply. They are wasted if covered in breadcrumbs and deep-fried, when the frozen variety would be perfectly adequate. Only the tails of these prawns are eaten.

2lb (900g) Dublin Bay prawns freshly caught

3oz (75g) butter

Sea salt and freshly milled pepper

Juice of 1 lemon

Triangles of hot brown toast to garnish

Steam the prawns over boiling water for about 15 minutes, then leave to cool. Shell them, removing their heads and claws and the black thread of gut. Melt the butter in a frying-pan and toss the prawn tails in the hot butter. Sprinkle lightly with salt and add a little pepper. Pour over the lemon juice and turn the prawn tails once again in the juices. Serve immediately with hollandaise sauce (see p.209) and garnished with triangles of hot brown toast.

Dublin Bay Prawns in Dill and Cream Sauce

(serves 4)

1lb (450g) Dublin Bay prawns, cooked and shelled

$\frac{1}{4}$pt (150ml) white wine

$\frac{1}{4}$pt (150ml) fish stock (see p.209)

Sea salt and freshly milled pepper

Sprigs of fresh dill and paprika to garnish

For the dill and cream sauce

1oz (25g) butter

1oz (25g) flour

1 tablespoon (15ml) fresh dill, finely chopped

2 tablespoons (2 × 15ml) double cream

1 tablespoon (15ml) medium sherry

Place the prawn tails in a saucepan with the wine and stock. Poach gently for a few minutes, then season with salt and pepper. Strain, reserving the cooking liquor, and put the prawns on one side.

To make the sauce, melt the butter in a saucepan and stir in the flour. Cook for a minute or two, then gradually add the reserved cooking liquor. Stir over a gentle heat until the sauce thickens and add the cream and sherry, followed by the prawns and the chopped fresh dill. Serve with sprigs of dill and a sprinkling of paprika on the top. This is good accompanied by fluffy rice and a green vegetable or salad.

Carrick-a-Rede Salmon

After the Giant's Causeway, the 60-foot rope bridge at Carrick-a-Rede is the most famous attraction on the Causeway Coast of Northern Ireland. The National Trust bought Carrick-a-Rede in 1967 with Enterprise Neptune funds.

Carrick-a-Rede means 'the rock in the road'; the road being that taken by the salmon as they return from the North Atlantic to their river spawning grounds. Recent research has shown that the main shoals reach the Irish coast between Rathlin Island and the Irishowen Head in Donegal and when winds are favourable, particularly during north-westerlies, the salmon swim close inshore seeking the fresh water of the Rivers Bush and Bann. At certain points where the tidal conditions are just right, the occurrence of salmon is very predictable and these have evolved over the centuries as the traditional fishery sites. Carrick-a-Rede is the most important site on this coastline and the rope bridge was first erected over 200 years ago by the salmon fishermen to reach the fishery as well as to allow the island to be used for sheep grazing. The original bridge was only a single hand-rope with a few slats of wood and, although the bridge is slightly more substantial now, it still sways in the wind and people cross it at their own risk.

The method of fishing salmon has changed over the years. In the 18th century a fixed draft net was used. Look-outs would perch on the edge of the cliffs, armed with a pile of small stones and watch for the approaching salmon. As the fish came within the bay, word was passed to the fishermen in their boats and while the look-outs threw stones to direct the salmon, the fishermen would surround the shoal with the net, dragging it into a tight circle until the fish were trapped and could be lifted out.

In the early 19th century the bag net of the type used today was introduced to North Antrim from Scotland. This net has two parts, a leader or vertical wall of net and a trap. The leader is attached to the shore and the whole net buoyed up with corks. The net is left set and the fish trap themselves by swimming into the bag. A great deal of skill is required to set the net correctly and judge the tide and wind for taking the best catch.

The fishing season is limited by law to between March and September. In practice, the bridge is usually put up as early in April as the weather will allow and the fishing rarely starts before mid May. It might be finished by July, although the bridge remains until the end of the season when it is removed for the winter.

Because of the rope bridge, the Carrick-a-Rede fishery attracts a lot of attention, but there is a second salmon fishery a little further west in Larrybane Bay.

Frances McCollum's way with Bush Salmon Steaks

(serves 4)

Frances McCollum gave me this recipe on BBC Radio Belfast when I asked listeners for traditional Irish fish recipes. She coats her salmon steaks in Indian meal which can be bought in most health food shops and good grocer's, although flour may be substituted.

4 thick salmon steaks

2oz (50g) seasoned Indian meal, or flour

3oz (75g) butter

2 teaspoons (2 × 5ml) lemon juice

1oz (25g) flour

½pt (300ml) milk

4 spring onions or scallions, finely chopped

4oz (125g) prawns, peeled

Sea salt and freshly milled pepper

2 tablespoons (2 × 15ml) double cream

Toss the salmon steaks in seasoned meal. Place the steaks in a piece of kitchen foil. Dot with 2oz (50g) butter and sprinkle with lemon juice. Make the foil into a parcel and bake in a moderate oven (350°F, 180°C, gas mark 4) for 20 minutes.

Melt the remaining 1oz (25g) butter in a small saucepan and stir in the flour. Cook for a few minutes, then gradually add the milk and the cooking juices from the fish. Continue cooking until the sauce has thickened, then add the chopped onions and prawns. Season to taste. Finally, stir in the cream.

Serve the fish with the sauce, buttered new potatoes and a green salad.

Baked Salmon with Spinach Sauce

(serves 6–8)

Apart from the two salmon fisheries at Carrick-a-Rede, salmon fishing is carried on at many places along the Causeway Coast where the fish congregate in the shelter of headlands. Bag nets are set at Blackrock, Portfad, Portmoon, and Dunseverick, where the National Trust purchased the harbour in 1968 with Enterprise Neptune funds. All these can be seen from the North Antrim Cliff Path, a 10-mile footpath from Blackrock to White Park Bay which crosses some of the most spectacular coastal scenery looked after by the National Trust. Near Blackrock is an old slipway which once served the salmon fishery. From the cliffs near the path at Portfad and Portmoon, the salmon nets may be seen in the sea below. An ice house, always an important part of an old fishery, is beside the path. Ice was formerly collected from the adjoining field which was flooded in winter when frost was expected.

However, fishing on this exposed and stormy coast gives a livelihood to only a few people. Farming is the mainstay of the local economy and farmers still have ancient rights to graze livestock down to sea level in the Causeway Bays and to collect seaweed for fertilising fields. Seaweed was also burned to produce ash for the preparation of iodine salts and soda in the 19th and early 20th centuries. There are many remains of old low stone kelp-drying walls and stone kilns on the shore in bays between Portnaboe and Dunseverick. Dense clouds of smoke from the kilns once filled Portnaboe and Port Noffer every June and July, but there is little collecting done on this stretch of coast today.

Whole rainbow, brown or sea trout or bass may be used instead of salmon in this recipe.

3lb (1.4kg) fresh salmon	Sprig of fresh fennel
2oz (50g) butter	
Sea salt and freshly milled black pepper	

For the spinach sauce

8fl oz (240ml) cream	8oz (225g) spinach
5oz (150g) butter	

Season the fish well and place on a piece of kitchen foil. Dot with butter and wrap in a parcel with the fennel. Bake in a moderate oven (350°F, 180°C, gas mark 4) for about 20 minutes or until tender. Meanwhile, put the cream in a frying-pan and boil down to about 1 tablespoon (15ml). Add the butter carefully in small pieces, stirring well to make a sauce. Cook the spinach in a little unsalted water for 5 minutes. Drain it well and chop roughly. Stir the spinach into the sauce.

When the salmon is cooked, remove it from the foil parcel and place on a warmed serving dish. Stir the fish cooking juices into the spinach sauce and adjust the seasoning if necessary. Serve immediately with buttered new potatoes and hand the sauce separately.

Salmon Head Soup   (serves 6–8)

The carcase of a salmon is put to good use in this recipe to produce a satisfying fish and vegetable soup that is ideal for lunch or supper. Cod or haddock heads can also be used.

Head, tail, bones and trimmings of 1 cooked salmon	$1\frac{1}{2}$ teaspoons ($1\frac{1}{2}$ × 5ml) salt
$1\frac{1}{2}$lb (675g) white fish bones	1 teaspoon (5ml) black peppercorns
2 large onions, one sliced and one chopped finely	$3\frac{1}{2}$pts (2 litres) water
2 celery sticks, chopped	1 bayleaf
	Sprig of tarragon

A few parsley stalks

Sprigs of basil

Strip of lemon peel

2oz (50g) butter

8oz (225g) courgettes, sliced

½pt (300ml) dry cider

1 teaspoon (5ml) vinegar

1 clove garlic, crushed

1 14oz (400g) tin tomatoes

A few flakes of cooked salmon

Fresh basil, chopped, to garnish

Put all the salmon and white fish trimmings in a large saucepan with the sliced onion, the celery, salt, peppercorns and water. Add the bayleaf, tarragon, parsley stalks, basil and lemon peel. Bring slowly to the boil and skim well. Cover the pan and simmer for 30 minutes. Strain through a sieve, and then through muslin. Boil the resulting stock to reduce to 2½pts (1.5 litres). Cool and skim off the fat.

Heat the butter in a large pan and gently fry the courgettes for a few minutes. Remove and reserve on one side. Gently fry the chopped onion. Add the garlic, cider and vinegar and boil vigorously for a few minutes. Stir in the roughly chopped tomatoes and their juice. Pour on the fish stock and bring to simmering point. Simmer for 15 minutes, then taste and adjust the seasoning. Add the reserved courgettes and the flakes of salmon. Heat through gently and garnish generously with fresh basil. Serve with crusty bread.

Scallop and Mushroom Pie *(serves 4)*

Both scallops and queenies are fished in Strangford Lough at the southern end near Portaferry. The queenie was held in high esteem as far back as the early 19th century and eaten in preference to its larger relatives, the scallop and the clam. Nowadays, queenies and scallops are usually sold opened and out of their shell. They both have a firm creamy-white flesh with a bright orange roe and are in season from September to March. Queenies can be used instead of scallops, but you will need 3 or 4 times the quantity, depending on their size.

8 large scallops, cleaned

4oz (125g) button mushrooms, sliced

½pt (300ml) milk

1½oz (40g) butter

1 small onion, finely chopped

1oz (25g) flour

A squeeze of lemon juice

4 tablespoons (4 × 15ml) medium sherry

1 tablespoon (15ml) fresh parsley, finely chopped

Sea salt and freshly milled pepper

1lb (450g) cooked potatoes, mashed

Cut the white part of the scallops in half, but keep the orange coral whole. Put the fish in a saucepan with the mushrooms and milk. Bring to the boil and simmer very gently for 1–2 minutes. Strain, reserving the milk. Melt 1oz (25g) butter in a saucepan and soften the onion without colouring. Stir in the flour and gradually add the flavoured milk. Cook until thick, then add the lemon juice, sherry and parsley. Finally, add the scallops and mushrooms. Season well. Pour into an ovenproof dish and cover with mashed potato. Dot with the remaining butter and bake in a moderate oven (350°F, 180°C, gas mark 4) for 20–30 minutes, or until the top is tinged with brown. Serve immediately with a green vegetable or salad.

Fried Queenies from Strangford   (serves 4)

Scallops may be used instead of queenies for this dish, but slice them in two across the white muscle leaving the orange roe whole.

32 queenies, or 16 scallops, cleaned	1 tablespoon (15ml) lemon juice
Milk	$\frac{1}{2}$ tablespoon (7.5ml) fresh parsley, finely chopped
2oz (50g) seasoned flour	
4oz (125g) butter	

Dip the queenies in milk and then toss them in seasoned flour. Heat 2oz (50g) butter in a frying-pan and fry the queenies very gently for 1–2 minutes on each side. Remove to a warm serving dish. Add the remaining butter to the pan and heat until it just begins to turn nut-brown. Add the lemon juice and parsley and pour over the waiting queenies. Serve immediately with crusty Irish soda bread.

Sea Urchins with Mayonnaise   (serves 4)

A special delight of Irish eating is the sea urchin, which takes its name from an old English meaning of urchin – hedgehog. Poor people living on the coast of Ireland and remote parts of Scotland often used the flesh of sea urchins instead of butter. The main demand now for Irish sea urchins comes from France, where it is common to see basketfuls on display alongside varieties from the Mediterranean. Usually one urchin is cut open to show the star-shaped orange ovaries, which are the edible part. In fact, in many European languages the sea urchin's name means 'sea-egg'.

Sea urchins are common in all the rocky areas of the Northern Ireland coast and in Strangford Lough. They are delicious eaten raw with lemon juice, crusty bread and plenty of white wine, or the bright orange creamy inside can be scooped out and added to sauces to serve with fish. They can also be cooked in the same way as a boiled egg and mixed with cream, mayonnaise or lemon juice. However you serve them, they must be very fresh or they are not worth eating. If you live in London they can be obtained quite easily most of the year from a fish merchant at Billingsgate who specialises in unusual fish and shellfish.

2 tablespoons (2 × 15ml) homemade mayonnaise (see p.210)
12 sea urchins

Cook the sea urchins for about 4 minutes in boiling water and remove the prickles from the top of the shell. Remove the plug with the point of a knife or kitchen scissors. Cut a large hole and scoop out the meat. Sieve it into a small basin and mix with the mayonnaise. Put back into the shells and serve chilled with fingers of warm buttered brown toast.

Ballycastle Dulse

'Did you treat your Mary Anne to dulse and yellowman
At the Ould Lammas Fair, at Ballycastle, O.?'

The Giant's Causeway on the treacherous north coast of Ireland was given to the National Trust in 1961. It is made up of thousands of strangely symmetrical basalt columns of varying colours, which jut out to sea between Port Ganny and Port Noffer. Legend has it that the whole Causeway was built by the Irish giant Finn McCool in order to travel across the sea to Scotland. In fact, the Causeway is a product of the prehistoric volcanic activity which altered the face of both Ireland and Scotland.

Near the Giant's Causeway is the town of Ballycastle, where at the end of August, a fair of several days' duration is held. This is called Lammas Fair and it has been held every year for over 350 years. Sheep and ponies are sold and there are the usual fairday delights. The two traditional foods are yellowman, a brittle yellow toffee, which has been made by the same family for hundreds of years, and dulse.

Also called dillisk and dillesk, dulse is a reddish-brown seaweed found on all coasts of Ireland. It is very common all around the British coast, but is only used as a food in the remoter parts of Ireland and Scotland. Seawater contains exactly the minerals and trace elements in the same proportions as our bodies. Growing in such a rich environment, seaweeds like dulse naturally absorb the minerals and are an excellent source of valuable iron, calcium and iodine. If gathering your own dulse, look for it growing on stones, or often on other seaweeds, fairly low down the tidal level on an unpolluted beach. The best months to gather it, as with most seaweeds, are April, May and June when the plant has produced new shoots. Cut the dulse leaving plenty of the stem-like part, which is attached to the stone, so that it continues to grow, or gather leaves, which have been washed free of their moorings. When you reach home, wash the dulse very thoroughly in fresh water to remove sand, shells and other beach debris which may have stuck to it.

Dulse used to be eaten raw in salads, but it is usually sold dried. To dry it yourself, leave the weed hanging outside on a sunny wall for a day or two until it is virtually dry, then bring it in and hang it for another day in a warm place, such as the airing cupboard. When it is crisp, store in airtight jars in a dry place. Eat as a vegetable with any meat or fish, or add a few fronds to vegetable and fish soups and stews to give them body and a wonderful flavour.

Dulse is gathered all over Ireland and can be seen drying on low stone walls and beaches. In Portaferry, at the entrance to Strangford Lough, it can be seen drying on the pavements.

To Cook Dulse

Soak the weed in cold water for 3 hours, then simmer in milk or water for 3–5 hours, or until tender. It is extremely tough, so the long cooking is really necessary. Add a good knob of butter and freshly milled pepper. Serve as a vegetable with any meat or fish.

Dulse Champ

Champ is a traditional Irish potato dish, particularly popular in the northern counties. It is basically mashed potato mixed with cooked spring onions, scallions or leeks, but can also be made with chopped parsley, chives, young nettle tops and freshly cooked young green peas or dulse. For a supper dish, scrambled eggs are often served with champ. A heavy wooden pestle or 'beetle' was used to mash large wooden tubs full of potatoes in the days when they were the staple food of many Irish people.

Cook the dulse in milk as before. Mash some potatoes, season to taste, then add the dulse with enough of the cooking liquor to make the dish creamy and smooth. You can add as much dulse as you like to suit your personal taste. Put the champ into a deep warmed dish, make a well in the centre and pour some hot melted butter into it. Dip the potato into the well of butter when serving.

Irish Sloke

The edible seaweed sloke, is found on rocks all over Ireland, and is the equivalent of Welsh laver. It is usually simmered in water for 4 or 5 hours, drained, then dressed with butter, cream and a squeeze of orange or lemon juice. Sloke is excellent served as a sauce with roast lamb, boiled ham and fish (see pp.78–80 for more details).

Sloke Cakes

Cook the sloke as before, then add butter, cream, pepper and salt. While hot, beat in as much medium oatmeal as it will take up. Form into small flat cakes. Roll them in oatmeal and fry them when you are cooking the breakfast bacon.

Carragheen Moss

The purplish-red fronds of this lovely marine plant are common on the rocks and stones of the western coasts of Scotland, but its real home is Ireland, where the village of Carragheen has provided the most common of the names used for it, Irish Moss. The plant is very popular in Ireland and many parents still think it is essential in the diet of growing children.

The Irish have found many ways of using carragheen in cookery. The women gather the seaweed from the rocky shores in large wicker baskets: it is found at the lowest tidal level and is easily recognised because its fronds have a distinctly flat stalk and branch repeatedly into a rough fan shape. Carragheen is best gathered young in April and May and either used immediately, or carefully dried. In Ireland it used to be spread out to dry on the cliffs, bleaching to a creamy-white colour. If you want to dry it yourself, wash it very well in fresh water, then lay it outside to dry somewhere out of the wind. Wash it from time to time with fresh water or simply leave it out in the rain until it changes colour. It is then ready to bring inside. Trim off any rough stalks, then dry thoroughly indoors. Store in paper bags hanging in a dry place. Once dried, carragheen can be used exactly as if it were fresh. Commercially prepared dried carragheen is available from health food shops and some chemists, but usually has not had the sea salt washed off and therefore has to be soaked in a bowl of water for 15 minutes, then drained, before use. The standard packet contains 3 handfuls of the dried moss.

Carragheen is a mucilaginous plant, an important source of alginates, or vegetable gelatines, so is useful for thickening fish or seafood soups and stews and setting sweet and savoury jellies, mousses, jams and marmalades. It can also be made into thin, durable film for use as edible sausage skins. Traditionally, however, it is used to thicken blancmange and milk drinks.

Irish Moss Blancmange (serves 6)

This pudding is reminiscent of junket. Most Irish people like to taste the gentle sea-tang of the carragheen and eat it with no extra flavouring, but with large quantities of rich farm cream. It may be flavoured if you wish with vanilla, almond, elderflowers, or fruit juice. Fresh or dried carragheen may be used.

2 good handfuls of carragheen	Sugar to taste
2pts (1.2 litres) milk	Chosen flavouring (optional)

Soak the seaweed in plenty of fresh water for at least 2 hours. Drain and pick over, removing any little bits of shell or grit. Put the seaweed into a saucepan with the milk. Bring to the boil and simmer gently for 30 minutes until most of the weed has dissolved. Strain through a sieve into a bowl, rubbing any jelly from the seaweed through into the milk below. Beat well until smooth and sweeten and flavour to taste. Pour into a mould or glass bowl, or individual glasses, and leave in the fridge to set. Serve with plenty of double cream. The blancmange is also good with fresh, lightly-stewed fruit.

Variation: Beat 1 egg yolk into the blancmange after straining and then fold in the whisked egg white once the mixture has been sweetened.

Irish Moss Fruit Jelly (serves 6)

This is another traditional use for carragheen. Any flavouring can be used instead of the fruit. Ginger is particularly successful – add the chopped root during the simmering of the weed. A savoury jelly may be made in exactly the same way by omitting the sugar.

1 cup fresh carragheen	Grated rind and juice from 1 orange
3 cups (750ml) water	6oz (175g) sugar
Grated rind and juice from 2 lemons	

Wash the seaweed well in fresh water, drain it and put into a saucepan with the water. Bring to the boil and add the grated rind of the lemons and orange. Cover and simmer for about 10 minutes.

Put the sugar into a 2 pint (1.2 litre) glass bowl and pour on the lemon and orange juice. Strain the carragheen mixture through a sieve into the bowl. Mix well to dissolve the sugar, then leave in a cool place to set. Decorate with whipped cream and serve.

Dublin Bay Prawns in Carragheen Jelly (serves 4)

Carragheen is particularly suitable for producing a seafood aspic as it tastes of the sea. The idea for this recipe came from Alan Davidson's *North Atlantic Seafood*.

1 good handful of carragheen	1 teaspoon (5ml) vinegar
1pt (600ml) water	Dublin Bay prawns, cooked and shelled
1 bayleaf	
2 cloves	Watercress or fronds of seaweed to garnish
Sprig of fresh parsley	
Sea salt	

Soak the carragheen in water for 15 minutes, then drain it. Put in a saucepan with 1pt (600ml) water and bring to the boil. Simmer gently for 1 hour with the bayleaf, cloves, parsley and a little salt. At the end of the cooking time, stir in the vinegar and leave to cool a little. Put the prepared prawns in a mould or bowl and strain the carragheen mixture over the fish. Chill until the jelly sets, then turn it out. Serve garnished with sprigs of watercress or fronds of seaweed.

Black Sole with Hotel Butter (serves 1)

There are two kinds of sole caught off the Irish coast; one is lemon sole which should be eaten very fresh; and the other is black sole, which has a better flavour if kept in a cool place for few days. Black sole, known as

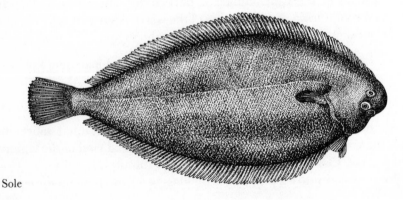

Sole

Dover sole in England, is so named because of its black skin which acts as a camouflage on the seabed.

Both types of sole are best cooked very simply to retain their full flavour, and they should be grilled or steamed rather than fried. Choose a fish which will fit neatly between two large dinner plates. Maître d'hôtel butter was known as 'Hotel butter' in 19th-century Ireland.

1 whole black sole, skinned	Maître d'hôtel butter to serve (see p.217)
1oz (25g) butter	
Sea salt	Watercress and lemon wedge to garnish
Freshly milled pepper	
Squeeze of lemon juice	

Cut off the head and tail of the fish if it will not fit neatly between two large dinner plates. Rub the centre of both plates with butter and sprinkle one of the plates with sea salt and pepper. Lay the fish on top of this and season again, adding a good squeeze of lemon juice. Invert the second dinner plate over the first so that the fish is sandwiched between the two. The rims of the plates should touch all the way round.

Choose a saucepan with a circumference slightly smaller than the dinner plates, and half fill with water. Bring to a fast boil. Place the plates with the fish on top and cook at a fast simmer for 12–15 minutes. When cooked remove the top plate carefully and garnish the sole with watercress and a lemon wedge. Serve with a generous knob of maître d'hôtel butter and crusty bread to mop up the buttery juices.

NORTH WEST

Whitehaven, fishing boats

Cumbria's magnificent and dramatic countryside has helped to preserve the local flavour of its cooking. Until comparatively recently, the
mountains, deep valleys and lakes plus the hardness of the winters made
travel difficult, so dishes tend to be very localised. People of the Central
Lakeland area traditionally eat freshwater fish from the lakes and the
rivers. The inhabitants of the coast consume a great deal of the excellent
seafish that is available: salmon and salmon trout from the Solway and
Morecambe Bay shrimps are world famous.

Walking around the industrial towns of Lancashire, it is easy to forget
that this is a county with a coastline. But a glimpse of the quality of the
fish reminds you that important fishing ports like Fleetwood land
excellent fish from the rich fishing grounds of the Irish Sea and Faroes.
Apart from Morecambe Bay shrimps, prawns, whelks, crabs and
lobsters are fished from here, and cockles are harvested from the miles of
sandy shores. Even with today's refrigeration and fast transport, the fish
supply in Lancashire tends to be determined by local resources. The
most characteristic fish in the markets during spring and early summer is
hake, later comes halibut sold in large chunks, plaice and cod.

The Vikings settled on the fertile green land of the Isle of Man 10
centuries ago, to enjoy the rich harvests from the sea and the land. The
island is best known for its delicious kippers, but mackerel and white fish
are caught and very good crabs, lobsters, scallops and queenies.

Scotland of course, is close by: in the fish shops of the North West hang rows of fresh filleted herrings, Arbroath smokies, Finnan haddocks and Scottish kippers.

Arbroath Smokies

Along the Angus and Kincardine coasts in Scotland are many former fishing ports. A few miles north of Arbroath, the picturesque village of Auchmithie sits perched on the edge of a steep sea cliff with the harbour, no longer in use, below. This is where the Arbroath smokie originated. Fish wives, using upturned barrels, produced the 'Auchmithie Luckens', 'Closefish' or 'Pinwiddies', as they were variously called. Today they are known simply as smokies.

For the cure, small fresh haddocks and sometimes whiting of the same size are gutted, headed and left whole. They are then dry-salted for about 1 hour, tied in pairs by the tails and hung over hot smoke for 40–50 minutes. The result is a delicious copper-coloured, mildly smoked cooked fish; no artificial preservatives or dyes are added.

Since the fish is hot-smoked and therefore already cooked, it can be eaten cold with brown bread and butter and lemon, but strangely enough, smokies are traditionally cooked and served hot. Brush or smear them with butter and lightly grill or bake in a hot oven for a few minutes, either wrapped in foil or left unprotected. Serve with a knob of butter in the middle. In the North West the fish is often eaten with a baked or boiled jacket potato as a favourite high-tea dish.

Potted Arbroath Smokie *(serves 4–6)*

This recipe makes a very simple starter for a dinner party, or a good dish for lunch or a picnic.

1 pair of Arbroath smokies	Pinch of cayenne pepper
3oz (75g) butter	Lemon juice
Sea salt and freshly milled pepper	

Skin and bone the two fish. Put the flesh into a blender or processor and add the butter. Blend or process to a smooth paste. Season to taste with salt, black and cayenne pepper and lemon juice. Turn into a china or earthenware pot and chill in the fridge for at least an hour before serving with hot wholemeal toast.

Cumbrian Fisherman's Pie
(serves 4)

Any fish, sea or lake, can be used in this recipe which was given to me by the Cumbria Tourist Board.

1lb (450g) poached fish	¼pt (150ml) milk
2 tablespoons (2 × 15ml) fresh parsley, chopped	¼pt (150ml) fish stock
2 hard-boiled eggs, chopped	Sea salt and freshly milled pepper
4 tomatoes, skinned	8oz (225g) shortcrust pastry
1oz (25g) butter	Beaten egg to glaze
1oz (25g) flour	

Flake the fish and mix it with the parsley and chopped hard-boiled eggs. Season well. Put half this mixture into a greased pie-dish and cover with a layer of sliced tomatoes. Top with the rest of the fish. Melt the butter in a small saucepan and stir in the flour. Cook for a few minutes then gradually add the milk and fish stock. Cook until smooth and thick and season to taste. Pour over the fish. Roll out the pastry and use to make a lid for the pie. Crimp the edges and decorate with pastry trimmings. Make a hole in the centre to allow the steam to escape, then brush with beaten egg. Bake in a fairly hot oven (400°F, 200°C, gas mark 6) for about 35 minutes, or until golden brown. Serve hot or cold.

Finny Haddie

In the 18th century, a few miles to the south of Aberdeen, haddocks were dried on the seashore, then smoked over peat or seaweed fires by the fish wives of Findon. These were the ancestors, albeit harder, drier and more salty, of the modern Finnan haddock, which is pale gold in colour. There are so many 'smoked fillets' on sale, which are neither haddock nor smoked; they have been dyed bright yellow and artificially flavoured. The way of recognising haddock is to look at the skin; there are two black marks said to be the fingermarks of St Peter when he drew the fish out of the water on the Sea of Galilee (though Yorkshire fishermen have another theory, p.163). Finnan haddock are split down the middle like kippers, but the backbone is usually to the right side, unlike the kipper which is to the left. The fish also have their tails left on.

One of the traditional ways of cooking Finnan haddock is to poach it very gently in milk in a large roasting tin, or flat pan, for about 10 minutes. Serve with a parsley, egg or butter sauce using the cooking liquor (see pp.207 and 216). The fish can also be steamed or baked, is superb as one of the fish in a fish pie, or as the main ingredient for kedgeree, soup, omelette, soufflé, paste, mousse and terrine.

Ham and Haddie
(serves 2–4)

This used to be a very popular dish in the North West. The traditional method of cooking is to fry the haddock and bacon together, but grilling prevents the fish drying out and preserves all the juices and flavour.

2 Finnan haddock	Sea salt and freshly milled pepper
2oz (50g) butter	1 tablespoon (15ml) double cream
6 rashers back bacon	

Grease a grill pan liberally, using half the butter. Place the fish in the pan, flesh side uppermost. Dot with the remaining butter. Lay the bacon rashers on the grid of the grill pan over the haddock. Cook under the grill, turning the bacon once, until it is crisp. Remove the bacon and the grid and keep the bacon warm. Continue to cook the haddock for about another 5 minutes, then remove to a warm serving dish. Season well and top with the bacon. Mix the cream with the pan juice, then pour over the haddock and bacon. Serve immediately with brown bread and butter, crusty bread or the traditional mashed potatoes.

Haddyanegg
(serves 2–4)

This is a special supper or high-tea dish in many parts of the North West. The egg is cooked in the rich salty juices from the fish.

1 large Finnan haddock	Sea salt and freshly milled pepper
1oz (25g) butter	2 eggs
Approx. ½pt (300ml) milk	

Using a little of the butter, grease a large plate which fits neatly over a saucepan of boiling water. Place the haddock on this plate, flesh side uppermost. Pour over the milk and season well. Cover with another plate and steam for about 20 minutes, or until almost cooked. Poach the eggs in the buttery juices and serve immediately on the plate with brown bread and butter and a pot of tea.

Cullen Skink
(serves 4–6)

Although a Scottish dish originating from Cullen, Cullen Skink has become more widely popular and is typical of fisher food all round the coast in the north of England. This soup-stew is traditionally made with the whole unboned Finnan, which undoubtedly makes the best soup, as the bones and skin have so much of the flavour. It can be made with fillet

121

of smoked fish as long as it is without artificial colouring and flavouring. 'Skink' was an old Scots word for 'soup' or 'broth'.

1 large Finnan haddock

1 medium onion, chopped

2pts (1.2 litres) water

Sea salt and freshly milled pepper

1lb (450g) potatoes, peeled

$\frac{1}{2}$pt (300ml) milk

2oz (50g) butter

4 tablespoons (4 × 15ml) double cream

Fresh parsley, chopped

Place the fish and onion in a saucepan with the water. Season well. Bring to the boil, cover and simmer for 10 minutes. Meanwhile, boil and mash the potatoes. Lift out the fish with a slotted spoon and leave to cool for a minute. Discard all the skin and bone. Strain the cooking liquor and return to the pan. Flake the fish and add it to the pan, with the milk, butter and mashed potatoes. Bring to the boil, cover and simmer for a few minutes. Taste and adjust the seasoning if necessary. Stir in the cream and garnish with parsley. Serve in bowls with crusty bread.

Fleetwood Hake and Shrimp Stew (serves 6)

The most characteristic fish in the markets of Lancashire and the North West during spring and early summer is hake – a fish often neglected. Fleetwood hake sold as whole fish, or as skinned 'silver' fillets, is very common and very good too, although it does lack the flavour of some other members of the cod family. It is best made into fish pies, stews, soups or served with a spicy, strong-flavoured sauce.

$1\frac{1}{2}$lb (675g) hake

1pt (600ml) unpicked shrimps or prawns

$2\frac{1}{2}$pts (1.5 litres) fish stock

2oz (50g) butter

8oz (225g) mushrooms, sliced thinly

3 cloves garlic, chopped

2oz (50g) flour

1lb (450g) potatoes, peeled and sliced

8oz (225g) peas

8oz (225g) carrots, thinly sliced

2 bayleaves

$\frac{1}{2}$pt (300ml) dry cider

Sea salt and freshly milled pepper

2–3 tablespoons (2–3 × 15ml) double cream

Skin and bone the hake and pick the shrimps or prawns. Simmer the heads and shells in the fish stock for about 15 minutes. Blend or process the stock, then sieve.

Melt the butter in a large saucepan and cook the mushrooms for a few minutes. Cut the hake into chunks and add to the pan with the garlic. Cook for a few minutes, then stir in the flour. Cook for 2 minutes, then gradually add the fish stock. Add the vegetables, bayleaves and cider. Simmer for about 20 minutes, or until the potatoes are just tender. Season to taste with salt and pepper.

Just before serving, stir in the cream and add the shrimps or prawns. Serve with crusty wholemeal bread.

Fried Flookburgh Fluke

These flatfish with longish tails are a speciality of Flookburgh and are really flounders. Their flavour is like that of plaice and thought to be finer by enthusiasts. Flukes are caught by being driven into stake nets on the sands around Flookburgh, which mark their dorsal side with 3 inch (75cm) diamonds. They are available from local fishmongers, but the majority are frozen immediately after landing at Flookburgh. There is really no better way of serving this fish than fried in butter, which is the local way. Allow 1 fish per person. Cut off its head and gut it. Dry the fish well. Season with pepper and fry gently in butter for a few minutes each side. Serve on a hot dish with melted butter and sprinkle with chopped parsley, or serve with a pat of savoury butter.

Flookburgh Flukes Baked with Shrimps   (serves 2)

2 fresh flukes, cleaned	1 egg
1oz (25g) butter	$\frac{1}{2}$pt (300ml) double cream
Sea salt and freshly milled pepper	1 tablespoon (15ml) fresh parsley,
2 small pots of potted shrimps	chopped

Dry the fish well with kitchen paper and slash them down the backbone on one side with a sharp knife. Season the fish and arrange them in a well-buttered dish. Top each fish with the potted shrimps and cover with buttered greaseproof paper. Bake in a moderate oven (350°F, 180°C, gas mark 4) for 15–20 minutes, depending on the thickness of the fish.

Beat the egg with the cream and season well. Heat the sauce very gently in a small saucepan. Do not let it boil, or it will curdle. When the fish is cooked, add the buttery cooking juices to the hot cream and pour over the fish. Brown under a very hot grill for 2 or 3 minutes and serve sprinkled with chopped parsley.

Baked Wild Lakeland Trout in Puffed Cheese Sauce
(serves 4)

Anglers who come to the Lake District to catch fish are principally in search of trout. The wild native brown trout lives in Lake Windermere and in other lakes in the region and they are also found in the small mountain streams. This recipe comes from Ullswater.

4 wild Lakeland trout	$\frac{1}{4}$pt (150ml) single cream
Milk	2 egg yolks
Seasoned flour	2oz (50g) Cheddar cheese, grated
5oz (150g) butter	Sea salt and freshly milled pepper
1 tablespoon (15ml) flour	Pinch of grated nutmeg
$\frac{1}{4}$pt (150ml) milk	6 egg whites

Cut the fins off the trout, but leave the heads and tails intact. Slit each fish right down the belly and press along the backbone to loosen it. Remove the bones and wash the fish. Fold the flesh together again. Prepare 4oz (125g) clarified butter for frying by melting butter slowly in a pan. Leave to stand until the sediment has settled, and strain through a muslin-lined sieve.

Dip the trout in milk and then in seasoned flour. Brown in sizzling clarified butter, but do not cook them through. Put them side by side in a lightly buttered ovenproof dish. Melt the remaining butter in a small saucepan and stir in the unseasoned flour. Cook for a couple of minutes, then gradually add the milk and single cream. Cook until smooth and thick. Remove from the heat and cool a little. Stir in the egg yolks, then the cheese. Season to taste with salt, pepper and nutmeg.

Whisk the egg whites until very stiff. Stir a little of the whipped egg whites into the sauce, then add this to the remaining egg whites. Cover the trout with this mixture and bake in a fairly hot oven (400°F, 200°C, gas mark 6) for about 10 minutes, or until puffed and golden brown. Serve immediately.

Fried Lakeland Charr
(serves 4)

The charr is the most unusual of the lake fish and the smallest member of the salmon family, very difficult to find in fishmongers because it is not fished commercially, but well worth the search. You have to go to Lake Windermere or Ullswater and make contact with a fisherman, or catch the charr yourself – having first checked that fishing for them is permitted. The charr is a most unusual fish, as big as a small trout, but more slender, silver and scarlet and olive green, the female being a deeper shade of pink inside.

About 1681 a Daniel Fleming of Ryedale wrote that Coniston Water produced 'many Pikes or Jacks, Bass or Perch, Trouts, Eels and Charrs; which last . . . is much esteemed and valued, being sold here [London] for ye most part at Two Pence apiece and many Charr-Pies being yearly in Lent (when this fish is in Season) sent unto London and other distant Places'.

This superb fish is best fried very simply and needs no sauce.

4 charr	Sea salt and freshly milled black
4oz (125g) butter	pepper
	Wedges of lemon

Wash, clean and dry the charr, but do not remove their heads or tails. Clarify the butter by melting it slowly in a small saucepan and leaving it to stand until the sediment has settled. Strain through a muslin-lined sieve.

Heat the clarified butter in a frying-pan, put in the fish and cook for a few minutes on each side. Season with salt and black pepper and serve immediately with wedges of lemon and plain boiled potatoes. Pour the pan butter over the fish.

Potted Lakeland Charr *(serves 6)*

Potted charr was a great delicacy which became very well-known in the 1770s when the Lake District experienced its first tourist explosion. With the recipe developed a very distinctive design in ceramics, the charr pot. The pots were shallow and white with hand-painted fish round the outside and were designed as non-returnable containers in which the fish could be prepared, transported and eaten. The charr would have been heavily encased in butter and the pots securely sealed to ensure that the contents withstood the jolting, discomfort and erratic temperature of an 18th-century mail coach trip from the Lakes to London. Most pots were originally made from 'delftware' or tin-glazed earthen-

Charr

ware and were supplied from factories in Liverpool; later on some were made from biscuit ware.

One of the few places that serves potted charr as a first course on its menu is Rothay Manor in Ambleside. Supplies, though, are dependent on the local fishermen around Lake Windermere who bring their catch to the hotel. They go out in boats between May and September to catch the fish using a rod and a series of lines, each ending in a hook and spinner. These spinners are the special trademark of each fisherman, hand made of brass, copper or silver and polished for hours. By using a number of weighted lines set at different depths in the water, the fisherman can find out where the charr are swimming. Some fish are caught 100 feet down and are often stunned by the pressure change when brought to the surface.

This recipe for potted charr was provided by the Cumbria Tourist Board and can be used for trout or salmon trout. Traditionally the potted charr would have been put in the fire-oven overnight.

2–3 charr	2 tablespoons (2 × 15ml) double cream
$\frac{1}{4}$pt (150ml) dry white wine	A little lemon juice
$\frac{1}{4}$ teaspoon (2ml) ground mace	Sea salt and freshly milled pepper
$\frac{1}{2}$ bayleaf	Clarified butter to cover
4oz (125g) butter	

Butter a casserole well and place the fish in it packed closely together. Pour over the wine. Tuck in the $\frac{1}{2}$ bayleaf and add the mace. Dot the fish with a little of the butter and bake in a slow oven (300°F, 150°C, gas mark 4) for about 30 minutes until tender. Drain the fish, cut off their heads and remove the bones and skin. Strain the cooking liquor and reduce by boiling to a strong syrupy essence. Stir in the rest of the butter so that it melts. Flake the fish into a blender or processor and add the butter mixture and cream. Season to taste with lemon juice and salt and pepper and blend or process to a paste. Check the seasoning and adjust if necessary, then pack into one large shallow pot or individual pots and chill.

When firm, cover with a layer of melted clarified butter and chill again. Cover with clingfilm and keep in the fridge for at least 24 hours before serving.

Serve with thin wholemeal bread and butter.

Manx Kippers

There was a small, but significant fishery in the Isle of Man in the 18th and 19th centuries. The original Manx boats, the square-sailed 'scowties' whose design had been influenced by their Viking ancestors, were replaced in the early 19th century by the more modern and larger cutter-rigged boats. Larger smacks cruised around the fleet taking the catch back to the island, to Liverpool or as far as the Mediterranean. By the 1820s, the Manx fleet comprised about 260 cutter or smack-rigged boats, crewed by 2,500 men, many of whom were also crofters.

The coming of the Cornish boats to the Manx summer fishing grounds for herring and mackerel in the 1820s also resulted in more efficient boats, called 'nickeys' because so many of the Cornish vessels being copied were called Nicholas, after the patron saint of fishermen. Local elm and Irish oak were used to build these boats, which were quite speedy. In the 1880s a smaller and more lightly rigged version, the 'nobby', was also developed. So many young men had departed from the island that there was the need for a boat which could be handled by a older, less numerous crew.

To the Manx, the herring is King of the Sea. Manx kippers, world famous and superb, are at their best during July and August. They are cured from very small herrings caught off the coast and landed at Peel and are especially delicate because they are smoked over oak sawdust. Manx law has always forbidden the use of artificial dyes in preparing them, although since 1983, under the Manx Kipper Rules for that year, 'approved colouring matter' has been allowed. However, the sweet Manx kipper is still a pale lemony fawn rather than the mahogany brown of the dyed varieties. There are three traditional curers on the Isle of Man whose kippers are worth asking for: John Curtis and Geo. Devereau in Douglas and Moore's in Peel, who supply Harrods.

Hot Manx Kipper Soufflé   (serves 3–4)

Some of the boarding houses and small hotels in Douglas make this dish as a speciality. It must be served straight from the oven either as a starter, or as a lunch or supper dish.

3 Manx kippers	Pinch of freshly grated nutmeg
2oz (50g) butter	4 large egg yolks, well beaten
2oz (50g) flour	5 large egg whites
$\frac{1}{2}$pt (300ml) milk, or single cream	$\frac{1}{2}$oz (12g) butter for soufflé dish
Pinch of cayenne pepper	

Jug the kippers (see p.146) and carefully remove all the bones and skin. Mash the flesh.

Melt the butter in a saucepan and stir in the flour. Cook over a moderate heat for 2 minutes, then gradually stir in the milk and cook gently for a few minutes until the sauce is thick and smooth. Season with pepper and nutmeg and stir in the flaked fish. Remove from the heat. Leave to cool a little, then stir in the beaten egg yolks.

Whisk the egg whites until they are very stiff and stir a tablespoonful into the sauce. Fold the rest in very carefully. Butter a 2½pt (1.5 litre) soufflé dish and pour in the mixture. Bake in a fairly hot oven (400°F, 200°C, gas mark 6) for 30 minutes. Serve and eat immediately.

Manx Queenies

Another speciality of the North West, fished off the Isle of Man, queenies are a small variety of scallop – the white muscle being only about the size of a two-pence piece across, but very sweet and full of flavour. Their eating quality is at its best from September until March. Queenies can be eaten raw served like oysters (see p.198) or used in any dish instead of scallops. The local fishermen at sea fry them in bacon fat and eat them with rashers of bacon and a generous helping of scrambled eggs.

Grilled Manx Queenies with Herb Butter

(serves 1–2)

10 Manx queenies in their shells	½ teaspoon (2.5ml) lemon juice
2oz (50g) butter	½ small clove garlic
1 teaspoon (5ml) fresh parsley, chopped	Freshly milled black pepper
½ teaspoon (2.5ml) fresh tarragon, chopped	

Scrub the queenies well. Beat the butter, herbs, seasoning and lemon juice together. Place the shellfish under a very hot grill until they open. Put a knob of herb butter on the meat of each one and grill for a few more minutes until the meat leaves the shell and the butter is bubbling. Serve immediately with warm crusty bread to mop up the buttery juices.

Artichoke and Queenie Soup (serves 6)

Queenies, like scallops, combine well with Jerusalem artichokes. The flavours of both are very delicate.

1½lb (675g) Jerusalem artichokes

2oz (50g) butter

1 large onion, chopped

2 medium potatoes, peeled and chopped

1½pts (900ml) chicken stock

Sea salt and freshly milled black pepper

12 queenies, removed from their shells

½pt (300ml) milk

2 tablespoons (2 × 15ml) fresh parsley, chopped

Double cream to garnish

Peel the artichokes, slicing them into a bowl of cold water to prevent them discolouring.

Melt the butter in a large pan and cook the onion until soft and transparent, but not coloured. Add the sliced artichokes and chopped potatoes, cover the pan and let the vegetables sweat for about 10 minutes on a low heat. Pour on the stock, cover again and simmer for another 20 minutes, then blend or push through a sieve. Return to the pan and season well with salt and pepper.

Poach the white part of the queenies very gently in the milk for 2 or 3 minutes and dice them, reserving the milk. Add the meat to the artichokes with the milk it was cooked in and heat through.

Just before serving, add the uncooked corals and chopped parsley. Check the seasoning again and serve garnished with a little cream.

Morecambe Bay Shrimps

The National Trust owns several hundred acres of pasture and woodland overlooking the flat sandy coast of Morecambe Bay, where the sea goes out for miles and from where the best shrimps in the North West, the small brown ones, are said to come. The shrimps are fished from Flookburgh and other villages around Morecambe Bay, to be exported all over the world.

Shrimp Teas 'up North'

Shrimp teas are very popular in the North of England. There used to be little seaside cottages with freshly-baked bread and fresh butter, where you could have shrimp teas. Dorothy Hartley in her book *Food in England* published in 1954 describes one such tea served by a Betsy Tattershall.

'Betsy brought out a pot of tea, with a woollen tea-cosy on it, sugar and cream, a cup and saucer each, two big plates of thin bread and butter – brown and white – a big green plate of watercress and a big pink plate of shrimps. And that was all, except an armoured salt cellar and a robin. Then you "reached to".' What a splendid meal and so simple, but do make sure your shrimps are really fresh and still smelling of the sea. Potted shrimps or shrimp paste can be served instead of fresh shrimps.

Morecambe Bay Potted Shrimps   *(serves 6–8)*

Since the 18th century the shrimps from Morecambe Bay have been potted with butter to preserve the surplus catch. Nowadays they are potted in tiny factories all along the coast, and the dish has taken its place alongside other tourist attractions in the region.

Most of the early recipes for potted shrimps produced something resembling a shrimp paste because the fish were picked, or shelled, pounded with butter and spices, then covered with a layer of melted butter. More recently, the shrimps have been left whole, stirred in melted butter with a little mace, nutmeg and cayenne, then packed into small pots or dishes. Finally, the buttered shrimps are covered with a layer of clarified butter which is left to set.

If you want to eat really delicious potted shrimps, make them yourself using freshly boiled and picked shrimps – preferably from Morecambe Bay. They make a super and easy topping for any grilled white fish.

1pt (600ml) picked shrimps	Pinch of cayenne pepper
8oz (225g) butter	Pinch of grated nutmeg
Blade of mace	

Melt 6oz (175g) of the butter slowly with the mace, cayenne and grated nutmeg. Stir in the shrimps and heat them through over a very low heat without boiling, stirring all the time. The butter will be absorbed by the shrimps. After discarding the mace, divide into little pots or fill one large one. Cool quickly and allow to set. Melt the remaining butter completely, then remove from the heat and allow to stand until the

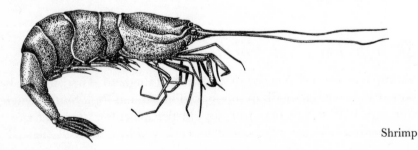

Shrimp

sediment sinks to the bottom. Strain through a muslin-lined sieve. Pour this clarified butter over the surface of the potted shrimps.

To serve, warm the shrimps slightly and eat with brown bread and butter or hot buttered wholemeal toast.

Shrimp Paste   (serves 6–8)

White fish and shrimps are used in equal quantities in this traditional fish paste, which has an excellent fish flavour. Serve for tea, as a starter at dinner, or for a summer lunch. Prawns can be used in the same way, but they should be roughly chopped.

12oz (350g) shrimps in their shells	Pinch of ground mace
12oz (350g) fresh haddock, cod or coley fillets	Cayenne pepper
	Dash of anchovy essence
Sea salt and freshly milled pepper	8oz (225g) softened butter

Pick or shell the shrimps. Put the heads and shells into a pan with water to cover. Bring to the boil, cover and simmer gently for 25 minutes. Blend or process briefly to crush and chop the shells, then strain every drop of the shellfish-flavoured stock through a fine sieve. Season generously with salt and pepper, then poach the white fish in the stock for about 8–10 minutes. Strain the shrimp stock again afterwards and use it to make a fish soup or stew, or freeze it.

Skin, bone and flake the fish fillets and chop or pound them very finely. Season to taste with ground mace, cayenne and anchovy essence. Add 6oz (175g) softened butter cut into little pieces and process or blend to make a smooth purée. Mix this purée with the shrimps in a basin, then check and adjust the seasoning if necessary. Pack into small china pots or one large pot and cool completely. Melt the remaining butter very slowly and leave to stand for a few minutes. Strain through a muslin-lined sieve and pour over the shrimp paste. Chill until shortly before serving, but make sure the paste is not too cold or the flavour will not come through. Serve with hot brown toast or warm crusty bread.

Dee Salmon and Shrimp Mousse   (serves 6)

Fine salmon is caught in the Dee, where the National Trust has about 40 acres of water-meadows, sandbanks and arable land at Heswall, on the Wirral, fronting the Dee Estuary with fine views across to North Wales. This land was bought in 1978 with the help of Enterprise Neptune funds. There is very little fishing in the estuary apart from the salmon, although the area used to be important for shellfish once caught in Liverpool Bay. Over the last 10 years, several salmon have been sighted in the River Mersey showing how much cleaner the river is becoming. Small bass, codling, grey mullet, gurnard, tope, dogfish and ray are all now being fished in the river, and grey seal are also back again. With the depressing story of increasing pollution that I have found all the way round the coast, it is so refreshing to find the opposite being true in one area at least.

Shrimps and prawns are fished from the beach at Formby, bought by the National Trust with Enterprise Neptune funds in 1967 and the nearest unspoilt coastline to the centre of Liverpool.

This is a very rich mousse and a tablespoon will be sufficient for one serving. It is not set with gelatine, so should be made in a soufflé dish or the equivalent as it will not turn out.

12oz (350g) freshly cooked salmon	Sea salt
8fl oz (240ml) milk	2 tablespoons (2 × 15ml) double cream
$\frac{1}{2}$ bayleaf	
1 blade mace	1 tablespoon (15ml) medium sherry or brandy
6 black peppercorns	$\frac{1}{2}$pt (300ml) aspic jelly (optional)
1 slice of onion	$\frac{1}{4}$ cucumber, thinly sliced (optional)
3oz (75g) butter	
1oz (25g) flour	

Remove all the skin and bones from the cold salmon. Put the milk in a small saucepan with the bayleaf, mace, peppercorns and onion. Heat very slowly until just under boiling point. Remove from the heat and leave to infuse for about 5 minutes.

Melt 1oz (25g) butter in a pan and stir in the flour. Cook for a few minutes, then pour in a little of the flavoured milk through a sieve. Beat until smooth, then continue to add the milk until you have a smooth sauce. Season with salt and stir over a gentle heat until boiling. Cook for 2–3 minutes, then leave on one side to cool.

Work the remaining butter until soft and lightly whip the cream. Pound, blend or process the salmon to break down the fibres of the fish so that it will then hold the sauce and butter without them curdling. Add the cold sauce and softened butter and blend together. Fold in the cream and the sherry or brandy and turn into a 6in (15cm) soufflé dish or suitable container. Smooth the top with a palette knife and set in a cool place for about 10 minutes to firm up. Pour over a thin layer of aspic jelly and when set arrange the cucumber slices in an overlapping circle on top, dipping each slice first in liquid aspic. When the cucumber slices are set in position fill the dish to the top with the remaining aspic. Serve slightly chilled with melba toast or brown bread.

Hot Poached Solway (allow 6–8oz [175–225g] per person)
Salmon with Shrimp Sauce

During the summer months, there is plenty of salmon to eat in the Lake District. Look out for signs saying 'Today's Special – Fresh Salmon', especially outside pubs.

Most of the fish comes from the Solway Firth and the estuary of the River Nith in Dumfries. Fishermen in these areas use a special purse net to catch salmon which they claim was introduced in Viking times, for the net is known as a 'haaf', the Norse term for the sea. The nylon net is draped over a wooden frame rather like a vast three-pronged fork, with a beam of pine often 14–18 feet across. The prongs or 'legs' are of greenheart – a wood with a good 'whip'. Some local men knit their own nets.

The National Trust holds 10 miles of coastline near Bowness on long lease and here, as at Bowness itself, it is not possible to fish the highest tides, because then the water is too deep and rough. When fishing the flow tide, a man looks for a good 'breeast' or slope of sand. A haaf-net fisherman may walk for $\frac{3}{4}$ hour before he reaches a good place for fishing. He may set off in sunshine and be overtaken by mist blowing in from the Irish Sea as the Firth is exposed to every wind that blows. Local fishermen say that 'Solway can catch a queer blast' and the sensible haaf-net fisherman wears warm clothes, oil skins and three pairs of socks inside his chest waders as he trudges over the sandbanks to gain the river channels. At a good fishing ground he may have to draw lots for his position in the river. There may be over 30 fishermen in a single line pulling out salmon. A haaf-netter stands in the water and holds the net upright against the tide; when he feels a salmon knock against the net, he has to tip and lift it out of the water to secure the fish. It is a clumsy instrument needing a lot of strength and skill and there are many variations in technique in different parts of the North West. Because this method is effective and could lead to over-fishing, licences are rigorously controlled by the local river authorities.

The thought of cooking salmon is always frightening and yet once mastered, it really is the simplest of all the fish. The problem is that salmon is nearly always overcooked, making it dry and tasteless. If you are not following a specific recipe here are a few simple rules to follow: if you are buying a piece of salmon rather than the whole fish, choose the tail-piece because it is moister and better flavoured; salmon should never go near water once it has been cut; the pieces should be wrapped in well-buttered paper or foil whether it is to be baked, poached or grilled, and the cooking time must be carefully calculated.

To Poach a Whole Salmon to Serve Hot

(allow 6–8oz [175–225g] per person)

1 fresh salmon, cleaned   Court bouillon (see p.208)

Stand the fish on the strainer of a fish kettle. Pour over enough cold court bouillon to cover the salmon. Put on the lid and bring the kettle very slowly to the boil. Cook the fish *very* gently, with the water *just* bubbling, allowing 1 minute to the lb (450g). Remove from the heat and leave the salmon to stand in the liquor with the lid on for about 30 minutes. Then, drain the fish for at least 5 minutes on its strainer covered with a clean tea-towel, to give it a chance to 'set'. Skin the fish if you wish and serve it with shrimp sauce (see p.216) and buttered new potatoes.

To Poach a Piece of Salmon to Serve Hot

(serves 12–15)

5lb (2.25kg) tail-piece salmon   Sea salt and freshly milled pepper
Butter

Brush an appropriately sized piece of foil well with melted butter. Season it generously. Lay the fish on the foil and make a tightly closed but baggy parcel. Fill a fish kettle half full of water and bring it to the boil. Lower the foil parcel of salmon into it on the strainer of the fish kettle. Bring back to the boil, turn down the heat at once so that the water is only trembling and allow 5 minutes per lb (450g), i.e. 25 minutes. Drain the fish for 10 minutes on its strainer, before removing it from the parcel and serving with shrimp sauce (see p.216) and buttered new potatoes.

For a 6–8lb (2.7–3.6kg) piece of salmon, allow 4 minutes per lb (450g), plus 5 minutes. For an 8–10lb (3.6–4.5kg) piece of salmon, allow 50–60 minutes total cooking time.

To Poach a Whole or a Piece of Salmon to Serve Cold

Cook as for a whole salmon until the cooking liquor has come to the boil, then remove *immediately* from the heat. Leave the salmon to cool completely in the cooking liquor, before removing. Skin carefully and decorate as you wish.

Lakeland Salmon Scouse

In most areas of the country where salmon has been an important fish, there is a traditional recipe combining salmon with potatoes. This one is an old Lakeland dish. It is simply freshly cooked salmon, skinned, boned and mixed with very buttery, well-seasoned mashed potatoes. Traditionally the dish is served with hot egg sauce.

Lune Smoked Salmon and Prawns   *(serves 6–8)*

The River Lune, flowing through the ancient picturesque city of Lancaster, provides what the locals say is the best salmon in the country. It is smoked locally by Lune Foods in Lancaster.

8oz (225g) smoked salmon, sliced

10oz (295g) shelled prawns

Generous ¼pt (150ml) home-made mayonnaise (see p.210)

Dash of Tabasco sauce

½ teaspoon (2.5ml) paprika

½ teaspoon (2.5ml) tomato purée

1 dessertspoon (10ml) double cream

Wedges of lemon to garnish

Sprigs of watercress to garnish

Roughly chop the prawns. Blend the mayonnaise with the Tabasco sauce, paprika, tomato purée and cream. Mix this with the prawns to bind them together and place the mixture on the slices of salmon, dividing it equally. Roll each slice up and serve on individual plates, with a wedge of lemon and a sprig of watercress. Provide plenty of brown bread and butter to eat with the salmon.

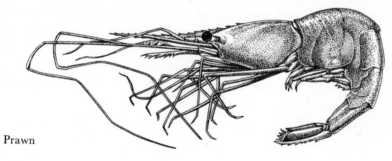

Prawn

Formby Asparagus

Asparagus farming has flourished on the Sefton coast in Merseyside for over 250 years and Formby asparagus, in particular, was very highly regarded by the connoisseurs who liked it for its crunchy texture, because it was grown on sand. At one time, local growers exported bundles all over the world, and it was served on Cunard liners. During the early part of this century, the cultivation around Formby peaked but there has been a steady decline ever since: 25 years ago about 250 acres of Formby coastline, just behind the sand dunes, were worked by 8 asparagus growers; today there are just 3 growers, farming little more than a couple of dozen acres, 2 on National Trust land.

Vegetables with a natural habitat on the shoreline seem to go particularly well with fish. This is certainly true of asparagus, which should be cooked with care – steam-boiled or steamed. The Romans always cooked asparagus upright and this is still considered one of the best ways. An asparagus pan, deep and narrow, fitted with a perforated basket, allows the tender tips to cook in steam while the stems boil gently in water. Failing a special steamer, you can improvise with a large saucepan and a glass jar.

To prepare the asparagus, use a knife to peel each stalk. Peel thickly at the butt end and thinly near the tip. Make bundles of about 10 stalks and tie up with string. Line up the tips and cut off the ends of the stalks. Stand the bundles in a glass jar almost filled with boiling water. Cover with perforated foil secured with a rubber band. Stand the jar in a large pan half-filled with boiling water. Steam for about 30 minutes. Use the cooking liquor for soup. Serve with any white fish, salmon, trout, or shellfish and accompany with melted butter or hollandaise sauce (see p.209).

Brown Shrimp Soup

(serves 6–8)

The National Trust owns several hundred acres of the Arnside/Silverdale Area of Outstanding Natural Beauty on the edge of Morecambe Bay, including the very attractive coastal fringe overlooking the salt marshes of the Kent Estuary. At high tide Morecambe Bay is a smooth blue semi-circle edged by green marshland dotted with sheep; at ebb tide, mile upon mile of sand and mud flats are revealed thronged with seabirds. This is the time the shrimpers set out with their tractors and nets across the sands.

2pts (1.2 litres) unpicked brown shrimps	2 egg yolks
2oz (50g) butter	$\frac{1}{4}$pt (150ml) single cream
2oz (50g) flour	Sea salt and freshly milled pepper
$2\frac{1}{2}$pts (1.5 litres) fish stock	1 tablespoon (15ml) fresh parsley, chopped
3fl oz (90ml) medium sherry	

Select 12 shrimps and reserve for garnishing. Melt the butter in a large saucepan and cook the rest of the shrimps, unpicked, for a few minutes. Stir in the flour and cook for a further 2 minutes, then gradually add the fish stock and the sherry. Simmer for 5 minutes, then pour the soup into a blender or processor. Blend or process and then sieve. Reheat gently. Mix the egg yolks in a bowl with a little of the soup, stirring thoroughly, then return to the soup. Let the soup thicken slowly over a low heat but do not allow it to boil. Pour in the cream and simmer for another minute. Season to taste.

Serve garnished with the reserved shrimps and parsley.

Solway Shrimp Puffs *(makes about 12)*

Another area in the North West where shrimps are caught is the Solway Firth. One fisherman operates from Allonby with a tractor and trawl seeking shrimps and the 'shoe net' is still employed, although it is now a curiosity. This net consists of a sandboard about 6 feet long with a 7-feet pole attached, forming the shape of a letter 'T', and a poke net. The operator wades in at low water, pushing the net ahead of him. Shrimps jump over the sandboard and enter the net. Such techniques are possible because at Allonby the Solway current is not strong inshore. The village itself was once a small fishing community with a fleet of 50 vessels early in the 18th century, but is now mainly devoted to the tourist trade with caravan parks and fields of chalets.

These shrimp puffs are traditional to the area. Serve as a starter or with drinks.

8oz (225g) flaky or rough puff pastry	Sea salt and freshly milled pepper
Beaten egg or milk	Dash of cayenne pepper
1oz (25g) butter	Dash of tomato sauce
1oz (25g) flour	4oz (125g) picked shrimps
5fl oz (150ml) single cream	A few whole shrimps to decorate

Roll out the pastry thinly to about $\frac{1}{8}$in (3mm) as evenly as possible. Using a 2in (5cm) cutter, cut out twelve rounds. Place these on a damp baking sheet and leave them to rest for 10 minutes in a cool place. Brush each one with a little beaten egg or milk and bake at the top of a hot oven (450°F, 230°C, gas mark 8) for about 10 minutes, or until golden brown. Remove them from the oven and transfer to a wire cooling rack. Split each one in half horizontally and scrape out any uncooked pastry from the centre. Melt the butter in a small saucepan and stir in the flour, then the cream to make a smooth thick white sauce. Season well with salt, pepper and cayenne and colour slightly pink with tomato sauce. Add the shrimps and check the seasoning again. Cool a little, then spoon into the warm puffs and sandwich them together. Warm up if necessary and serve, decorated with a few whole shrimps.

NORTHUMBRIA

Bamburgh Castle, Northumbria

Northumberland boasts a wealth of beauty in its windswept countryside and coastline. This is essentially a Celtic area with a predominantly Viking heritage.

The National Trust owns some of the most beautiful wild areas of coastline in Northumberland including two castles – Dunstanburgh and Lindisfarne, a complete fishing village – Low Newton-by-the-Sea, and a group of islands – the Farnes. Travelling north from the port of Blyth via the fishing village of Newbiggin to Amble, the gleaming golden sweep of Druridge Bay contrasts strongly with the scene of devastation caused by open-cast coal mines a mile or two inland. Some mines have now been grassed over, but Butterwell still has two or three working years left. The Trust bought a mile of coastline, consisting of 99 acres of windswept sand dunes and grass hinterland, in the centre of this bay in 1972 with Enterprise Neptune funds. A few miles north of Amble, near Alnmouth, the Trust owns a similar, smaller piece of coastline at Buston Links. The rest of the dunes and saltings at Alnmouth have been leased to the Trust by the Duke of Northumberland.

Further north, a grassy track leads from the picturesque fishing village of Craster along the edge of the sea to the dramatic ruins of Dunstanburgh Castle. The castle perches on an isolated hill on what is the eastern end of the Great Whin Sill, the basaltic backbone of this part of Northumberland. The craggy cliff on which the castle is built is a fine habitat for seabirds. Several hundred pairs of kittiwakes breed here and eider ducks, oyster-catchers and rock pipits nest in the grounds. The present great castle was begun in 1313 on the orders of Thomas, 2nd Earl of Lancaster and enlarged and considerably fortified by John of Gaunt in 1380. In the Wars of the Roses the castle was badly damaged and it fell rapidly into ruin providing stone, timber and lead for the repair of other castles and buildings in the area. The castle still remains a splendid ruin, the stone pitted and eroded by the sand-laden wind, unspoilt by modern buildings of any kind. It was given to the National Trust in 1961 by Sir Arthur Sutherland of Newcastle.

The National Trust also owns Embleton Links, the dunes and foreshore including the golf course, extending round the back of the bay. The calcium-rich sand provides ideal conditions for such plants as bloody cranesbill, burnet rose and pyramidal orchid. At the north end is Newton Pool, a freshwater lake behind the dunes protected as a nature reserve by the Trust. Breeding birds include the black-headed gull, mallard, teal, coot, mute swan, dabchick, sedge warbler and reed bunting. A footpath from the lake leads to Low Newton-by-the-Sea.

From Seahouses, Billy Shiel's motor boat *Glad Tidings*, or one of the other motor boats, will take visitors to the wild and windswept Farne Islands. Thirty treeless rocky islands, covering up to 80 acres depending on the state of the tide, divide into two main groups, the Megstones to the west and the Crumstones to the east. Each group has a lighthouse; the Longstone well out into the North Sea and the Inner Farne Light. It was from the Longstone in 1838 that Grace Darling and her lighthouse-keeper father rowed in appalling conditions to the wrecked SS *Forfarshire* to rescue survivors; a night that made her a national heroine.

The magnificent Farne Islands are possibly Europe's most important seabird reserve. To safeguard the birds only two of the islands are open to the public, Inner Farne and Staple Island. For nearly 900 years hermits and monks lived on Inner Farne, including St Cuthbert, who ended his days on the island. His influence made Inner Farne a place of pilgrimage and a Benedictine monastery was established there in the 13th century; with the exception of the lighthouse, all the buildings on Inner Farne date from the Middle Ages. St Cuthbert provided a *hospitium* for his visitors and the monks subsequently built a guesthouse on the site. All that now remains is the small stone 'Fishehouse' near the landing place.

At least 235 species of birds have been recorded on the Farnes, but they are best known for some 20 species of breeding seabirds. St Cuthbert was in fact the first person in this country to carry out bird protection, as he had a particular affection for eider ducks; they are still known locally as 'Cuddy's Ducks'! Now the National Trust has the awesome responsibility of managing the islands to ensure that the birds, grey seals (one of the largest breeding colonies) and visitors all get the maximum benefit from their stay without in any way endangering the habitat.

Magnificent views of the Farne Islands can be gained from St Aidan's and Shoreston Dunes, a 6-acre stretch of coastline between Seahouses and Bamburgh, also owned by the National Trust and very popular with visitors. On leaving Bamburgh, Lindisfarne Castle on Holy Island dominates the skyline; an incredibly romantic outline. In 1901 the owner and founder of the magazine *Country Life*, Edward Hudson, was enjoying a holiday in the North East when he was captivated by the sight of the decaying 16th-century castle on Holy Island. He bought the ruins and set his young architect friend Edwin Lutyens the difficult task of rebuilding the romantic castle and transforming it into a comfortable country house, which he triumphantly achieved. Gertrude Jekyll designed a little walled garden, with carefully chosen plants that would stand up to the rough climate and flower at their best in the summer, when the castle was full of guests. The original plans for the garden were recently discovered in California and the National Trust, with the University of Durham, has recreated the garden with more than 50 of the plant species originally selected by Gertrude Jekyll.

The windy coastlines and chilling rugged terrain of Northumberland have encouraged the meals of plain and wholesome food designed to feed well the inner man. The typical 15th-century Northumbrian breakfast of 'one loaf of bread, a quart of beer, a quart of wine, a dish of butter, piece of salt-fish and a dish of buttered eggs' would have sustained any warrior. As in Yorkshire, an extra fish and chip supper is often eaten as late as 10 p.m. Fresh fish from the local seaports figure in many of the traditional Northumbrian dishes. Although the herring industry has disappeared and the whole coast is suffering from over-fishing and pollution, fishing is still important to the economy.

The traditional east coast coble is the most popular boat with the working fisherman of Northumberland, who fishes for salmon and sea trout from March to August, pots for lobster and crab, catches prawns and, at various other times of the year, fishes the seabed with tangle nets for cod and other white fish.

Northumberland Fisherman's Chowder (serves 4–6)

This is the sort of soup-stew made and eaten at sea with some of the filleted fresh catch. It is served up steaming hot in pint mugs. The inclusion of bacon in this soup again shows the Viking influence on North East Britain. Any white fish can be used, such as cod, haddock, whiting, pollock and coley.

1oz (25g) butter	¾pt (450ml) water or fish stock
1 large onion, finely chopped	¾pt (450ml) milk
4oz (125g) streaky bacon, chopped	2–3 potatoes, scrubbed and diced
1oz (25g) flour	10oz (275g) white fish fillets

10oz (275g) Craster kipper fillets	Pinch of ground mace
4oz (125g) prawns, peeled	Freshly milled black pepper
3 tablespoons (3 × 15ml) double cream	Cayenne pepper
	Fresh parsley, finely chopped

Melt the butter in a large pan and cook the onion with the bacon until soft, but not coloured. Stir in the flour and cook for a few minutes. Add the water or fish stock and milk and heat until it is just gently simmering; then add the diced potato. Cover and simmer gently for 5–8 minutes, then add the white fish chopped into bite-sized pieces. Continue to cook for another few minutes and then add the kipper cut into bite-sized pieces, followed by the prawns. Cook until the kipper and prawns are heated through and then stir in the cream. Season with the peppers and mace and add the parsley. Serve with crusty wholemeal bread or toast for lunch or supper.

Cod with Mustard Sauce   (serves 4–6)

Almost the entire village of Low Newton-by-the-Sea, with 12 cottages, the Square including the Ship Inn, the beach and other land and buildings adjoining, is owned by the National Trust. It was bought in 1980 and 1982, partly from Enterprise Neptune funds.

In 1200 there were three boats engaged in full-time fishing and the Newton fishermen were brought up before the local bailiff for illegally claiming exemption from the payment of the toll of 'cayriefish'. Fifty years ago there were 12 boats operating in the summer and 7 in the winter. The Square housed the fishing families, all of whom assisted in hand hauling the boats to and from the sea. There used to be a little herring fishing but line fishing for cod and other white fish, with the daily, monotonous baiting of the lines, was the main occupation until the 1940s. This usually was done ashore by the women and children, often by candlelight. Lines baited with mussels on hooks at regular intervals were left on the seabed for a while, then hauled up. These charming fishing villages must have been very smelly places, littered with mussel shells and fish guts.

Today there is only one boat operating from the village, but the Square of cottages has become extremely popular with summer visitors.

As in all fishing communities, people on this coast found themselves eating a great deal of their catch. Most of it was simply cooked, but one Northumbrian housewife's recipe has emerged which obviously evolved out of the need to do something more interesting with cod.

1½lb (675g) small cod fillets

3 tablespoons (3 × 15ml) fresh parsley, chopped

1 medium onion, finely chopped

¾pt (450ml) water

Sea salt and freshly milled black pepper

Cut the cod into even-sized pieces and place in a large saucepan. Add the parsley and onion and cover with water. Season with salt and pepper and bring gently to simmering point. Cook the fish for about 5 minutes. Drain and keep warm on a serving dish.

Serve immediately with mustard sauce (see p.216) and jacket potatoes.

Beadnell Dressed Crab *(serves 4)*

The picturesque fishing village of Beadnell also has an agricultural history. To provide lime for the fields at the end of the 18th century, a huge lime kiln was built on the pier by a certain Richard Pringle. Later, 3 more kilns, stoutly built of sandstone, were added. When lime-burning fell off, the kilns were used for herring curing, until the herring industry died out. Now the kilns have another use; they are owned by the National Trust and local fishermen use them to store their lobster pots, which are quite unlike those used in other parts of the country. They are rectangular, made partly of metal and look more like huge rat-traps.

Preparing a crab is time-consuming, but the result is so much better than when you buy a crab already dressed that it is worth the effort.

1 freshly boiled crab, approx. 1–1½lb (450–675g)

1 tablespoon (15ml) mayonnaise

Salt and freshly milled black pepper

1oz (25g) fine brown breadcrumbs (optional)

1 hard-boiled egg

1 tablespoon (15ml) fresh parsley, finely chopped

Break off the claws and legs of the crab and put on one side. Holding the front of the shell towards you, push the body of the crab away from you using your thumbs, until it detaches itself completely. Remove the grey feathery gills, known as 'dead men's fingers', which lie on either side of the body and discard them. There should be 7 on each side. Also remove the stomach sac which lies behind the crab's mouth and discard this. The rest of the crab is edible. Cut the body in half with a sharp knife and remove all the white meat using a skewer into a bowl. Any brown meat adhering to the body should be put into a separate bowl.

Crack open the claws with a hammer or rolling pin and remove the white flesh with a skewer or knife. Add to the bowl of white meat. Treat the legs in the same way if they are reasonably large, otherwise use them to garnish the final dish.

Scoop out any soft brown meat left in the shell and put in the brown meat bowl, including the darker brown skin against the shell – it is all edible. To prepare the shell as a container for the finished crab, use a hammer to tap away at the clearly marked line on the underside, until the rough-edged part breaks away and can be discarded. Wash and dry the shell thoroughly.

Mix the brown meat of the crab with the mayonnaise and seasoning, and add breadcrumbs if the mixture is a bit soft. Flake the white meat finely. Spoon the brown meat into the centre of the shell and arrange the white meat either side. Finely chop the egg yolk and egg white separately and use to decorate the crab. Garnish with chopped parsley and the crab legs if they have not been used. Serve with thin brown bread and butter.

Eyemouth Pales   (serves 6)

Although the attractive village of Eyemouth lies just over the border in Scotland, there has always been an association with Northumberland. As early as the 11th century, a colony of monks from near Berwick decided that the Bay of Eyemouth was the only safe landing place in the area from which they could conduct their trade. Eyemouth became a busy port with a steady trade, particularly in grain, until the 18th century when fishing was the main source of livelihood.

Eyemouth, still a true fishing port with its picturesque sheltered harbour, has given its name to a special method of curing fish. The name 'Pales' is an apt description for a haddock smoked over sawdust to a pale golden colour quite distinct from the darker colour of the better known Finnan haddock. The haddock, after splitting and brining, take only 4 hours in the smoke-house to develop their delicate smoky flavour. The bone in this cure is not removed and this greatly enhances the flavour.

Pales are best left whole and slowly grilled with butter and seasoning, or poached, either on top of the stove or in the oven, in lightly boiling milk or water for 5–8 minutes depending on their size. The cooked fish can also be used to make the most delicious breakfast, lunch or supper dishes as in the following recipes. Finnan haddock may be substituted.

4 large Eyemouth Pales	1pt (500ml) double cream
1oz (25g) butter	Freshly milled black pepper

Poach the fish in lightly boiling water for 4 minutes and drain. Remove the skin and all the bones and flake the fish. Butter an ovenproof dish and arrange the fish in it. Pour over the cream, completely covering the fish. Sprinkle black pepper on top and bake in a moderate oven (350°F, 180°C, gas mark 4) for 10 minutes. Brown quickly under the grill and serve immediately with hot brown toast.

Eyemouth Fish Pudding
(serves 3–4)

Fish pudding recipes made with either breadcrumbs or potatoes are many and varied in this area of Northumberland. Again the Eyemouth Pales can be substituted by Finnan haddock or any smoked haddock without artificial colouring and flavouring.

2 large Eyemouth Pales	Salt and cayenne pepper
2oz (50g) fine white breadcrumbs	1oz (25g) butter, melted
2 eggs, separated	$\frac{1}{4}$pt (150ml) single cream
1 tablespoon (15ml) fresh parsley, chopped	

Poach the fish in boiling water for 4 minutes, then remove the skin and all the bones. Flake the flesh into a bowl. Add 1$\frac{1}{2}$oz (40g) breadcrumbs, the egg yolks, parsley, salt, cayenne pepper and melted butter. Lastly stir in the cream and mix together well. Beat the egg whites until stiff and fold gently into the mixture. Turn into a buttered ovenproof dish and sprinkle with the remaining breadcrumbs. Stand in a roasting tin half-filled with hot water and bake in a moderate oven (350°F, 180°C, gas mark 4) for 35–40 minutes, or until the top is lightly browned. Serve immediately.

Northumbrian Herrings in Oatmeal
(serves 4)

In the 19th and early 20th centuries the herring fishing industry was very important to Northumberland. Most of the east coast ports and villages were involved in catching and salting down herrings. The memory of the local fishergirls who gutted and salted the fish still lingers on. They were a hardy breed, usually recruited in February and travelling the whole of the east coast during the herring season. They all knew the cry 'Get up and tie your fingers'. Old cloths or 'clooties' were used as bandages to protect their fingers against the sharp knives and coarse salt, and as the season progressed old bits of sacking were utilised. The work was cold and very hard, and in the early 1900s the girls were paid 8d a barrel, or 3d an hour, shared amongst three of them. They worked a 12-hour day and had certainly earned every penny by the end of the season. In spite of the messy work, the fishergirls took a pride in keeping clean and were proud of their jerseys made to traditional patterns. Many of them wed fishermen whom they met on their travels.

Serving fish with bacon is another reminder of the Viking influence. The chief grains of this area were rye and oatmeal until the 18th century when more and more corn was produced. There are still many local recipes using oatmeal. Trout can be cooked in the same way.

4 fresh herrings

Milk

3oz (75g) coarse oatmeal

Sea salt and freshly milled black
pepper

Approx. 3oz (75g) lard or bacon fat
for frying

4 rashers streaky bacon, with rind
removed

Remove the heads of the fish and clean them. Scrape off the scales with
the back of a blunt knife, or a scallop shell – the traditional fish scaler.
Press each fish down firmly to open it out and remove the backbone,
taking out as many bones as possible. Dip the herrings into milk and
then into the oatmeal mixed with plenty of salt and black pepper,
patting it in well, particularly on the outside.

Make the bacon into small rolls. Heat a little of the lard or bacon fat in
a large frying-pan. When it is hot, fry the bacon rolls and the herrings
two at a time if there is room in the pan. Fry for a few minutes each side
depending on the thickness of the fish until brown and crisp on the
outside and soft and juicy inside, turning the herrings carefully, but do
not overcook. Serve immediately with hot mustard sauce (see p.216)
and brown bread and butter or oatcakes.

Baked Herrings in Lindisfarne   *(serves 6)*
 Mead

Lindisfarne, or to use its more modern name, Holy Island, lies 6 miles
north of Bamburgh and is linked to the mainland by a 3-mile causeway
which is under water for several hours at high tide. A small hut on stilts
has been provided by the side of the causeway for travellers unfortunate
enough to be caught by the incoming sea.

In 635 St Aidan came from Iona, the great Celtic centre of
Christianity, as bishop to preach the Gospel in the North of England. He
chose to found his monastery on the magic island of Lindisfarne or Innis
Medcaut. Perhaps his most famous successor was St Cuthbert, who was
transferred to Lindisfarne to teach the new Catholic faith following the

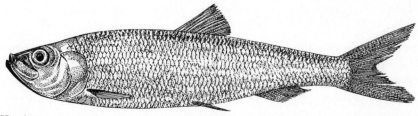

Herring

great Synod of Whitby. Viking and Scots raids eventually drove the monks away in 875, leaving the island virtually to nature. Two centuries later Benedictine monks arrived and renamed it Holy Island. The monks devoted themselves to clearing the ruined abbey and building the present priory. The fishing grounds had always been good and the monks took advantage of this, building their own boats using local labour. With the Dissolution of the Monasteries in the 16th century the priory in turn fell into ruins.

Shortly before 1800 a Bill of Enclosure settled the layout of the island and it has changed little since then. Fishing became really well established: in 1863 there were 37 herring boats and 17 white fishing boats. The wives and daughters of the fishermen worked hard at packing and gutting the fish, and they were so busy at times that help was brought from the mainland, on a half-share basis. This share system was, and still is, a method of payment for many Northumbrian fishermen, with one share for the boat and the rest for the crew.

Lindisfarne mead is still produced by the Lindisfarne Liqueur Company, who have a small distillery on the island. The mead can be sampled daily throughout the season at the Winery Showroom.

6 fresh herrings	$\frac{1}{2}$ teaspoon (2.5ml) salt
$\frac{1}{2}$oz (12g) butter	Freshly milled black pepper
4 bayleaves	1oz (25g) flour
Lindisfarne mead	1oz (25g) butter
Water	

Clean the fish well, then remove their heads and tails. Open them up and press down on each one to remove the backbone. Roll up each fish keeping the skin to the outside. Pack tightly in a buttered ovenproof dish with the bayleaves. Pour over the mead and water and season with salt and a little pepper. Sprinkle with flour and dot with butter. Bake in a moderate oven (350°F, 180°C, gas mark 4) for about 40 minutes, basting occasionally. Serve cold as a starter, or for lunch, with crusty brown bread.

Jugged Craster Kippers (serves 2)

In 1856, 5 smoke-houses for turning herrings into kippers were built in the charming village of Craster. Ever since, Craster has been famous throughout the world for its pale juicy kippers. Now there is only 1 factory using 3 of the old smoke-houses, started in 1906 by the grandfather of the Robson brothers, Kenneth and Alan, who keep it going today. At one time, Craster's own fishing fleet brought in the herrings for kippering, but now the fish are caught off the west coast of

Scotland and collected from Edinburgh daily. Only the best herrings are used for Craster kippers.

The Craster method of curing was invented by John Woodger from Seahouses, a few miles further north, who adapted the original salmon kippering technique to herring. The fish are first gutted and split down the back before being soaked briefly in brine. Much of the splitting is now done by machine, but some very skilled workers still do it by hand. The herring are then hung on tenterhooks in rows for loading into the old smoke-houses, some 5,000 at a time. The walls of the smoking sheds glisten blackly as you enter, shiny with the deposit of many years, with the rails for hanging the herring set high above your head. The method of smoking is by a base of white wood chips covered with oak sawdust and takes about 12 hours, with fresh fires lit every 2 to 3 hours. The smoke from the sawdust gives the kippers a characteristic mild smoky piquant flavouring; no artifical dyes are used.

Craster kippers are best cooked simply: grilled, fried in pairs, baked, poached or jugged as in the following recipe. A very old method of cooking kippers, it is nevertheless very easy and eliminates cooking smells.

| 1 pair of Craster kippers | 1oz (25g) butter |
| Boiling water | |

Remove the heads of the fish and stand them tail up in a tall heat-proof jug. Pour over boiling water to cover the fish. Leave for about 6 minutes, when they will be perfectly cooked. Remove them from the jug by the tail and dry them with kitchen paper. Serve immediately with a knob of butter, mustard and thin brown bread and butter. Jugged kippers are also excellent with creamy scrambled eggs.

Craster Potted Kippers (serves 6)

This can be served as a starter for lunch or with hot toast for supper. The kippers can be cooked in any way you like, but this recipe for baking them cuts down the cooking smells.

10oz (275g) kipper fillets	Ground mace
6oz (175g) unsalted butter	Freshly milled black pepper
Lemon juice	A little tomato purée

Place the kipper fillets on a piece of kitchen foil, dot with 1oz (25g) butter and sprinkle with lemon juice. Loosely wrap the fillets in the foil and bake in a moderate oven (350°F, 180°C, gas mark 4) for 15 minutes. Remove from the foil and remove the skin and bones, reserving the cooking juices. Melt the remaining butter and mash or blend well with the kippers. Add the kipper juice and melted butter. Season to taste with the mace, pepper and tomato purée, and more lemon juice if necessary. Blend or mix well and pile into a suitable pot or pots. Cover and chill for at least 8 hours before serving, making sure that you remove the pot from the fridge in plenty of time for the flavour to come out. Serve with hot brown toast.

Craster Kipper Dip
(serves 6–8)

4 Craster kipper fillets

2oz (50g) unsalted butter

1–2 tablespoons (1–2 × 15ml) single cream

1 tablespoon (15ml) lemon juice

Freshly milled black pepper

$\frac{1}{4}$pt (150ml) mayonnaise (see p.210)

Place the kipper fillets in a shallow pan or frying-pan of gently simmering water and poach for 4–5 minutes until tender. Drain and chill. Remove the skins and any bones from the fillets and blend in a food processor or liquidiser or flake into a bowl. Add the butter and single cream and blend well. Stir in the lemon juice and season with pepper, then finally add the mayonnaise. Mix well and chill before serving.

Serve with a selection of fresh raw vegetables such as cauliflower sprigs, baby turnips, peppers, new carrots, for a starter or party dish.

Cragside Lobster Pie
(serves 2–4)

Cragside is situated at Rothbury, the 'capital of Coquetdale' on the banks of the famous salmon- and trout-fishing River Coquet. Cragside House is a magnificent Victorian mansion designed by Norman Shaw and set in 900 acres of country park with fine rhododendrons, millions of trees, streams, lakes and waterfalls, now owned by the National Trust.

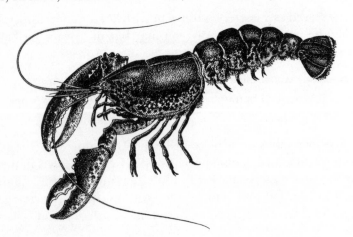

Lobster

The house was built for Lord Armstrong, the inventor of hydraulic machinery, the Armstrong gun and other armaments, and was the first house in the world to be lit by electricity generated by water-power. The lift, kitchen spit and many other pieces of machinery on the property were all run by hydraulic power.

This lobster pie recipe was given to me by John Forrest, who manages the National Trust restaurant at Cragside. John says that white fish can be included to make the lobster go further; it assumes a lobster flavour. He also sometimes uses kirsch instead of white wine. The pie is rich and delicious.

1 large freshly-boiled lobster	Salt and cayenne pepper
2oz (50g) butter	1 bayleaf
2oz (50g) flour	Freshly grated nutmeg
$\frac{3}{4}$pt (450ml) fish stock	2 hard-boiled eggs, sliced
$\frac{1}{4}$pt (150ml) white wine	8oz (225g) puff or flaky pastry
$\frac{1}{4}$pt (150ml) cream	Beaten egg to glaze

Remove the flesh from the lobster and cut it into cubes. Boil the shell in some good fish stock and reduce the liquid to give about $\frac{3}{4}$pt (450ml) finished fish stock. Melt the butter in a saucepan and stir in the flour. Cook for a few minutes before gradually adding the stock and the wine. Stir well until smooth and thick and then add the cream. Season with salt, cayenne pepper, the bayleaf and nutmeg. Add the lobster and sliced hard-boiled eggs to the sauce, then pour into an earthenware pie-dish. Roll out the prepared pastry and use to make a lid for the pie in the usual way. Decorate with the pastry trimmings and brush with beaten egg. Bake in a fairly hot oven (425°F, 210°C, gas mark 7) for about 30 minutes, or until the pastry is golden brown and well-risen. Serve immediately.

Newbiggin Poached Salmon (*serves 2–3*)

Of all the fishing places in Northumberland, the name of Newbiggin would probably come first to mind. Indeed, by the late 1300s it was being mentioned as a busy port with a pier. Fishing continued to grow in importance and by the end of the 19th century, encouraged by the opening of the Blyth and Tyne Railway, there were 30 to 40 cobles fishing from Newbiggin with most of the fish going to Carlisle and Newcastle. But in 1908 a colliery was sunk and this changed the face of the village. While mining increased, fishing decreased. By the late 1920s the promenade was under construction and the village had become a small town.

Many factors have affected Newbiggin fishing over the years; pit-falls on the seabed and developments to the south have caused material to be swept around from the Lynemouth area into Newbiggin Bay. Today there are only 8 or 9 cobles fishing on a full-time basis, some still operated by locals whose families have been fishing out of Newbiggin for generations.

Most of the villages along this coast have their own traditional ways of cooking salmon as it used to be so plentiful. Newbiggin was no exception. This particular recipe is from an old Norwegian lady who lived there all her life and was given to me by June Palmer, secretary to the Information Officer for the National Trust in Northumbria. The salmon stays very moist and succulent and can be served hot or cold.

1lb (450g) salmon	$\frac{1}{2}$ tablespoon (7.5ml) spring onion or chives, finely chopped
1 tablespoon (15ml) lemon juice	
$\frac{1}{4}$ teaspoon ($1\frac{1}{2}$ml) marjoram	Sea salt and freshly milled black pepper
1 bayleaf	2 tablespoons (2 × 15ml) oil
1 teaspoon (5ml) brown sugar	$\frac{1}{2}$pt (300ml) water

To serve cold, place the salmon in a pan which fits it snugly. Add the other ingredients and pour over the water. Cover and bring slowly to the boil. Remove from the heat and leave the salmon to cool in the liquid. Serve either in one piece or cut into steaks with a salad of thinly sliced cucumber and a light dressing.

If you want to serve the salmon hot, bring all the ingredients, apart from the fish to the boil. Lower the salmon into the water and bring back to the boil. Boil rapidly for 1 minute and then remove from the pan and serve.

Potted Newcastle Salmon   (serves 4–6)

Before salmon could be delivered fresh to the markets, it was usually pickled. Beer was the secret of the famous 18th-century Newcastle pickled salmon, which came not from Newcastle, but from the River Tweed. The fish was carried 60 miles by pack-horse to the salt pans of South Shields, where it was simmered in the characteristic pickle of beer, salt, and water, then potted with spices. It was claimed that salmon treated in this way would keep for a whole year.

The following recipe is based on this traditional way of potting salmon with spices. It makes an unusual starter or is delicious for lunch, tea or supper.

8oz (225g) filleted fresh salmon,
skinned

2 blades of mace

Pinch of ground cloves

6 black peppercorns, crushed

$\frac{1}{2}$ small bayleaf

A little freshly-grated nutmeg

Sea salt

6oz (175g) butter

Place the salmon in a shallow ovenproof dish which fits it tightly. Add all
the spices and the $\frac{1}{2}$ bayleaf and season with salt. Slice the butter and lay
it over the salmon. Bake the salmon in a moderate oven (350°F, 180°C,
gas mark 4) for about 15 minutes, or until cooked through. Drain the
fish and pour the juices through a sieve into a glass measuring jug. Blend
or process the warm salmon with the butter from the top of the glass jug,
but do not add the cooking juices at the bottom of the jug. Pack the
salmon into a china or earthenware dish and leave to get cold. Cover
with a thin layer of clarified butter. When this has set, cover tightly with
foil or greaseproof paper and leave to chill in the fridge for 24 hours
before serving with hot brown toast or crusty brown bread.

Traditional Berwick Salmon (*allow 6–8oz [175–225g] per person*)

As far back as the 14th century, the salmon fisheries of the Berwick area
were of note; on the north side of the River Tweed was Crown land with
the 'Kings Fisheries'; on the south side was Church land with the
'Bishops Fisheries'. Thousands of barrels of salmon annually were
exported from Berwick.

By the early 1500s the guilds of Berwick had been set up and laws were
laid down regarding the salmon trade; only guild members could rent a
fishery, or salt the fish, or export it. Perhaps this was why there was so
much poaching. The famous 'Newcastle salmon', so well known in
London at the time, was in fact poached Berwick salmon.

By 1800 there were about 300 men employed in the salmon trade and
the rental of the fisheries was worth about £10,000 a year, with July as
the best month for catches. By then the idea of packing fish in ice had

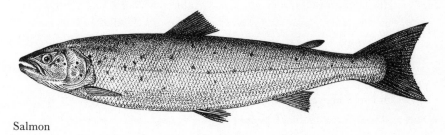

Salmon

151

been adopted and ice houses built, thus doing away with the old method of boiling in salty water and pickling.

The present Berwick Salmon and Fisheries Company is one of the oldest in Britain and began life in the 18th century when a group of local men took shares in a small fleet of sailing ships; these Berwick 'smacks' were fast and could travel from Scotland to London in three days, carrying large quantities of boiled and salted salmon. With the coming of the railway in the mid 19th century, the shipping trade declined, so the directors of the company decided to concentrate instead on improving their salmon fisheries. With seven to a crew, the fishermen now work on a share basis during the season from 14 February to 14 September. They use a sharp-nosed, square-sterned, flat-bottomed coble type of boat, partly decked so that 40–50 fathoms of net can be easily let out. The fish caught is taken to the company's premises in Berwick, where it is washed, graded, packed and then sent by rail or road to markets all over the country.

To Cook Tweed Salmon

The traditional Berwick way of cooking Tweed salmon is peculiar to the valley. Take a whole fresh salmon and weigh it. After gutting and cleaning, cut the fish along the back and then cut into half steaks about 1 inch (2.5cm) thick. Place the fish on the tray of the fish kettle. Fill the kettle with well-salted water and bring to the boil. Lower the tray of fish into it and quickly bring back to the boil. Boil rapidly, allowing 1 minute for every 1lb (450g) of the original weight of fish. (If cooking a half-steaked 7lb (3kg) fish, boil for 7 minutes.) Remove the tray from the fish kettle and drain. Allow the fish to cool.

The salmon should be served cold with a little of the cooking liquor, or 'dover' as they say in Northumberland.

Tweed Kettle   (serves 4–6)

In the 19th century, this type of dish was commonly known as salmon hash and was sold in cook-shops in Edinburgh with mashed potatoes.

2lb (900g) fresh salmon	2 tablespoons (2 × 15ml) dill, finely chopped
Water to cover	
$\frac{1}{4}$pt (150ml) fish stock	1oz (25g) butter
$\frac{1}{4}$pt (150ml) dry white wine	4oz (124g) mushrooms, finely chopped
2 tablespoons (2 × 15ml) shallots or chives, finely chopped	4oz (125g) shrimps or prawns, cooked
Salt and freshly milled black pepper	
Pinch of mace	

Put the salmon in one piece into a pan which just fits it. Cover with water and bring slowly to the boil. Simmer for 1 minute and remove the salmon from the pan with a draining spoon, reserving the cooking liquor. Peel off the skin and remove the bones and put on one side. Cut the fish up into pieces about 1in (2.5cm) square.

Return the skin and bones to the cooking liquor and simmer for 15–20 minutes. Strain and reserve the stock. Measure $\frac{1}{4}$pt (150ml) of the fish stock and put in a new saucepan with the wine. Add the salmon and shallots. Season with salt, pepper and mace and bring to the boil. Cover and simmer very gently for 3–4 minutes. Add the dill and adjust the seasoning if necessary.

Melt the butter in a small saucepan and cook the mushrooms gently until soft. Add to the fish with the shrimps or chopped prawns and serve hot with creamy mashed potatoes.

Marinated Trout Fillets   (serves 6)

Fresh trout is found in many of the rivers of Northumberland. Marinated for several hours in a creamy dressing, it makes a delicious summer lunch or starter.

3 river trout

Sea salt and freshly milled black pepper

3 tablespoons (3 × 15ml) lemon juice

2 tablespoons (2 × 15ml) shallot, finely chopped

A pinch of powdered English mustard

$1\frac{1}{2}$ teaspoons ($1\frac{1}{2}$ × 5ml) sugar

8fl oz (240ml) double cream

2 teaspoons (2 × 5ml) ·bland nut-oil

1 tablespoon (15ml) fresh dill, chopped

Fillet the trout and skin them, removing any bones. Cut each fillet diagonally into 6 or 7 strips, following the natural grain of the fish. Season well with salt and pepper. Mix the lemon juice, shallot, mustard, sugar and cream in a small basin with the oil and whisk until very lightly thickened. Stir in the chopped dill and the seasoned trout strips. Cover with foil and leave to marinate in the fridge for at least 3 hours, preferably overnight.

Serve decorated with sprigs of dill and accompany with fingers of buttered rye bread.

Coquet Riverside Kedgeree

(serves 6)

The River Coquet is famous for its salmon, sea trout and river trout. Kedgeree is one of the easiest and best ways of using up cooked salmon or trout, although smoked haddock is also very good. It was a very popular breakfast dish in Victorian and Edwardian times, having been brought back from India. There are dozens of variations; this particular one is made with brown rice and includes prawns and peas – do experiment with other ingredients for yourself, such as dried fruit. Kedgeree is excellent for lunch or supper, as well as for a special breakfast.

12oz (350g) cold cooked sea trout, salmon or river trout	1 tablespoon (15ml) lemon juice
2oz (50g) butter	Salt and freshly milled pepper
1 small onion, finely sliced	6oz (175g) brown rice, cooked
4oz (125g) button mushrooms, finely sliced	4oz (125g) young peas, cooked
1oz (25g) flour	3 hard-boiled eggs, cut into eights
Pinch of curry powder	8oz (225g) prawns, peeled
1pt (600ml) milk	3 tablespoons (3 × 15ml) fresh parsley, chopped

Remove any skin and bones from the fish and flake into big chunks. Melt the butter in a large saucepan and gently fry the onion until soft, but not coloured. Add the mushrooms and fry for a few minutes. Stir in the flour and curry powder and cook for another few minutes. Gradually add the milk until the sauce is smooth. Slowly bring to the boil and stir in the lemon juice. Season well with salt and pepper. Add the cooked rice and peas followed by the chunks of fish. Reheat gently, making sure that the fish does not disintegrate. Just before serving, stir in the prawns and hard-boiled egg segments. Check the seasoning again and transfer to a warm serving dish. Sprinkle with parsley and serve immediately with a large green salad.

Alnmouth Whiting with Cream and Herbs

(serves 6)

Although never really a busy fishing village, Alnmouth still warrants a mention when talking of Northumbrian fishing. The converted granaries recall its past history as a grain-exporting port in the 17th century. The fishing rights of the area originally belonged to the Church, but with the Dissolution of the Monasteries they passed first to the Crown and then to the Duke of Northumberland.

Now there is only one full-time fisherman at Alnmouth, but the lovely little village is considered a very desirable place to live and a great place for a holiday. The National Trust has covenants over 272 acres of fantastic duneland and saltings adjacent to the river, which can be reached by a track from the main road just south of the village. This land was leased to the National Trust in 1966 by the Duke of Northumberland whose family seat is Alnwick Castle, which dominates the town of the same name, a few miles inland and famous for its summer International Music Festival. From Alnmouth Dunes a public footpath and bridle way leads on to Buston Links, a further $18\frac{1}{2}$ acres of sand dunes. Sand quarrying in the 1950s and 60s threatened the existence of these dunes, but the fencing of vulnerable areas, the planting of marram grass and the laying of paths by the National Trust have saved the situation.

Whiting is one of the white fish commonly caught off this coast and was often 'wind blown' by the fishermen. After salting briefly, the fish were hung up on pegs at the side of the house out of the sun and left overnight to sharpen the flavour. They were then cooked simply with butter. For this recipe, which is a popular way of cooking in the North East, the whiting must be very fresh, otherwise the flavour of the fish deteriorates rapidly.

6 small fresh whiting, whole	$\frac{1}{2}$ tablespoon (7.5ml) chives or shallot, finely chopped
Milk	
Seasoned flour	$\frac{1}{4}$pt (150ml) fish stock or milk
2oz (50g) butter	2 tablespoons (2 × 15ml) double cream
1 tablespoon (15ml) fresh parsley, finely chopped	

Clean the fish if necessary and remove the eyes. Curl each whiting round, with the tails through the eye sockets. Brush with milk and dust with well-seasoned flour. Melt the butter in a frying-pan and slowly fry the fish. Add the chopped parsley and chives or shallot to the fish stock or milk, followed by the cream. Mix well and pour over the whiting before they are cooked. Continue to simmer until the fish is cooked. Serve the fish with creamy mashed potatoes or buttered new potatoes.

YORKSHIRE

Robin Hood's Bay, N. Yorkshire

Forty-five miles of the North Yorkshire coast have been identified as worthy of protection, and currently the National Trust owns only 8. A great deal of this land is in little pieces spread along the coast, so additional Enterprise Neptune funds are urgently needed to buy more coast when the opportunities arise.

Recently Enterprise Neptune acquired Newbiggin, just north of Filey, an area of 25 acres of extremely beautiful cliff top popular with nesting guillemots. The Cleveland Way, a long distance footpath of 100 miles, runs across this land and actually starts at Filey. It follows the coast all the way up to Saltburn-by-the-Sea, before cutting inland to cross the North Yorkshire Moors, ending at Helmsley. Several of the National Trust's coastal properties are reached only from the Cleveland Way; one of these being Knipe Point and the small beach of Cayton Bay below.

Another small but very attractive bay overlooked by high cliffs, a few miles north of Scarborough, is Hayburn Wyke, reached by a woodland path running beside a stream, which climbs down the cliff face in a waterfall cascading on to the rocky beach below. Further north again the Trust owns another two miles of superb cliff top at Stainton Dale above the remote and beautiful undercliff at Beast and Common Cliff.

The most spectacular bay along this stretch of coast is Robin Hood's Bay. National Trust ownership includes most of the southern headland at Ravenscar and all the northern headland beyond the village of Robin Hood's Bay, known locally as Bay Town. Most of this coastline was acquired between 1979 and 1982 under the Enterprise Neptune Campaign.

Ravenscar is a tiny scattered community perched on the great south headland, overlooking the wide sweep of the Robin Hood's Bay. It used to be called Peak, until 1900 when its name was changed to Ravenscar and it became 'the town that never was'. From the late 19th century to World War I, a company attempted to create a second Scarborough here. Sewers and roads, still traceable, were laid down, but the people never came because of the high winds on this exposed cliff-top site. Eventually the development company went bankrupt. The Trust have an information centre and shop at Ravenscar where details of the Ravenscar Trail may be obtained. This trail has been established to illustrate some of the unique geological features and land forms of the area, and the way-marked route starts outside the Trust shop. The complete walk takes about two and a half hours at a leisurely pace.

Adjoining the village of Robin Hood's Bay is another area of fine coastal land and cliff bought for Enterprise Neptune in 1976 and known as Rocket Post Field. Nearby, Bay Ness Farm and Ness Point, with nearly 70 acres of superb cliffs, form the northern headland of Robin Hood's Bay, all belonging to the National Trust. Further up the coast is the very well-known local landmark of Saltwick Nab, 1 mile east of Whitby, consisting of several acres of cliff and a low, rocky point or nab jutting out into the sea and owned by the Trust. Access to this wild and beautiful spot is from the Cleveland Way.

The harvest of the sea has been one of the chief concerns of the inhabitants of the North Yorkshire coast since time immemorial. Although most of the villages have generally been too poor to provide themselves with man-made harbours, the innumerable creeks and bays have afforded enough protection for the launching and landing of small boats or cobles unique to the east coast. All along the Yorkshire coast from Filey to Staithes the sturdy little cobles still fish the waters. The coble has changed little since the 16th century and is descended from the Viking longboat, which brought the Norsemen first to plunder, then to settle in this region. Its distinguishing features are a deep bow, high shoulders and a low sloping square stern with a long detachable rudder ideal for launching into the waves. From the beach it heads into the sea, but is landed stern first with rudder unslipped. In the days before the petrol engine, the coble's brown square sail must have made a fine sight as it sped out to sea with a stiff westerly behind it. All kinds of fish are caught by coble fishermen; haddock, cod, mackerel, ling, halibut, catfish or 'woof' as it is known locally, as well as lobster, crab and salmon. Larger boats known as 'keel boats' work from the bigger fishing ports of Whitby and Scarborough. Using trawls, seine nets, drift nets or lines, they catch cod, haddock, plaice, whiting and skate, while some concentrate on crab and lobster. Although these keel boats now carry a mass of modern equipment they still bear a close resemblance to the old Humber keels from which they sprang.

The area of the North Sea lying between the Dogger Bank and the Yorkshire coast has been one of the most productive of all the fishing grounds in England. Fresh fish has always formed an important item of diet in Yorkshire, with seafish readily available from these east coast ports and freshwater fish from the unpolluted streams and rivers that drain from the Pennines and the Moors. Indeed, fish consumption in the county is 49% above the national average. Even in towns too small to hold a regular market there is inevitably an excellent fishmonger's shop where quality and choice is good.

Scarborough Woof Pie *(serves 4–6)*

A delicious fish, caught off the north coast of Yorkshire, is called locally 'woof', supposedly from the sound it makes when thrown on to the deck of a boat. It is, in fact, catfish, also known as wolf-fish, rock turbot or rock salmon, and is usually sold in fillets without the head and skin as it is such a fierce looking creature. The flesh is firm and pinkish white with only a central bone and is very good to eat. Woof pie is a dish traditional to many places along the north coast, but 'Scarborough Woof' is particularly famous in Yorkshire.

1½lb (575g) fillets of catfish	1 medium onion or 1 large leek, finely chopped
1oz (25g) butter	
Salt and freshly milled black pepper	½pt (300ml) milk
About 1 tablespoon (15ml) flour	8oz (225g) shortcrust pastry
8oz (225g) streaky bacon, chopped	Beaten egg to glaze
4 hard-boiled eggs, sliced	

Skin the fish if necessary and cut into small pieces. Generously butter a pie-dish and put in a layer of fish. Season well and sprinkle with a little flour. Add a layer of bacon, a layer of sliced egg, and a layer of onion (or leek). Repeat the layers, seasoning well, until the dish is full. Pour over the milk. Roll out the pastry and use to make a lid for the pie. Cut a slit in the top of the pastry to allow the steam to escape during cooking. Bake in a fairly hot oven (375°F, 190°C, gas mark 5) for about 50 minutes, protecting the pastry with greaseproof paper if it is browning too quickly. Serve hot or cold.

Cod and Bacon Pot *(serves 4)*

The 'Cod of Grimsby' has been famous since early medieval days and it was early in the 15th century that the distant-water fishermen of the region, who had larger boats than the inshore fishermen, pursued cod on the Dogger Bank and for the first time moved towards Iceland. They left in March, taking provisions for the summer and salt. When they reached Icelandic waters they caught cod, salted it on board, before drying it. At the end of the summer when all their salt had been used up, they sailed for home and the autumn markets.

Not all the cod was salted and dried; some was barrelled in salt and left in its own pickle until the boat came home. Fish in this state was known as green fish, and sometimes was taken out and dried at the end of the voyage, after spending several weeks in brine. The salted and dried cod was known as stock-fish and required drastic treatment to make it edible. 'And when it is desired to eat it, it behoves to beat it with a wooden hammer for a full hour and then set it to soak in warm water for a full two hours or more, then cook and scour it very well like beef; then eat it with mustard or soaked in butter.' The stock-fish hammer was a regular kitchen item, even in Elizabeth I's reign, but the fish was eaten more from necessity than pleasure.

Interestingly, salt cod and stock-fish still come from Norway and Iceland where they are hung up to dry on racks in huge open sheds. The main market for salt cod are the Mediterranean countries, especially Portugal, although it is available here from some specialist food shops. If you should come across it, the fish must be soaked for at least 24 hours with several changes of water before being simmered in water for about 15 minutes. The flesh is good served cold with a garlic mayonnaise or can be used in various fish stews.

The inshore fishermen on the north-east coast still fish for cod in the winter and if you are buying from a fishmonger, always ask for inshore cod; it has a much better flavour. This recipe is a typical north-eastern dish bearing a close resemblance to New England coastal recipes, where salt pork is used instead of bacon.

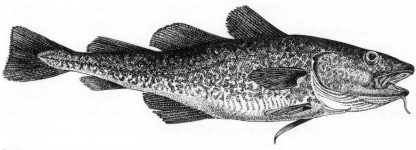

Cod

4 cod steaks (about 6oz (175g) each)

Sea salt and freshly milled pepper

2oz (50g) butter

1 large onion, very thinly sliced

2 tablespoons (2 × 15ml) fresh
parsley, chopped

$\frac{1}{2}$ teaspoon (2.5ml) dried thyme

4 rashers back bacon, chopped

4oz (125g) haricot beans, cooked

Approx. $\frac{1}{2}$pt (300ml) milk or single
cream

1lb (450g) potatoes, very thinly
sliced

Pinch of grated nutmeg

Season each cod steak. Butter an ovenproof dish using half the butter and cover the bottom of the dish with slices of onion. Arrange the fish on top of the onions and sprinkle over the parsley and thyme. Add the bacon and cooked haricot beans. Pour over enough milk or cream just to cover and top with thin slices of potato. Dot with the remaining butter and bake in a moderately hot oven (400°F, 200°C, gas mark 6) for about 45 minutes, or until tender. Serve immediately.

Bay Town Crab   (serves 4)

The village of Robin Hood's Bay, known locally as Bay Town, was once a thriving fishing centre. In the mid 19th century there were still 35 cobles and 5 yawls working from the village, but now there is just a handful of cobles catching sole, plaice, halibut, lobsters, crabs and shrimps. It is a picturesque place, with narrow streets leading down to the sea and an attractive collection of red-roofed cottages huddled around the slipway at the foot of a steep ravine.

In the early 19th century, crabs and lobsters were caught using bag-nets or 'trunks' fixed to iron hoops about 20 inches in diameter. From around the 1850s, these were replaced by crab and lobster pots, baited and dropped on to the seabed from cobles; lines and floats enabling them to be drawn up to remove the catch.

This crab recipe was a famous 18th- and 19th-century dish in Yorkshire. It makes a delicious starter or supper dish.

1 freshly boiled crab

2$\frac{1}{2}$oz (60g) butter, softened

Sea salt and cayenne pepper

Pinch of grated nutmeg

1 tablespoon (15ml) breadcrumbs

1 tablespoon (15ml) double cream

2 tablespoons (2 × 15ml) dry white
wine

1 anchovy fillet or essence

Fresh parsley to garnish

Remove the crab meat from the shell (see p.142) and flake. Mix the meat in a bowl with 2oz (50g) softened butter, seasoning and nutmeg. Add the breadcrumbs, cream and wine, and then the mashed anchovy fillet or anchovy essence. Blend thoroughly and put back in the cleaned crab shell. Dot with the remaining butter and cook under the grill for about 10 minutes. Garnish with parsley and serve with hot buttered brown toast. Alternatively, pile the blended mixture straight on to the toast.

Yorkshire Fish and Chips

'Fish and Chips' are an institution which is said to have originated in Yorkshire and the North West and Northerners still insist that only in their part of the kingdom is there real fish and chips.

Fish was first fried to preserve it for a day or two longer and in 19th-century London was sold already cooked with baked potatoes or bread, but there were no chips. About 1870, the practice of combining the sale of fried fish with unpeeled chipped potatoes, was introduced from France and revolutionised the trade. Although London makes claim to being the first fish and chip centre in the country, in the North they have different ideas! Certainly, the organisation of the trade as we know it began in the North, the first co-operative on record being in Hull in 1893.

'T' biggest chip 'oile i' Yorkshire' and the biggest fish and chip shop in the world is Harry Ramsden's at Guiseley, between Leeds and Ilkley, a vast place employing 200 people in shifts and visited with a mixture of reverence and fanaticism by millions of people each year. You can either go to the takeaway side and eat on the rows of benches out in front, or sit inside in the bright bustling restaurant with its cut-glass chandeliers, plush decor, soft fitted carpet, banks of fresh flowers and waitress service. Ramsden's thrives and maintains its reputation by producing very good food; chips that are crisp and light and made from fresh potatoes; fresh best quality fish from Grimsby which is skinned and fried in beef dripping with a thin covering of crisp and succulent batter. Plaice and halibut are on the menu, but 80% of customers choose haddock, the Yorkshire man's favourite. All this is traditionally served with a plate of bread and butter and a pot of tea.

The history of the place is fascinating. In 1928 Mr Harry Ramsden borrowed £150 to open a small green and white painted hut as a fish shop. He stood at the serving hatch in front of two pan friers – a large man in a wing collar, Arthur Askey glasses, starched apron and a ribboned straw boater. The coming of the motor car and the potential of the location, a natural gateway to the Lake District and the Yorkshire Dales, inspired Mr Ramsden to embark on an ambitious scheme to build the largest fish and chip shop in the country, which he achieved in 1931. In 1954 Harry decided to sell out to Eddie Stokes, a restaurateur from Blackpool, who changed Harry Ramsden's from a popular attraction into the unique establishment it is today. In 1965 the business was acquired by Associated Fisheries and is now managed by Tony Bramwell, well qualified to run the place as he was born across the road from Ramsden's and employed in the shop as a boy.

Madge's Special Fish Batter   *(enough for 4 large pieces of fish)*

Madge is my sister's mother-in-law and a Yorkshire woman. She worked in her mother's fish and chip shop until they sold out to Bryan's: the shop has since become famous in Leeds. This is the batter recipe they used, light and really crisp. Some recipes suggest using beer, yeast, lemon juice and eggs, but this is the best fish batter I have tried and, as Eddie Stokes used to say, 'nowt's right, unless the batter's right'.

4oz (125g) plain or self-raising white flour

Pinch of salt

3 teaspoons (3 × 5ml) malt vinegar

Approx. $\frac{1}{4}$pt (150ml) water

4 haddock fillets

Seasoned flour

Dripping or oil for frying

Sieve the flour and salt into a bowl, then gradually beat in the vinegar and enough water to make a smooth batter which will coat the back of a spoon. Remove the skin from the fish and rinse under cold water. Dry well with absorbent kitchen paper and dip in seasoned flour before lightly coating the fish in batter. Deep-fry or shallow-fry in dripping or oil until the batter is puffed, golden brown and crisp. (The fish is steamed inside the batter.) Serve immediately with freshly-fried chips, vinegar, bread and butter and a pot of tea. 'Mushy peas' are also a favourite accompaniment in Yorkshire.

Yorkshire Fish Scallops   *(serves 4)*

These 'fish cakes' can be bought already cooked in many of the fish and chip shops in Yorkshire, but they are also very popular as a homemade dish. I think they are quite delicious and look forward to my first Yorkshire fish scallop when visiting my sister.

4 small fillets of haddock

Salt and pepper

8 slices of potato, the same size as the fish and cut $\frac{1}{4}$in (5mm) thick

Madge's special fish batter (see above)

Remove the skin from the fish and season well with salt and pepper. Sandwich the seasoned fish between two potato slices. Dip each sandwich into the prepared batter and deep-fry in dripping or oil for 8–10 minutes, or until the potato is tender. Serve immediately with fresh tomato sauce, vinegar, bread and butter and a pot of tea.

Filey Brigg Haddock   (serves 4)

The seaside resort of Filey is famous for its Brigg, a long shelving strip of rock extending out to sea, which is covered at high tide. According to legend it belongs to the Devil who wanted to make it stretch across the North Sea but, tiring of the effort, he dropped his hammer into the sea. In trying to find it, he grabbed a fish instead – locally caught haddock are said to be marked with his fingerprints to this day.

4 thick haddock steaks or fillets	1 egg, beaten
Approx. 4oz (125g) butter	Flour
Sea salt and freshly milled pepper	

Line the grill pan with lightly oiled cooking foil and place the steaks or fillets on top. Dot with butter and season well. Cook under the preheated grill until the butter has melted. Then brush the fish generously with beaten egg and sprinkle with flour. Dot with more butter, before continuing to cook the fish. Turn the fish over once and baste with the butter in the pan. Test to see if the fish is cooked through by sticking the point of a knife into the flesh next to the central bone. It should fall away easily. The cooking time will obviously depend on the size and thickness of the fish. Serve immediately with shrimp sauce (see p.216).

Pan-fried Halibut   (serves 4)

Halibut is in season all the year round and lives in the cold deep waters of the North Sea. It is the largest of all the flat fish and can grow as long as 10 feet. The biggest ever landed was at Hull and weighed 660lb (300kg), but the ideal size to produce good steaks is said to be about 3lb (1.3kg). Halibut is highly nutritious, full of vitamin D and has a valuable liver oil. The main problem with cooking it, is to make sure that the fish does not dry out, so it should be treated with care. The steaks should be grilled with plenty of herb or savoury butter, baked in lightly buttered foil, poached or fried gently as in the following recipe. Halibut is excellent poached and eaten cold with mayonnaise. When buying the fish, try to avoid the tail, which can be particularly dry.

4 halibut steaks

Lemon juice

Seasoned flour

Salt and freshly milled black pepper

2oz (50g) butter

1 tablespoon (15ml) fresh parsley,
chopped

1 tablespoon (15ml) oil

Dip each steak in seasoned flour, shaking away any that is surplus. Melt the butter and oil in a frying-pan, tipping the pan from side to side to ensure that it is melting evenly. When the fat is foaming and giving off an almond-smelling haze, lower each steak into the pan. Fry the fish on both sides until cooked and then remove to a warm serving dish. Squeeze a little lemon juice into the pan, add a little salt and pepper and the chopped parsley (with a little more butter if necessary), and stir vigorously over the heat for a few seconds. Pour the sauce over the waiting fish and serve immediately with boiled or creamed potatoes. Decorate with deep-fried parsley sprigs if you wish.

Ravenscar Baby Halibut   (serves 4)

Baby or chicken halibut is a young and smaller than normal halibut, about the size of a large plaice, but fatter (2–3lb [900kg–1kg]). This recipe was given to me by Valerie Russell, the manageress of the National Trust Information Centre at Ravenscar, who regards baby halibut, quite rightly, as a delicacy.

4 baby halibut fillets

Fish cooking liquor

Salt and freshly milled black pepper

$\frac{1}{4}$pt (150ml) whipping cream

2oz (50g) butter

Tomato ketchup

$\frac{1}{4}$pt (150ml) dry white wine

A squeeze of lemon juice

4oz (125g) prawns (with their shells
if possible)

1 tablespoon (15ml) fresh parsley,
chopped

$\frac{1}{4}$pt (150ml) milk

Lemon slices to garnish

1oz (25g) flour

Skin the fillets of halibut, season the cut side of each fillet and roll up. Secure each roll with a cocktail stick to keep its shape. Using half the butter, grease a fireproof dish which is just large enough to hold the rolled-up fish. Place the fish in this dish and pour the white wine over it.

Bring to the boil on top of the stove, cover with foil or greaseproof paper and cook in a moderate oven (350°F, 180°C, gas mark 4) for about 10 minutes, or until tender, turning the fillets once. Meanwhile, peel and chop the prawns and place the shells in a small saucepan with the milk. Bring the milk to the boil and simmer over a gentle heat for 10 minutes to extract the flavour from the shells. Strain the milk and reserve for the sauce. Melt the remaining butter in a saucepan and stir in the flour. Cook for a few minutes and then gradually stir in the flavoured milk and enough cooking liquor from the fish to make a thick sauce. Continue cooking before adding the cream, just enough tomato ketchup to colour the sauce a delicate pink, the lemon juice and chopped parsley. Lastly add the chopped prawns and adjust the seasoning as necessary. Pour the sauce over the cooked fish, garnish with lemon slices and serve.

Yorkshire Herring Pie   (serves 4)

The herring fishery began in Britain in the late Roman period. It expanded during the 9th and 10th centuries receiving fresh impetus from the Viking invaders whose arrival in England, it has been claimed, may even have been connected with the temporary disappearance of the herring from their own home waters. By the time of the Norman Conquest, herring fishing was important in England's economy.

The season began in early June off the Shetland Isles where the shoals first appeared. On the Yorkshire coast fishing commenced about August and was very productive. To catch the herrings, the drift net was used; a long net which hung down into the water from a series of cork floats spaced along its upper edge, one end being made fast to the boat while the other reached out across the current. The main herring season lasted from mid-September to early November, when boats left their local harbours to join the great fishing fleet which assembled down the coast at Yarmouth. Just before their departure, the fishermen sent a piece of sea-beef on shore from each boat to their friends at the public houses. As a result, a 'bit of supper' was held, at which those who were going away could enjoy a good evening in the company of those who were staying behind. Similarly the Sunday just before they set sail was called 'boat Sunday', when all their friends from the neighbouring villages came to bid them farewell. In the course of just a few weeks, each boat might catch 300,000 herrings. On returning home, the boats were then laid up for the winter, although cobles carrying three men might continue to fish through to the following spring.

There are many recipes for herring pie in Yorkshire, most combining herring, potato and apple, showing the Viking influence on the area.

4 herrings, filleted	1 tablespoon (15ml) fresh parsley, chopped
4 medium potatoes, parboiled	
2oz (50g) butter	Salt and freshly milled black pepper
1 large cooking apple	$\frac{1}{4}$pt (150ml) water
1 small onion, sliced finely	

Cut the herrings into three and soak them in salted water for about 20 minutes, then drain them. Slice the potatoes and the apples thinly and grease a lidded ovenproof dish generously with half the butter. Line the dish thickly with some potato slices, then add half the fish followed by half the apple and onion. Season well and sprinkle with parsley, then repeat the layers, finishing with a layer of potato. Flake the remaining butter on top of the potato and pour on the water. Cover with a lid and bake in a moderate oven (350°F, 180°C, gas mark 4) for 30 minutes. Remove the lid and cook for a further 15 minutes to brown the potatoes. Serve immediately.

Solomon Gundie *(serves 4–6)*

A salmagundy was a substantial Elizabethan salad made of a mixture of fish, cold meat, poultry, herbs and vegetables. It continued to be very popular until the beginning of the 19th century. This recipe is based on a Yorkshire version dating back to 1741 when Solomon Gundie was prepared for Lent or other fasting days without using meat. Boiled white or salted herrings were originally used, but soused herrings make a delicious salad. The finished dish would have been garnished with pickled oysters, mushrooms and capers.

4 medium herrings	$\frac{1}{2}$ small onion, finely grated
1 large onion, sliced	Grated rind of 1 lemon
6 black peppercorns, crushed	Approx. 4 tablespoons (60ml) cream or vinaigrette dressing
6 cloves	
2 bayleaves	Fresh parsley, chopped
$\frac{1}{4}$pt (150ml) malt vinegar	Salt and pepper
$\frac{1}{4}$pt (150ml) water	Lettuce
12oz (350g) new potatoes, cooked	1 lemon and anchovies and capers for garnish
2 large Cox's apples	
2 beetroot, cooked	

Clean and wash the herrings and dry them. Put them in a large ovenproof dish. Sprinkle over the sliced onion, crushed peppercorns, cloves and bayleaves. Cover with the vinegar and water mixed together and bake in a moderate oven (350°F, 180°C, gas mark 4) for 20–25 minutes. Allow the fish to cool in the cooking liquor, then remove them carefully. Skin the herrings and remove the flesh without breaking the backbone or removing the heads or tails; keep the fish skeletons in reserve. Dice the cooked potatoes, apples and beetroot and mix them together in a bowl. Add the the grated onion and lemon rind. Moisten with cream or vinaigrette dressing and add plenty of chopped parsley.

Shred the reserved fish and fold into the vegetables carefully. Season to taste and chill well. Place the fish skeletons on a large bed of lettuce and lay the fish mixture over the bones in the shape of the original fish. Cut some lemon peel into long strips and place these over the 'herrings'; garnish with a few anchovies and capers. Serve well chilled.

Whitby Oak-Smoked Kippers

Families in Yorkshire ports have been concerned with curing herrings for many years. By the 1830s, locally caught herrings were being preserved by kippering and were known as 'soldiers' in Yorkshire. They were described as – 'red herring – sea beef wi' forty ribs tul t'inch; can be scented hawf a mile off, or a mile wi' a stiff breeze blowin' fro' t'quarter it's in!', and were sold inland by men on donkeys. Having been cleaned and split, the fish were packed overnight in coarse-grained salt, the coarser the better, since it prevented the herrings from lying too close together. Next morning long sticks were passed through their eyes and thus, arranged in rows, they were hung from beams in specially built smoke-houses where the fumes from smouldering oak chips slowly changed their colour from silver to burnished copper. However, the present Whitby method of curing was adapted from the herring cure developed by John Woodger of Seahouses in Northumberland, based on an old system of curing salmon. He adopted the salmon technique of splitting the fish down the back, before salting them briefly and then smoking them over an oak fire. Whitby kippers are a pale silvery gold, unlike the artificially-dyed deep brown kippers available all over the country. The old curing houses, which are still being used, are situated in Henrietta Street at the foot of the 199 church steps.

Correctly cured kippers have a mild smoky-salt flavour and are delicious grilled or fried with butter, jugged (see p.146) or eaten raw.

Kippers

Golden Ling

Ling, known locally as 'the drizzle', has been caught off the North Yorkshire coast since medieval times although the name was often used to refer to dried cod generally. It is the largest of the cod family, growing to a maximum length of about 6 feet, although the smaller fish have more flavour. Ling can be cooked like cod, but does need extra flavourings such as bacon, herbs or spices.

This particular recipe is very old and is said to originate from Scarborough, but all the fishing villages of the north-east coast had their own ling specialities. Oatmeal is used to coat the fish, because oats were the traditional staple food in North Yorkshire.

Any white fish can be used instead of ling.

1pt (600ml) fish stock

Pinch of saffron

4 ling fillets

Salt and freshly milled black pepper

2oz (50g) fine oatmeal

2–3oz (50–75g) butter

1 medium onion, finely chopped

1 large parsnip, finely chopped

1 carrot, finely chopped

$\frac{1}{2}$ tablespoon (7.5ml) mixed fresh herbs, finely chopped

$\frac{1}{2}$ tablespoon (7.5ml) fresh parsley, chopped

Heat the fish stock to boiling point and pour it on to the saffron. Leave until cold to infuse, then strain and reserve on one side (it will have turned golden).

Season each fillet of ling well and coat them with oatmeal. Heat the butter in a frying-pan and fry the fish quickly until golden brown, but not cooked through. Place in a lidded ovenproof dish and fry the chopped vegetables gently in the remaining fat. Sprinkle them over the fish and add the herbs. Pour over the fish stock, cover with a lid and bake in a slow oven (325°F, 160°C, gas mark 3) for about 35 minutes. Serve hot with a green vegetable.

Staithes Ling Pie

Ling pie was a speciality of all the northern fishing villages on the Yorkshire coast. It was also a great favourite in large Yorkshire households in Victorian days and in many seaside boarding houses. The cooking of it was particularly important in the tiny village of Staithes where no girl was considered a good wife unless she could make a really good ling pie! 'A dish fit for anny King Is yan o' them ling pies; Steeas women – an they're wise Knows what ti deea wi ling'. The 'Steeas women' also had to be tough to help push out or haul in the coble boats in rough weather and bait hundreds of hooks with mussels and limpets.

Originally the pie would have been made of dried and salted ling, and was baked traditionally at Lent when the fish was mixed with eggs, herbs, spices and butter. In Elizabethan times, the pastry lid would have been coated with sugar after baking. The pie became associated with Good Friday in more recent times at Filey.

Any white fish may be used and in some of the old recipes a little warm cream is poured into the pie just before serving, as is traditional in the West Country.

1lb (450g) ling	2oz (50g) onion, finely chopped
1oz (25g) butter	Pinch of ground mace
Salt and freshly milled pepper	$\frac{1}{2}$pt (300ml) milk
1oz (25g) flour	8oz (225g) puff, flaky or shortcrust
4oz (125g) back bacon, chopped	pastry
2 hard-boiled eggs, sliced	

Cut the ling into even-sized pieces. Grease a pie-dish with the butter and arrange half the fish in the bottom. Season with salt and pepper and sprinkle with flour. Add half the bacon, half the egg and half the onion, then repeat the layers to fill the pie dish. Sprinkle with the mace and pour the milk over. Roll out the pastry to make a lid for the pie and decorate if you wish. Bake in a hot oven (425°F, 210°C, gas mark 7) for 10 minutes to set the pastry and then at 350°F, 180°C, gas mark 4 for a further 20–30 minutes or until cooked through and golden brown. Serve immediately with parsley sauce (see p.216).

Staithes Mackerel in Wine   (serves 4)

A few miles north of Whitby is the quaint village of Staithes. In the 19th century it was a very busy fishing port, its fishing fleet being one of the most important on the whole Yorkshire coast for the capture of codling, haddock and mackerel. In the height of the herring season, the fleet went as far as Great Yarmouth with other vessels from northern ports and there were 400 men directly employed in fishing. The women also took an active part, mending nets and baiting hooks. Today the women of Staithes still wear the traditional fishergirls' bonnets.

Mackerel has been popular in Yorkshire for some centuries, either potted or pickled to preserve it. Family recipe books of the 19th century also suggest ways of cooking the fresh fish stuffed with fennel, then buttered and baked. This recipe is a combination of pickling and baking. Any dry white wine or cider can be used.

4 large mackerel, cleaned	$\frac{1}{4}$pt (150ml) water
2oz (50g) butter	1 bayleaf
1 medium onion, chopped	Salt and cayenne pepper
$\frac{1}{2}$oz (12g) flour	Pinch of ground mace
$\frac{1}{4}$pt (150ml) dry white wine	1 teaspoon French mustard

Grease an ovenproof dish with half the butter and place the fish head to tail in the dish. Melt the remaining butter in a small saucepan and cook the chopped onion gently until soft, but not coloured. Stir in the flour, then the wine and water. Add the bayleaf and cook until the sauce is smooth. Season to taste with salt, pepper and mace. Pour over the fish and bake in a fairly hot oven (400°F, 200°C, gas mark 6) for about 25 minutes, or until the fish is cooked. Remove the fish to a warm serving plate and stir the mustard into the sauce. Boil up to reduce a little, and pour over the fish. Serve immediately.

Dished North Sea Plaice   (serves 4)

Plaice has always been a very popular fish in Britain. A recipe from the 12th century gives details for a 'Plaice boiled. Take a plaice, and draw him in the side by the head; And make sauce of water, parsley, salt and a little ale; and when it beginneth to boil, skim it clean, and cast it thereto, and let seeth.'

From records, it appears that as far back as the 15th century, the inshore fishermen of Scarborough, Whitby and the other coastal villages of north-east Yorkshire fished for plaice in winter, for lobsters and cod during Lent and for skate and more lobsters in the summer. North Sea plaice is said to be the best in the world.

Mussels are also common on this coast. They can be bought from traditional quayside stalls selling the 'fruits of the sea' – oysters, cockles, winkles, whelks, crabs, lobsters, kippers and fresh fish. Cockles and mussels were both so popular in Yorkshire in the 19th century that impressive, covered dishes were made specially to serve these hot cooked shellfish at the table.

2pts (1.2 litres) fresh mussels	2 tablespoons (2 × 15ml) fresh parsley, chopped
4 large fillets of plaice	Juice of $\frac{1}{2}$ a lemon
Sea salt and freshly milled pepper	3 tablespoons (3 × 15ml) dry white wine
3oz (75g) butter	
2 shallots or 1 small onion, finely chopped	2oz (50g) white breadcrumbs
4oz (125g) button mushrooms, finely chopped	Fresh parsley, chopped, to garnish

Clean the mussels as usual (see p.171). Put them in a large saucepan and shake it gently over a high heat with the lid on for about 3 to 5 minutes, until the mussels start to open. Remove them as they open with cooking tongs, reserving all the juice you can. Throw away any mussels that refuse to open and remove the others from their shells. Strain the juice through a muslin-lined sieve and reserve.

Season the plaice fillets with salt and pepper. Melt 2oz (50g) butter in a small saucepan and gently fry the chopped shallot or onion, until soft. Add the chopped mushrooms and cook for a few minutes, before adding the parsley. Season with salt and pepper and spread the mussels out on the bottom of a buttered ovenproof dish. Put the seasoned plaice fillets on top and add the lemon juice, wine and reserved mussel juice. Bake in a moderate oven (350°F, 190°C, gas mark 4) for 15 minutes, basting from time to time. When the fish is cooked, remove it from the oven and place the cooked mussels around it. Sprinkle with the breadcrumbs and dot with the remaining butter. Cook under a hot grill for a few minutes until the breadcrumbs are brown. Serve immediately garnished with chopped parsley.

Scarborough Coble Stew   (*serves 6–8*)

In the 18th century a fish market was held on the sands adjoining the harbour at Scarborough, but this was a small-scale operation until the arrival of the railway. Since then, the expansion of the fishing industry has been enormous and, nowadays, a whole quay is devoted to the landing and selling of the catch. Alongside Bridlington, Scarborough is now Yorkshire's second largest port with a total landing, including shellfish, in the region of £4 million. Cod and other members of the cod family – coley and saithe – continue to be the bulk of the catch of local vessels, but fairly substantial quantities of whiting, halibut, ling and haddock are also landed.

This delicious stew is made like a chowder, using a variety of local fish and shellfish. It is a combination of one served regularly at the Royal Hotel in Scarborough, with a recipe given to me by Mr Alexander, Director of Tourism and Amenities for Yorkshire.

Any firm-fleshed fish such as monkfish, skate nobs, woof (catfish), dogfish (huss) or ling can be used, together with any shellfish that is available. If you want to use softer fish, such as cod, halibut or haddock, reduce the cooking time. Vegetables other than those given below, such as carrots, celery or tomatoes can also be added. Scarborough coble stew makes a substantial dish for lunch or supper. It is too robust for a starter.

1oz (25g) butter or oil

2oz (50g) streaky bacon, finely chopped

2 medium onions, chopped

1oz (25g) flour

2 medium potatoes, diced

1pt (600ml) fish stock

1lb (450g) mixed firm-fleshed fish

4oz (125g) whelks, chopped

4oz (125g) cockles

4oz (125g) queens

4oz (125g) mussels

4oz (125g) white crab meat, chopped

Salt and freshly milled black pepper

$\frac{1}{4}$pt (150ml) double cream

Fresh parsley, chopped

Melt the butter or oil in a saucepan and fry the chopped bacon to extract all the fat. Add the chopped onions and cook until soft, but not brown. Sprinkle over the flour and mix to form a roux. Cook for a few minutes without browning, then add the diced potatoes. Gradually add the fish stock and mix to a smooth consistency. Bring to the boil, then simmer for about 5 minutes. Skin and bone all the white fish and cut into bite-sized pieces. Add to the saucepan with the chopped whelks and whole cockles and cook for a further 10–15 minutes, stirring occasionally. A few minutes before serving, add the queens, mussels and crab and cook gently. Season to taste and stir in the double cream. Add plenty of parsley and serve in soup bowls with water biscuits or hot crisp rolls.

Scarborough Witch with Lobster Sauce   (serves 6)

Witch or Torbay sole is not a true sole but a flounder and its flavour is not as good, but it is much cheaper and, dressed up with a sauce as in this recipe, can be quite delicious.

As well as being Yorkshire's second largest port, Scarborough is also the county's biggest holiday resort. In Edwardian days, when holidays at the seaside were very fashionable, the fishermen's wives sold fresh fish and shellfish from trestle tables on the beach to the tourists. Oysters were particularly popular, advertised for sale 'Fresh from the beds'.

6 sole fillets, skinned

Salt and freshly milled black pepper

1oz (25g) butter

$\frac{1}{4}$pt (150ml) dry white wine

$\frac{1}{4}$pt (150ml) water or fish stock

Juice of $\frac{1}{2}$ a lemon

Lemon slices and parsley to garnish

For the lobster sauce

2oz (50g) butter

2oz (50g) flour

$\frac{1}{2}$pt (300ml) milk mixed with fish cooking liquor

Salt and cayenne pepper

3 tablespoons (3 × 15ml) lobster meat, chopped

$\frac{1}{2}$ teaspoon (2.5ml) anchovy essence

Season the sole fillets. Butter an ovenproof dish and arrange the fish in it. Pour over the wine and water, or fish stock, and lemon juice. Bake in a moderate oven (350°F, 180°C, gas mark 4) for about 15 minutes, or until cooked, basting occasionally. When the fish is cooked, strain off the cooking liquor into a saucepan. Place the fish on a warm serving dish. Boil the cooking liquor rapidly to reduce by half.

To make the sauce, melt the butter in a saucepan and stir in the flour. Cook for a few minutes, but do not brown. Gradually stir in the cooking liquor mixed with milk and the cream until the sauce is smooth and thick. Continue cooking for 5 minutes and then stir in the chopped lobster. Season well with salt, cayenne pepper and anchovy essence. Pour the sauce over the waiting fish and serve immediately, decorated with lemon slices and parsley.

Traditional Yorkshire Fish Cakes   (*serves 4–6*)

Fish cakes make a cheap and satisfying meal, and can be made with either left-over or freshly cooked fish. They have always been very popular in Yorkshire and are excellent for 'high tea'. Most recipes suggest using the same quantity of fish and mashed potato, but you can increase the amount of fish if you like. Do experiment with seasoning and try a rasher of bacon with the fish cakes – this is very good. Kipper fillets or smoked trout fillets can be used instead of the white fish, but do not season with salt.

1lb (450g) fillets of white fish

$\frac{1}{2}$pt (300ml) milk

1lb (450g) potatoes, cooked and mashed

1oz (25g) butter

Pinch of cayenne pepper

Pinch of ground mace or nutmeg

1 tablespoon (15ml) fresh parsley, chopped

$\frac{1}{2}$ teaspoon (2.5ml) mustard

A few drops of vinegar

$\frac{1}{2}$ teaspoon (2.5ml) anchovy essence

Salt and freshly milled black pepper

1 egg, beaten

Seasoned flour

For the coating

Beaten egg

Approx. 6oz (125g) dry white breadcrumbs

Fat for frying

Skin the fish and place it in a saucepan with the milk. Poach gently for 5–7 minutes, or until just cooked. Reserve the cooking liquor. Flake the cooked fish and combine with the potatoes, butter, seasonings and parsley. Check the seasoning again and mix well. Bind the mixture together with half the beaten egg and some of the cooking liquor. Shape into small cakes and dip in a little seasoned flour. Brush the cakes with beaten egg and roll them in breadcrumbs. Fry the fish cakes in smoking hot fat until golden brown on both sides. Serve immediately while crisp on a warm serving dish for breakfast, high tea or supper.

Fish and Oatmeal Cakes (serves 4)

1lb (450g) filleted white fish, cooked

3 teacups oatmeal, cooked

2oz (50g) butter

½ onion, finely chopped

Salt and freshly milled pepper

Pinch of mace

1 tablespoon (15ml) fresh parsley, chopped

1 large egg

For the coating

1 egg, beaten

Approx. 6oz (175g) dry breadcrumbs

Melt the butter in a small saucepan and fry the chopped onion until soft. Mix the fish, oatmeal and onion together and season well with salt and pepper and the pinch of mace. Add the parsley and beaten egg. Shape into flat cakes on a floured board. Dip each cake into beaten egg and then roll in breadcrumbs. Fry in smoking hot fat until slightly browned on each side. Serve immediately.

Whitby Fish Pie (serves 4–6)

Perched on a high cliff overlooking the sea, are the ruins of Whitby Abbey, founded in 657 by St Hilda and run as a mixed sex community until the Synod of Whitby in 664. The monastery collected dues from the fishing boats when Whitby first became a port in 1088 and the ruins still dominate the town, clustered on both banks of the River Esk linked by a bridge between the west and east cliffs. The most spectacular way to approach it is from the ruins of the abbey. The colourful scene with the quaint red-roofed houses, brightly painted fishing boats, yachts and sea is quite delightful.

Whitby has had a spectacular history as a seaport since the 17th century when vast quantities of alum were shipped out. By 1828, it ranked seventh in England. Captain Cook grew up in Whitby and the harbour saw his departure as apprentice on his first ship. Later, Whitby was to build the Captain's ships, HMS *Endeavour*, *Resolution*, and *Adventure* for his great world-wide voyages of discovery.

From 1753 to 1837, Whitby was an important whaling port and the jawbone of a whale still forms an unusual arch on the west cliff. Much of the other fish landed on the north Yorkshire coast was handled by Whitby market. Before the railway arrived, great quantities of fish were carried inland by teams of pack ponies equipped with panniers, first to Pickering, Malton and York and then across to the towns of the industrial West Riding.

The modern fish quay was built in 1957 and is still a busy place early in the day, as the cobles and keel boats unload their catches. Today, the fishing fleet is around 22 keel boats, 40 motor cobles and about 14 salmon cobles. Although the herring fishing has largely disappeared, and with it the crowds of Scottish keel boats, the total value of fish has increased. Cod, halibut, plaice, whiting, woof, ling, mackerel and herring are caught and some of the cobles concentrate on crab, lobster and salmon in the summer.

This recipe for fish pie is a traditional one from Whitby and any white fish can be used.

1lb (450g) cooked white fish	$\frac{1}{4}$pt (150ml) fish cooking liquor
4oz (125g) lean ham	Salt and freshly milled black pepper
2 hard-boiled eggs	6oz (175g) shortcrust pastry
1oz (25g) butter	Beaten egg to glaze

Remove all the bones and skin from the cooked fish and flake. Cut up the ham into small pieces and slice the hard-boiled eggs. Butter an ovenproof dish generously and fill with alternate layers of the three ingredients. Moisten with a little of the cooking liquor from the fish and season well. Roll out the pastry to make a lid for the pie in the usual way, making a slit in the top to allow the steam to escape. Decorate with pastry trimmings if you wish and brush with beaten egg. Bake in a hot oven (425°F, 220°C, gas mark 7) for 10 minutes, then reduce to 350°F, 180°C, gas mark 4 for a further 20 minutes, or until the pastry is golden brown. Serve hot or cold.

Mike's Favourite Moorland Trout   (serves 1)

This recipe was given to me by Mike O'Donnell, who runs Moorland Trout farms at Pickering in North Yorkshire, and is his favourite way of eating trout. He recommends one 8–10oz (225–275g) trout per person for a main meal.

1 fresh trout, 8–10oz (225–275g)	2 tablespoons (2 × 15ml) single cream
Salt and freshly milled black pepper	
1oz (25g) butter	Beurre manié to thicken (see p.207)
$\frac{1}{4}$pt (150ml) dry cider	$\frac{1}{2}$ teaspoon (2.5ml) tomato purée
Dash of brandy	

Season the inside of the fish well with salt and pepper. Melt the butter in a frying-pan and add the cider and brandy. Place the fish in the pan, cover with a lid and cook gently for 20 minutes, turning over after 10 minutes. Remove the trout from the pan to a serving dish and keep warm. Make a sauce by pouring the cream into the frying-pan and bringing gently to the boil. Thicken with beurre mainié, stirring continuously. Remove the pan from the heat, stir in a little tomato pureé and adjust the seasoning if necessary. Pour the sauce over the trout and serve.

Moorland Oak Smoked Trout Paste

Trout smoked with oak chippings are a Moorland Farms speciality. First, the fish are gutted and cleaned, then brined for several hours, after which they are left to hang overnight. Smoking, using only oak chippings, takes place the following day and again takes several hours. Originally, only oak sawdust from the nearby Kilburn workshops of 'Mousey' Thompson, a wood carver who always carved a tiny mouse on each piece of work, was used. The smoking is mild so that the taste of the trout comes through.

1 smoked trout, approx. 6oz (175g)	2 teaspoons (2 × 5ml) cream
1½oz (40g) butter	Salt and freshly milled black pepper
1oz (25g) cream cheese	Squeeze of lemon juice

Remove all the flesh from the trout and blend with all the other ingredients until smooth. Pile into a suitable china or earthenware pot and chill. Serve with hot brown toast as a starter or snack.

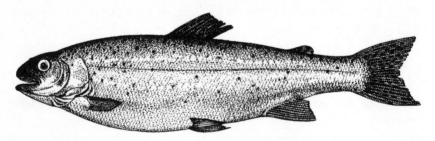

Rainbow trout

EAST ANGLIA

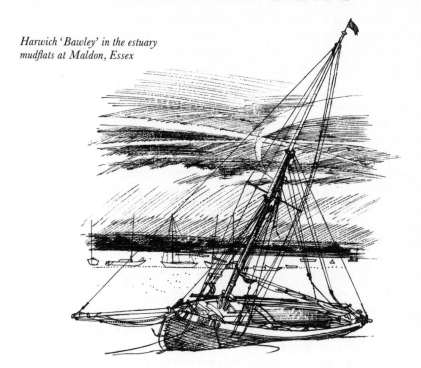

Harwich 'Bawley' in the estuary mudflats at Maldon, Essex

Throughout history the flat coasts of the east have fought against an ever-encroaching North Sea. Shingle and mud is removed and deposited further up the coast on Norfolk's northern shores, developing this area into the finest complex of sand and mudflats, marshes, shingle ridges and dunes in the country.

The coastline between Hunstanton and Sheringham is not only one of great beauty, but is also of exceptional interest to naturalists and specialists in many other branches of science. Since 1912, when Blakeney Point, a shingle spit leaving the coast at Cley and stretching miles to the east, was acquired by the National Trust, the Trust has steadily increased its ownership of areas important for their wildlife and natural beauty along this North Norfolk coast. Today, the Trust protects over 6,000 acres of marshes, dunes and foreshore from Sheringham to Brancaster. Apart from Burnham Overy, all this land is included in the Heritage Coast and is subject to a special management plan adopted by the Trust.

The shingle banks and dunes of Blakeney attract many breeding birds such as the shelduck, oyster-catcher, ringed plover and tern. The Point is open to the public all the year round free of charge and can be reached along the shingle bank from Cley, or by boat from Morston or Blakeney

Quays. The ferries operate in the season on the tides and will drop visitors off on the Point, near the Lifeboat Station, or take them round the sand bars to the west of the Point to see the seals.

The network of creeks and salt marshes that forms the coast opposite Blakeney Point is invaluable as a habitat for the specialised flora and bird population. The old undisturbed salt marshes to the west at Stiffkey lie behind shingle ridges that provide ideal nesting sites for terns. The marshes themselves, covered with mauve sea-lavender and sea-aster in the summer, provide winter feeding grounds for brent geese, widgeon and teal, and hunting grounds for others. Morston Marshes, to the east, attract large populations of redshank, shelduck and brent geese and has a variety of salt-marsh flora. There is a wooden lookout, known locally as 'The Pagoda', on Morston Quay, opened two years ago, which houses displays and information about the marshes.

Further round the coast is Scolt Head Island, which has been a Nature Reserve since 1923 and is owned by the National Trust and Norfolk Naturalists' Trust. In 1953 it was leased to the Nature Conservancy Council and the island is now looked after by a joint committee of representatives of the three organisations and local residents. Nearly 4 miles long, the island consists of about 1,500 acres of sand dune and salt marsh, surrounded by shingle and mud, all constantly changing shape as the tides and currents course around the coast. The sand is washed up and down the beaches and stabilised above the high-water mark by a wide variety of grasses and plants such as glasswort, sea-blite and sea-aster. In summer the marshes are covered with a carpet of mauve sea-lavender. The island is particularly noted for its large nesting colonies of sandwich and common terns at its western end. Widgeon and brent geese winter in large numbers, feeding on the eel or widgeon-grass on the salt marsh.

Local boatmen at Brancaster Staithe will take visitors to Scolt Head Island from April to September, but it is very dangerous to walk across the marshes without local knowledge. A self-guiding nature trail operates from the landing point at the western end of the island, and an explanatory leaflet is available from the Warden at Brancaster Staithe, where there is a National Trust information centre. Shoals of sea trout visit inshore waters and enter the harbour in late summer. This area is also the centre of a thriving shellfish industry. Whelk-pots are laid on a big stone bed lying some way off Scolt Head Island and the gathering of winkles is carried on in a small way during the summer. There are mussel beds in the creeks worked by the boatmen who use for their equipment an old line of sheds on the east side of the harbour, owned by the Trust.

The wide, sandy beach, backed by lines of high dunes and the salt marsh at Brancaster are part of the Manor of Brancaster and were acquired by the National Trust in 1967 through a local appeal and Enterprise Neptune funds. Shining mud lines the maze of creeks and brown water comes lapping in and out with the tide. On the higher parts of the marsh, special plants like samphire grow, trap more silt and make dark soil. The lines of sand dunes are blown up the beach by the strong northerly winds which are a feature of this coast. High spring tides often erode the dunes, revealing the ironwork of maritime defences. Much of this has been removed recently by the National Trust; marram grass has been planted and brushwood fences erected to try to trap and stabilise the shifting sand. When the tide is out black peaty lumps can be seen on Brancaster beach; the remains of a great forest, which grew across the bed of the North Sea before the ice melted and Britain became an island.

Eleven miles north of Yarmouth the Trust owns another interesting property where the coast is undeveloped and unspoilt; this is Horsey, which includes Horsey Mere, marshes and Horsey Hall. The Hall is not open, but there is restricted access to the mere on which, it is said, Lord Nelson learned to sail.

Dunwich Heath is the only area on the Suffolk coast owned by the National Trust. It was acquired in 1968 with a grant from H. J. Heinz & Co. Ltd, as one of their contributions to Enterprise Neptune. The Heath lies to the south of Dunwich, which began to be devoured by the sea in the 14th century. Despite the efforts of the inhabitants, the sea continued its advance until after 600 years, all that remains of the important medieval city and port is now a village. In King John's reign the Borough of Dunwich paid charges of 5,000 eels and 8,000 herrings to the Crown and in 1565, 60,000 herrings and £50, which shows how prosperous it once was and how important was its fishing. Dunwich was sending boats to fish in Icelandic waters as early as the 16th century. Today, only 4 boats go out regularly catching cod and whiting by long-lining from October to May, sprats by netting in December and Dover soles, plaice and dabs by trawling from May to September or October. During the winter some good sea fishing can be had from the beach at Dunwich Heath.

The National Trust is carrying out a great deal of work on the Heath to try to protect it from the erosive effects of wind, rain and sea. Marram grass is being planted on the cliffs to anchor the soil and rainwater is being diverted, but it is a hard struggle against the elements.

Further south, in Essex, the National Trust owns Northey Island, 300 acres lying near the head of the Blackwater Estuary, east of the port of Maldon. The island was given to the Trust in 1978 and the sea-wall and saltings are now a nature reserve. Access to the island is via a causeway, the original probably being Roman, which is covered at high tide. There are no parking facilities on the island so cars must be left in the car park past South House Farm. Although the exact site is unknown, the Battle of Maldon was fought near here on 11 August 991, when the Vikings defeated the Saxons. Millennial anniversary plans include a tapestry, 325 feet long, depicting the battle.

In May and June the salt marshes of Northey Island are a sheet of flowering sea-pink, followed in July by mauve sea-lavender. In late summer oyster-catchers and shelduck are protected while they are nesting. It is hoped that by avoiding artificial fertilisers, a small triangular field near the sea-wall will revert to a meadow attracting many species of butterflies. There are footpaths on the island and a hide for watching birds.

At one time, the populations of coastal communities from the Wash round the East Anglian bulge to the Thames Estuary, lived largely on or from the sea. The sea itself is unpredictable and the coast is treacherous: bars or sandbanks running across harbour mouths have increased the difficulties of navigation and the open unprotected beaches are notoriously dangerous. Not only is it difficult to push boats off against an oncoming wind, but it requires masterly precision to land them up the steep slope of the shelving beaches. The sea defences are by no means impregnable. Periodically villages lying behind the saltings have been inundated by scouring tides, or in places, entirely lost to the sea. Yet despite all these hazards, men have launched crab boats from open beaches or sailed cobles and smacks from creeks and harbours. They have dredged for oysters, set pots for crabs, lobsters or whelks, raked cockles and, in season, gone musseling, trawling for shrimps and flatfish, long-lining for cod, and seine-netting for mackerel and herring.

The steward's accounts for Hunstanton Hall in North Norfolk from 9 October 1328 to 4 February 1329 included 150 to 200 'stockfish', which were sun-dried and salted cod and ling. In addition he bought a lot of herring, also mullet, haddock, plaice, smelt, winkles and mussels. Interestingly enough, the servants' food in these accounts includes 28 stock-fish, but no fresh fish, even though Hunstanton is right on the coast. Two hundred years later, the purchases of fish for Hunstanton Hall included a porpoise, herring – pickled, white and red – ling, cod, turbot, tench, haddock, plaice, smelt, brill, salmon, salmon trout, conger eel, sturgeon, whelks and shrimps.

By the 17th century, the variety of fish was enormous. The steward's accounts for Oxnead Hall, Norfolk, some miles inland and home of Sir William Paston, mention the purchase of lobsters and crabs from 'the old man of Sheringham', 'sea fish from Cromer', '$2\frac{1}{2}$ hundred oysters from Cley', barrels of oysters from Colchester and Burnham and dozens of other types of sea and freshwater fish. Some interesting local names of fish were used, such as 'sandling', which was probably a dab and 'mudfish', probably a skate. Turbot was often referred to as 'brett' or 'bretcock' locally. Sir William Paston was very interested in food and had a cookery book dedicated to him.

There have always been strong links between the fishing ports and agricultural villages in East Anglia. People living along the immediate coastal fringe had for centuries combined an interest in both fishing and farming, but with the expansion of the English herring industry in the 19th century, more labour was required to crew the boats and work in the fish-curing houses. Once the harvest was over, many farmworkers went to work in Yarmouth and Lowestoft for the home herring fishing season. By the end of the century, these country 'joskins' or 'half-breed fishermen' as they were called in North Suffolk, played an important part in the East Anglian fishing industry, trawling as well as drifting. Many of them became full-time fishermen finding the sea more profitable and secure than the land.

But the tide is turning now and the men employed in fishing are disappearing. Each year the average age rises, for as the older men retire, their places are no longer being filled. Where there were hundreds of boats a century ago, today there are dozens; where there were dozens, only one or two remain. If they are not converted into pleasure yachts they lie rotting in the mud. Having said all this, there are glimmers of hope. There has been massive investment in new fishing methods, which has changed the face of the main Lowestoft trawler fleet over the past 3 years and it is now beginning to pay off with a succession of big catches of high value species. However, catch restrictions in the North Sea and restrictions on the number of vessels in a fleet continue to cast a shadow over the fishing future of Lowestoft.

The shellfish industry in North Norfolk is small, but valuable nevertheless and increasing all the time with careful farming. Fresh fish and shellfish of excellent quality can be bought regularly straight from the boats or from fishermen's beach huts or from improvised stalls outside their cottages. Wonderful smoked fish and shellfish can also be purchased directly from local smokehouses.

Indeed fish lovers can have a wonderful time in East Anglia.

Yarmouth Bloaters

The name bloater is said to come from the Old Norse 'blautr' meaning soft and swollen or plump, which is a good description of this lightly salted and lightly smoked herring. Bloaters have a silvery sheen to them and a mild delicate, but unmistakable gamey flavour, as they are cured whole and ungutted.

The herrings are steeped in salt overnight before being smoked for from 12 to 18 hours over oak logs to achieve this light cure. The bloater's origin is said to go back to 1835, when Mr Bishop, a fish curer from Yarmouth, was annoyed to find that his workers had gone home one day leaving a batch of fresh herring unattended. Determined not to let them go to waste, he threw salt over them, ungutted as they were, and left them to smoke overnight. Next morning, the results were very pleasing and far less salty and dry than the traditional red herring, so he began marketing them.

To Cook Bloaters

The old method of cooking bloaters was to boil or grill them on a gridiron rubbed with a piece of mutton fat, over a gentle fire for a few minutes.

Simple grilling is still the best way of eating a bloater in my opinion. Cut off its head and split open down the back. Remove the guts, then lay it flat. Place under a hot grill for 3–4 minutes on each side. Rub over with a good knob of butter and serve on its own or with a pile of creamy scrambled eggs, brown bread and butter and a little mustard if liked. Bloaters can also be fried with a little butter, or baked in foil or buttered paper in a slow oven for about 20 minutes and served with a potato salad.

Betty's Special Bloaters   (serves 6)

Betty Nice has recently taken over the running of the Guildhall Tea Rooms at Lavenham in Suffolk for the National Trust and she sent me this recipe for bloaters which is delicious and reminds me of the traditional West Country combination of pilchards and clotted cream.

6 bloaters	1 tablespoon (15ml) fresh dill, chopped
½pt (300ml) double cream	

Prepare the fish as above. Place them in an ovenproof dish and cover with cream. Sprinkle over a little dill and bake in a fairly hot oven (400°F, 200°C, gas mark 6) for 10–15 minutes or until cooked. Serve immediately with crusty brown bread.

Buckling

This is the luxury fish of the herring trade. Like bloaters, buckling are cured ungutted, but are lightly hot-smoked, which means that the herring has been cooked as well as flavoured in the curing process. They have the slightly gamey flavour of a bloater, but in a milder form. Serve as you would smoked trout, with brown bread and butter, lemon juice and horseradish sauce. Buckling will not keep for long, even in the fridge. They can be served hot if you wish; warm them through under the grill or in the oven and eat with a herb butter.

Stookey Blues

The North Norfolk coast has always been famed for its cockles and is now one of the 3 main fisheries for cockles in Britain. The best were, and still are, found at Wells and Stiffkey, where they are known as 'Stookey' or 'Stewkey Blues' because of their blue-black shells. These are very large succulent cockles, living a few inches below the surface in the mud-flats and sands of this stretch of coast, and can be gathered easily at low tide. Cockle gathering used to be a very hard life in the old days, usually done by the women. With layers of clothing to protect them from the treacherous winds, they would dig for the cockles, carrying them home in sacks and baskets. Cockling today is men's work and they travel to and from the beds by boat, setting out from Boston, King's Lynn or Heacham to work the sands with their short-handled rakes. Once collected, the cockles are put into nets and taken back to sheds on the quayside to be boiled. The National Trust owns a group of early 19th-century cockle sheds at Brancaster, which are rented to the local fishermen for boiling cockles and whelks.

If you want to gather cockles yourself, walk out at low tide onto the flats around Stiffkey, Blakeney, or just around the coast on the main Brancaster beach, with a bucket and rake and look for the tell-tale signs in the sand; a rich vein of mud or a streak of green plankton over the sand usually indicates the presence of cockles. Handle them carefully to avoid cracking the shells and don't gather any which are less than 1 inch (2.5cm) across. When you return home, wash the cockles free of sand and mud in fresh water. Drain them and cover with more fresh water. Add two or three handfuls of plain flour and a pinch of salt. They should then be left like this for a few hours, or preferably overnight. The cockles will clean themselves of sand and grit and at the same time take in some of the flour to make them fat and soft. Next morning, rinse them well again and throw out any that are open or damaged. Cockles can be eaten raw like oysters or cooked.

To Cook Cockles

Place the cleaned cockles in a large saucepan and just cover with fresh boiling water or court bouillon (see p.208). Set them on a low heat and cook for about 5 minutes, shaking the saucepan from time to time until their shells open. Be careful not to continue cooking after the shells have opened, or the flesh will be tough. Discard any that do not open. Drain off the water, pick the cockles out of their shells whilst still hot. Serve immediately with melted butter or leave to cool. Serve with a dash of vinegar, a little black pepper and brown bread and butter and you have a feast fit for a king.

An old method of cooking cockles was to lay them on a dustpan and cook them over an open fire. This can be simulated by cooking them in a large saucepan covered with a lid without adding water; just shake them over the heat until the shells open.

Cockles, like mussels, can be put into stews and soups as well as being included in stuffings for pork, lamb and mutton joints, and white fish. They also make excellent pies and supper dishes as in the following recipes.

Stookey Blue Cockle Pie *(serves 2–3)*

This recipe comes from a lady living at Stiffkey.

1pt (600ml) cockles with shells	1oz (25g) butter
½pt (300ml) vinegar	2 medium tomatoes, sliced
½pt (300ml) white sauce	1oz (25g) fresh white or brown breadcrumbs
1 tablespoon (15ml) fresh parsley, finely chopped	
Sea salt and freshly milled black pepper	

Place the cockles in a heavy pan and add the vinegar. Cover with a lid and heat for a few minutes until the cockles open. Drain off the liquid and shell the cockles. Stir them into the white sauce and add the parsley. Season to taste. Butter a pie-dish well and pour in the sauce. Arrange the sliced tomatoes on top and sprinkle with the breadcrumbs. Bake in a moderately hot oven (400°F, 200°C, gas mark 6) for about 15 minutes. Serve with thin brown bread and butter.

Stookey Blues in Garlic Butter
(serves 4)

Serve as a simple starter. 'Stookey Blues' are excellent but any fresh cockles may be used.

1pt (600ml) freshly boiled cockles, shelled

4oz (125g) softened butter

4 cloves garlic, crushed

½ tablespoon (7.5ml) fresh parsley, chopped

Freshly milled black pepper

2oz (50g) fresh brown breadcrumbs

Parsley to garnish

Divide the cockles between four individual heatproof dishes. Pound the softened butter and garlic together until well mixed, then beat in the parsley. Melt the butter and pour it over the cockles. Season with black pepper and sprinkle with breadcrumbs. Grill until the breadcrumbs are brown and crisp. Serve immediately garnished with parsley.

Fish Dinner from Yarmouth
(serves 6)

The Yarmouth fishermen's wives used to go to the quayside and collect the broken fish and shellfish left after the catch had been sorted for the fish market. They would make a meal out of whatever was available.

1½lb (675g) fresh cod, hake or whiting fillets

½pt (300ml) shrimps or prawns, unpeeled

1pt (600ml) milk

2 onions, sliced

1 bayleaf

Sprig of fresh fennel

2 fresh mackerel, cleaned and filleted

½pt (300ml) water

2½oz (60g) butter

8oz (225g) crab meat

4oz (125g) mushrooms, sliced

2oz (50g) flour

Sea salt and freshly milled pepper

2 tablespoons (2 × 15ml) fresh parsley, chopped

2oz (50g) fresh breadcrumbs

Peel and chop the prawns, reserving the peelings. Put these peelings into a saucepan with the milk, half the onion, bayleaf and fennel. Bring to the boil, then simmer for 15 minutes to make a fish stock. While this is cooking, poach the mackerel in the water with the rest of the onion until tender. Drain and reserve the cooking liquor. Butter a shallow oven-proof dish with ½oz (12g) butter and arrange the poached mackerel in it.

Strain the milk, discarding the peelings, onion and herbs. Poach the white fish in this stock very gently for about 8 minutes, then drain it, reserving the cooking liquor, and remove all the skin and bones.

Arrange the white fish on top of the mackerel fillets and sprinkle over the chopped prawns, followed by the crab meat. Melt the remaining butter in a saucepan and gently fry the mushrooms. Stir in the flour and cook for a few minutes. Gradually add the reserved cooking liquors and cook until thick and smooth. Season to taste with salt and pepper and add the parsley. Pour over the waiting fish and sprinkle on the breadcrumbs. Bake in a moderate oven (350°F, 180°C, gas mark 4) for 20–30 minutes, or until brown on top. Serve immediately with buttered boiled potatoes.

Cromer Crab

Crabs are a North Norfolk speciality and those from around Cromer and nearby Sheringham are the most special and justly famous. Although the crabs from this area tend to be smaller than those from the rest of the country, they are also fleshier and more succulent because they do not change their shells so often. Unfortunately, because of their size, marketing is a problem. Billingsgate prefers the larger crabs from Devon and Cornwall where the water is warmer and the crabs therefore grow twice as quickly, but a Norfolk crab is very special. Most fishermen cook and sell their own catch, so from March to October, chalked or handprinted boards stand outside their flint cottages and houses almost anywhere along the coast roads advertising 'Fresh boiled crab daily'.

Cromer became a fashionable seaside resort in Victorian days with the coming of the railway and its 19th-century hotels and boarding houses stand alongside the rows of modern retirement bungalows. Holidaymakers still flock to the town, probably unaware of its long and important maritime history and the hazardous lives led by its fishermen, who operate off the dangerous beaches of Cromer and Sheringham. The first half mile of the coast is the most treacherous with the breakers hitting the beach and in the past, the most common fatalities among fishermen occurred within 200 yards of the shore. Further out to sea this stretch of coast is notorious for its submerged rocks and unpredictable tides and the weather can be extremely bad during the winter.

Sadly, the fishing from both Cromer and Sheringham, like the rest of the North Norfolk coast, has declined rapidly over the last 50 years, but the reputation of the Norfolk crab boat is still considerable. The boat is small, about 20 feet long, light, clinker-built and double-ended with a motor now, of course, instead of sails. The ribs of the boats are always of oak, while the planking is larch and there is a metal rim around the boat to stop the edge wearing when the crab pots are dragged up from the bottom of the sea bed. The pots are wooden or iron cages covered with tarred string and were originally made at Sheringham. In fact, crab pots were not used in Cromer until 1863, when a man called Sandford saw a crab pot being used on the South Coast and introduced it. Prior to that, hoop nets with a net bag attached to a circular metal ring were used.

Dressed Cromer Crab

The traditional way of dressing a Cromer crab is to remove the meat as detailed on p.142, keeping the brown and white meat separate. Mix the brown meat with a little vinegar and salt and cayenne pepper to taste. Replace it in the shell and pile the white meat on top. Serve with salad. Crab meat can also be devilled, made into soups, sauces, stuffings, omelettes, soufflés, casseroles and mousses. Cromer crab is frequently on the summer menu of the National Trust restaurant at Felbrigg Hall, 2 miles from Cromer and one of the finest 17th-century houses in Norfolk, given to the Trust in 1969.

Crab Casserole   (serves 4)

This makes a very good hot starter or a tasty dish for lunch or supper.

2oz (50g) butter

1oz (25g) flour

½pt (300ml) milk

Sea salt and freshly milled pepper

½ teaspoon (2.5ml) grated nutmeg

1lb (450g) freshly boiled crab meat, brown and white mixed

4 tablespoons (4 × 15ml) double cream

2 tablespoons (2 × 15ml) Parmesan cheese, grated

3oz (75g) fresh brown breadcrumbs

Melt half the butter in a saucepan and stir in the flour. Cook for a few minutes before adding the milk and stirring to make a thick smooth sauce. Season with salt, pepper and nutmeg and stir in the crab meat. Bring very gently to the boil and stir in the cream. Check the seasoning again and pour into individual buttered ovenproof dishes. Mix the cheese and breadcrumbs together and sprinkle over the crab. Dot the top of each dish with the remaining butter and stand in a roasting tin filled with about ½in (1cm) water. Bake for about 10 minutes in a fairly hot oven (400°F, 200°C, gas mark 6) until golden brown and crisp. Serve immediately with thin slices of buttered rye or wholemeal bread or strips of raw vegetables, such as carrot, baby turnip, celery, fennel, pepper and sprigs of cauliflower.

Cromer Crab Cocktail

(serves 6)

1½lb (675g) freshly boiled crab meat, brown and white mixed

½pt (300ml) shrimps, cooked and peeled

½pt (300ml) homemade mayonnaise

2 tablespoons (2 × 15ml) double cream

A little curry paste

Lemon juice

Cayenne pepper

A few samphire tips, cooked (see p.202), or watercress to garnish

Divide the crab meat and shrimps between six individual dishes. Mix the mayonnaise and cream together and add a very little curry paste. Season with lemon juice and cayenne pepper. Pour over the crab and shrimps and mix in gently. Decorate with a few cooked samphire tips or watercress. Serve chilled with wholemeal bread and butter.

Crab and Shrimp Soup

(serves 4–6)

In North Norfolk, crabs are so cheap and plentiful in the summer that they are ideal for this rich soup and shrimps are also easily available in this part of the world. Prawns could be used instead if you wish. This recipe was given to me by the Sea Fish Industry Authority.

1oz (25g) butter

1 medium onion, finely chopped

1 stick of celery, finely chopped

¼pt (150ml) dry white wine

1pt (600ml) fish stock

1 bouquet garni

1 bayleaf

Salt and freshly milled black pepper

8oz (225g) shrimps, peeled

1½lb (675g) crab meat (brown and white kept separate)

¼pt (150ml) single cream

1 tablespoon (15ml) brandy

¼pt (150ml) natural yoghurt

1 tablespoon (15ml) fresh dill, finely chopped

Melt the butter in a large saucepan and fry the onion and celery until soft and transparent. Add the wine, fish stock, bouquet garni and bayleaf. Season to taste. Bring to the boil and then simmer gently for 5–10 minutes to allow the flavours to infuse.

Stir in the peeled shrimps, followed by the brown crab meat and half the white crab meat. Simmer for another 10 minutes, then liquidise in a blender or food processor. Return to the pan and heat again. Add the cream, brandy and remaining white crab meat. Check the seasoning. Just before serving, stir in the natural yoghurt and sprinkle with dill. Serve with hot crusty wholemeal bread or rolls.

Blakeney Dabs with Samphire
(serves 1)

Dabs are a separate species from other flatfish, although they look like the young of a larger fish. They are rather like a rough-skinned plaice or flounder and the delight of inshore anglers. A traditional way of catching them off the North Norfolk coast, especially from the shallow water of Blakeney channel, is by spearing them with a long bamboo pole which needs a steady hand and very quick reflexes. If the dabs are large, they may be skinned and filleted and cooked like plaice or lemon sole, but if they are small, plain grilling or frying is best. The smaller fish, in particular, have a delicate and sweet flavour and are ideal for breakfast or tea. Allow at least 1 fish per person depending on its size and the occasion. An egg and breadcrumb coating may be used instead of flour if you prefer. Only the stringless green tips of the samphire are used here (see p.202).

2 small dabs	Fresh tarragon, chopped
Seasoned flour	A handful of samphire tips
2–3oz (50–75g) butter	Melted butter

Cut the heads off the dabs and clean them if necessary. Leave on the skin but scale the fish on their rough side. Dip them into the seasoned flour. Melt the butter in a frying-pan and gently fry the fish until golden brown. While the fish is frying, wash the samphire well and blanch it in boiling water for about 5 minutes. Drain well and keep warm. When the fish is cooked, sprinkle over a little chopped tarragon and serve immediately with the samphire dressed with a little melted butter.

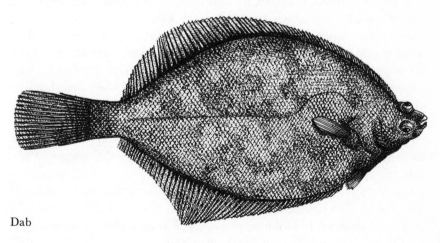

Dab

King Herring

Herring was the great fish of the Middle Ages, when fasting meant no meat on at least two days of the week. Salted in barrels, salted and smoked, they could be transported inland, or exported overseas as part of the massive trade in salt fish from the North to the Mediterranean.

By the 12th century, Great Yarmouth had become the centre of the herring trade, and indeed remained so right up until the end of the fishing in the 1960s. It was ideally sited; there were salt workings nearby, which were vital for the curing of the fish; it was convenient, near to the shoals and even before the town was built, it was a meeting place for fishermen and buyers every autumn. This continued as the Free Fair from Michaelmas to Martinmas, 29 September to 11 November, which went on well into the 18th century.

Before the final sad years when over-fishing reduced the great shoals to a pitiful remnant and the drifter fleet dwindled season by season until it was non-existent, herring provided a staple food for the people of East Anglia. Once the drifters had returned safely the whole of Yarmouth and Lowestoft came to life. According to George Ewart Evans in his fascinating book about fishing in East Anglia *The Days That We Have Seen*, the whole place would be alight with flares, on both carts and boats, the horses would be stamping, men shouting, loose herrings flying all over the place. There were no hours of work; boats came in and were unloaded and the fish carted away to the fish-houses for curing; people worked until it was done. All the fish-houses had fires blazing and the towns of both Yarmouth and Lowestoft smelt of oak fires.

Each fish-house was a working unit with its own stables, horses, carts, copper's shop for making barrels for the herring, out of season, salt stores, smoke-houses and stacks of oak shavings for smoking. A fish-house would open on 1 September and work through until the end of the herring season on 30 November. Many farm workers worked in fish-houses after the harvest was safely gathered in, and then went back to work on the land at the end of the herring season.

One of the features of the Yarmouth and Lowestoft scene during the herring season was the Scots 'girls' who came down to do the salting of the herring and some splitting of the kippers in the fish-houses. They were always referred to as 'girls' despite the fact that some of them were grandmothers. They used to arrive on special trains from Scotland bringing all their belongings in great wooden boxes. Local people would give them lodgings to make extra money, but they always stripped the rooms bare, because the girls' working clothes, covered in herring scales, smelt pretty awful. They always dressed in shawls and long skirts covered with oil-skins, or 'balm-skins', which made them creak as they walked. The work was very hard, but these girls displayed awesome skill as they gutted and packed the herring in sheds open to the wind blowing off the North Sea.

Things changed after World War II and the herring catch suddenly dropped and has continued to drop. The once great ports of Lowestoft and Yarmouth have been taken over by the big processors of frozen fish and vegetables and there are only memories of the time when the 'Silver Darlings' swam up and provided bumper catches.

However, to look on the bright side, herrings are now reappearing in the shops as a ban on herring fishing to conserve stocks was lifted in 1984. They are once again probably the cheapest and most highly nutritious food available to us. Herrings, like mackerel and sprats, are rich in oil and are best cooked simply; boiled, grilled, fried, barbecued or, of course, pickled or soused.

Fried Fresh Herring   (serves 4)

This is how the East Anglian fishermen used to like their herring cooked for breakfast. The fish were slit along the side in several places called 'snatches' and fried. It is still the finest way to cook a really fresh herring and was recommended in a cookbook from Great Yarmouth and Lowestoft dated 1866, which is now in the fishing museum at Great Yarmouth. The book says about herrings, 'no fish is apt to be handled more carelessly in cooking', so beware! The advice continues: 'The fire should not be too fierce; the frying-pan should be clean and thick-based; the butter, lard or oil fresh; the cooked fish should never be covered up or it will not be crisp; and should be served well-drained and very hot.'

4 fresh herrings	Wedges of lemon
Seasoned flour	Fresh parsley to garnish
Approx. 4oz (125g) butter or lard	

Scale the fish and clean them, but do not remove their heads and tails. Reserve the roes, which must be fried separately. Wipe the fish dry and score them diagonally across the belly three or four times on each side so that they cook through evenly. Coat them in seasoned flour. Melt the fat over a moderate heat and fry the herrings until they are crisp and brown. Lightly coat the roes with seasoned flour and fry them gently for a few minutes until they are light brown and crisp. Drain the fish and the roes well in kitchen paper and serve immediately with lemon wedges and garnished with parsley.

The traditional way of presenting fried fish was in a warm white napkin and this does look very appetising.

191

Blakeney Boiled Herrings (serves 4)

This was another traditional way of cooking herrings in East Anglia.

4 fresh herring

Approx. 1pt (600ml) water

6 black peppercorns

Sea salt

1 dessertspoon (10ml) lemon juice

Scale the fish and cut off their heads. Open them out and clean them, leaving the roes intact. Place the fish in a pan and barely cover them with water. Add the peppercorns, salt and lemon juice. Heat very slowly to boiling point, then simmer gently for about 8 minutes until tender. Drain well and serve with hollandaise sauce or a creamy herb sauce (see pp.209 and 215).

Herring Roes

Soft herring roes can be bought separately at the fishmonger's because so many herrings are gutted and turned into kippers. Fresh herring roes are very different from frozen, which tend to be rather wet, but are more difficult to find. In either form they are cheap and highly nutritious.

Dipped in a little seasoned flour and lightly fried in butter until crisp and light brown, they make a very good starter either served hot or cold in a little French dressing. They also make an unusual breakfast dish on buttered toast.

Herring Roes with Cream and Tarragon (serves 4)

Served either hot or cold, this recipe makes an excellent summer starter.

12oz (350g) soft herring roes

Seasoned flour

1½oz (40g) butter

8fl oz (240ml) dry white wine

Grated rind and juice of a lemon

8fl oz (240ml) single cream

Fresh tarragon, finely chopped

Lightly coat the herring roes with seasoned flour. Melt the butter in a frying-pan and gently fry the roes so that they are just beginning to cook, then add the wine and the lemon rind and juice. Cook for a few minutes until the wine reduces by half, then add the cream. Stir to make a sauce and adjust the seasoning if necessary. Sprinkle with fresh tarragon and serve immediately with wholemeal toast.

Yarmouth Red Herrings

These were the great mass-produced food of the Middle Ages; herrings heavily salted without splitting or gutting, dried and smoked over slow oak fires until they were hard, dry and coloured a rich mahogany. The process would take several weeks and was essential because the fish were very perishable. Yarmouth was the traditional centre of the herring curing industry.

With the development of refrigeration in the 19th century, the red herring virtually disappeared in favour of less harshly cured fish and since World War II most of the curing-houses have fallen into disuse, although there are notable exceptions. Sutton's of Great Yarmouth still cure reds, although they are less dry and salty than their ancestors. The Raglan Smokehouse in nearby Lowestoft, run by Gordon Buckenham and David Mullender, also produces good quality red herrings as well as kippers and other smoked fish, which are sold direct from the smoke-room.

To Cook Red Herrings

Florence White in *Good Things in England* includes a recipe for cooking red herrings from Great Yarmouth dated 1823, which involves soaking the fish in beer or milk for 30 minutes before toasting them in front of the fire and serving with butter. Traditionally the fish was served with egg sauce or buttered eggs and mashed potatoes.

Certainly, red herring do need to be split open and soaked unless you like their very strong salty taste. I have tried them soaked in milk for an hour, then grilled, and still found them a trifle salty for my taste, but they are fine used raw instead of anchovies.

Red Herrings Rob Roy

This way of dealing with red herrings was sent to me by Trevor Westgate, who writes for the *Lowestoft Journal*, and is currently working on a book of traditional East Anglian fish recipes.

The red herrings are split open, soaked in whisky and then set alight. When the flames go out, the fish is ready to eat. I have yet to try this out as my husband guards the whisky bottle!

Yarmouth Kipper Soup
(serves 6)

The word 'kipper' comes from the Dutch 'kuppen' meaning to spawn. It referred originally to salmon that had spawned and were in poor condition. These fish were of little use fresh, but after drying and smoking they could be made reasonably palatable. John Woodger of Seahouses (see p.147) came to Yarmouth where he started special curing-houses to produce kippers.

1lb (450g) filleted kippers	$\frac{1}{4}$pt (150ml) milk
2 14oz (400g) tins tomatoes	Freshly milled black pepper
2 cloves garlic, crushed	2 tablespoons (2 × 15ml) natural yoghurt
2 tablespoons (2 × 15ml) tomato purée	Fresh parsley, chopped to garnish
$\frac{3}{4}$pt (450ml) jugging liquor	

Place the kipper fillets in a tall jug. Pour on boiling water to cover and leave to stand for 5 minutes. Drain, reserving the jugging liquor.

Skin the kippers and flake the fish into a blender or processor. Add the tomatoes, garlic and tomato purée and blend until smooth. Pour the mixture into a large saucepan and add $\frac{3}{4}$pt (450ml) of the reserved jugging liquor together with the milk. Bring to simmering point and continue to simmer for 5 minutes. Serve hot with a swirl of yoghurt and chopped parsley to garnish.

Mussel Soup Moorings Style
(serves 8)

This recipe is from the Moorings Restaurant in Wells-next-the-Sea in North Norfolk. Owned by Bernard and Carla Phillips, a *Sunday Times* 'Cook of the Year', they specialise in dishes using local fish and shellfish. They also do most of their own smoking apart from the kippers, which come from the Cley Smokehouse. Carla sometimes uses a Suffolk dry cider by James White instead of wine, but any good, still, dry cider will do.

A handful of unpeeled shrimps	Celery leaves
1 large carrot, grated	1 tablespoon (15ml) fresh parsley, chopped
2 medium onions, chopped	
2 leeks, finely chopped including the green tops	Freshly milled black pepper
	2 teaspoons (2 × 5ml) Herbs de Provence (optional)
1 bottle dry white wine or good, dry, still cider	2oz (50g) butter
1pt (600ml) water	2 shallots, chopped
2pts (1.2 litres) fresh mussels	$\frac{1}{2}$ bulb Florentine fennel, finely chopped
1 clove garlic, crushed	

194

1 celery stick, finely chopped

2 tomatoes, skinned, deseeded and chopped

Juice and grated rind of 1 orange

½pt (300ml) double cream

Chop up the shrimps without peeling them and put them in a saucepan with a little of the carrot, onions, and leeks, a dash of the wine or cider and the water. Simmer to make a stock for about 10 minutes. Strain and reserve. Put the mussels in a large pan with three-quarters of the remaining wine or cider, the garlic, half the remaining onions, the celery leaves, parsley, some black pepper and the herbs and steam them open. Discard the mussel shells when they are cool and reserve all the liquid.

Melt the butter in a large casserole. Add the remaining carrot, onion and leeks and the shallots, fennel and celery. Cook the vegetables for about 5 minutes or until soft, then add the tomatoes and the orange juice and grated rind. Lastly, add the shrimp and mussel stocks and any remaining wine or cider. Bring the soup to the boil, lower the heat and allow the mixture to simmer for about 10 minutes. Then stir in the cream. Taste and add more pepper if necessary. Just before serving, add the mussels and cook for a few more minutes. Garnish with chopped parsley and serve with freshly made croûtons.

Baked Staithe Mussels (serves 4)

It was the exquisite, slightly sweet flesh of mussels which first attracted prehistoric man to the shores and estuaries of East Anglia. Mussels remained extremely popular right up to Victorian times as a welcome addition to the diet of salt and dried fish. Then overpicking suddenly made them more expensive, like oysters.

Fortunately, mussels have again become cheap and plentiful and there are a number of mussel beds around the East Anglian coast, especially in North Norfolk. Mussels are best purchased from a trustworthy fishmonger rather than gathered yourself, because they can be dangerous if living in polluted water. The mussel is a little pumping machine, which passes at least 10 gallons of water a day through itself and normally needs to be purified in fresh seawater for a few hours before being eaten.

There are vast areas of mussel lays of excellent quality at Brancaster Harbour, owned by the National Trust. The mussel seed is collected from The Wash when it is ½ inch long and dumped in specific places in the harbour and left to grow for 2 to 3 years.

The harbour is the only E.E.C.-recognised, pollution-free harbour in England and Wales, and consequently the mussels are clean and wholesome. These mussel lays are rented out to Brancaster fishermen by the National Trust, so the shellfish must not be gathered by the general public; mussels from the main beach at Brancaster, however, can be.

Allow 1 pint (600ml) or 1lb (450g) of mussels per person, which will give 3–4oz (75–125g) mussel meat.

4 pints (2.4 litres) fresh mussels	1 tablespoon (15ml) lemon juice
6oz (175g) softened butter	Sea salt and freshly milled black pepper
4 cloves garlic, crushed	
1 tablespoon (15ml) fresh parsley, chopped	

Give the mussels a rigorous scrub under cold running water and scrape them free of barnacles. Pull out as much as you can of the wiry beard known as the 'byssus', which the mussel uses to cling to the seabed or rock and discard any mussels that are broken or any that remain open when tapped. Put some of the mussels in a large pan, cover with a lid and shake gently over heat for 3–5 minutes until they open. You will need to cook the mussels in several batches rather than over-fill the pan. Discard any that do not open. Mix the butter, crushed garlic and parsley together, then season with lemon juice, sea salt and pepper. Remove the mussels from one half of their shell and discard the surplus shells. The juice can be used as a base for a fish soup or stew. Set the mussels in their half-shells on a baking tray filled with a thick layer of sea salt to prevent them tipping over. Put a generous knob of garlic butter on top of each mussel and grill or bake them in a hot oven (450°F, 230°C, gas mark 8) for 5–10 minutes until the butter begins to bubble. Serve immediately with plenty of wholemeal bread to mop up the garlicky juices.

Mussel and Shrimp Soup   *(serves 4–6)*

1pt (600ml) shrimps, unpeeled	$\frac{1}{2}$oz (12g) flour
1 medium carrot, chopped	1 heaped teaspoon curry powder
1 large onion, chopped	1 small glass medium or sweet sherry
A few sprigs of fennel	Sea salt and freshly milled black pepper
1$\frac{1}{2}$pts (900ml) cold water	
1pt (600ml) fresh mussels	A few drops of Tabasco sauce
2oz (50g) butter	2–3 tablespoons (2–3 × 15ml) single cream
1 celery stick, finely chopped	

Peel the shrimps, reserving the shells and heads. Set them aside, then put the peelings into a saucepan with the chopped carrot, half the chopped onion and the sprigs of fennel. Pour over the water, cover with a lid and bring to the boil. Simmer for at least 30 minutes to make a well-flavoured stock. Meanwhile scrub the mussels well, removing any barnacles and the beards. In a large saucepan, melt half the butter and add the chopped celery, the remaining chopped onion and lastly, the mussels. Cover with a lid and cook for 3–5 minutes over a moderate heat, shaking the pan from time to time, until all the mussels are open. Remove the mussels from their shells, reserving the liquor, and add them to the shrimps.

Melt the remaining butter in the same saucepan and stir in the flour and curry powder. Cook for a few minutes, then strain in the shrimp stock followed by the mussel liquor. Bring to the boil and then add the sherry. Season to taste with salt, pepper and Tabasco sauce. Lastly, stir in the shrimps and the mussels followed by the cream. Serve immediately with crusty wholemeal bread or rolls.

Brancaster Staithe Oysters

Oysters have been eaten since the earliest days of man and were the particular glory of Britain in Roman times. Legend has it that one of the reasons the Romans invaded Britain was for its oysters! The Romans were indeed the first to cultivate them and started oyster farms in British coastal waters which still exist; the most famous being at Colchester; Hundreds of oyster shells have been found at Branodunum, the site of a Roman fort owned by the Trust just west of Brancaster Staithe.

Oysters continued to be the favourite food of both rich and poor alike. They could be kept alive in brackish water for as long as 12 days, so they were carried quite long distances inland and, pickled in vinegar, they lasted for several weeks. A suggested menu for a large fish day feast in the 1630s has stewed oysters in the first course; oysters fried, pickled and baked in a pie in the second course. This liberal use of oysters in cookery continued into Victorian times, while pickled oysters were the staple diet of the poor in London and other towns, sold from barrows for pennies.

Then, quite suddenly, the oyster beds became exhausted, mainly through over-fishing to satisfy the demands of these same large industrial towns, and oysters became a rare luxury. It was only by deliberate artificial breeding that they were saved from complete extinction. Today the main supplies of native oysters come from areas around the south-east corner of England, especially Whitstable and Mersea near Colchester and are in season from 4 August to 14 May. The famous 'Oyster Feast' at Colchester Town Hall is still held once a year.

Although native oysters are farmed, they are still vulnerable and have suffered in recent years from bad winters, pests and in 1983 from a disease called bonarnia. Consequently they have become more expensive than ever and made the production of Pacific and Portuguese oysters more attractive. These are larger although their flavour is not so good, but they do have two advantages: they are not susceptible to bonarnia, and are available all the year round since they are bred in hatcheries. Our waters are too cold for them to reproduce naturally.

Brancaster Staithe, bought by the National Trust with Enterprise Neptune funds in 1967, is an ideal oyster ground with its mixture of salt and fresh, unpolluted water. Pacific oysters are artificially reared here from seed, in rafts standing about one foot above the sea bed, rented from the National Trust by one fisherman. The oysters mature in 2 or 3 years and are mostly exported to the Continent.

To Open or 'Shuck' an Oyster

If you intend eating your oysters raw, the shells should be opened immediately before and this requires a certain knack. I recommend asking your fishmonger to show you how, because it is quite difficult. You need a bowl, a tea-towel and a strong short-bladed knife, or a special oyster knife. Wrap the tea-towel round one hand to help you get a grip on the oyster. Grasp the oyster firmly, flat side up in your palm. Insert the knife into the hinge of the oyster and move it about to cut the oyster free of the upper shell and to prise the shells open. Do this over the bowl, so the oyster juices are not lost. Remove the top shell, leaving the oyster in the bottom shell with its liquor. Remove any flakes of shell that may have fallen on top of the oyster, which is now ready to serve raw or to cook.

Raw Native Oysters

The larger Pacific or Portuguese oysters are ideal for cooking and are especially good deep-fried but English oysters are best served raw.

Allow at least 4 oysters per person and serve them freshly opened with their liquor. Arrange them on a bed of crushed ice decorated with a layer of seaweed, pointed end inwards. Chill on the ice for about 15 minutes before serving. Accompany with wedges of lemon, cayenne pepper, brown bread and butter and a glass of dry wine or stout. Provide small forks to eat the oyster, but drink the juice from the shell, or the oyster can be sucked out of its shell.

Oysters may be grilled, fried, stewed, made into soups, sauces, soufflés, omelettes or added to meat pies and puddings, traditionally steak and kidney; or to Lancashire Hot Pot.

Oyster Loaves
(serves 6)

This recipe is based on one for stewed oysters by a Mary Eaton from Bungay in Suffolk, dating back to 1823 and given in Florence White's *Good Things in England*, who suggests that the oysters may be used to fill patty cases of puff pastry or cases made from stale dinner rolls. Mussels, cockles, scallops, clams or queens could be used instead.

6 soft rolls	Cayenne pepper
Approx. 6oz (175g) butter	Freshly milled black pepper
24 oysters	A little lemon juice
$\frac{1}{2}$pt (300ml) double cream	Fresh parsley, finely chopped

Roughen the outside of the rolls on a grater and cut a piece off the top of each for a lid. Hollow out the inside crumb to form 6 little cases. Brush the rolls and their lids inside and out with melted butter and bake in a fairly hot oven (400°F, 200°C, gas mark 6) for a few minutes until crisp and golden. Keep the cases warm. Clean and open the oysters in the usual way, reserving the liquor carefully. Put the oysters and their liquor into a saucepan and simmer for a few seconds until slightly stiff, but be careful not to overcook. Drain the oysters and reserve. Boil the juices down for a few minutes, then stir in the cream and boil until thick, seasoning with the peppers and a little lemon juice. Add the parsley and the oysters to reheat for a couple of seconds, then divide between the rolls. Serve immediately.

East Anglian Oyster Soup
(serves 6–8)

You cannot write about oysters in East Anglia without mentioning the Butley-Orford Oysterage in Suffolk, which is famous for its home-grown Pacific oysters and smoked fish. Richard Pinney started his oyster beds in 1955 and has been curing and smoking seafood since 1960. The restaurant is the only one in England with its own oyster hatchery, established on an 8-acre stretch of the nearby river.

Oyster soup is one of the dishes served regularly.

24 fresh oysters	$\frac{1}{4}$pt (150ml) double cream
2oz (50g) butter	Sea salt and freshly milled black pepper
2oz (50g) flour	A little lemon juice
$\frac{1}{2}$pt (300ml) milk	Fresh parsley, finely chopped to garnish
$\frac{1}{2}$pt (300ml) white stock	
$\frac{3}{4}$ teaspoon (4ml) anchovy essence	
Cayenne pepper	

Clean and open the oysters in the usual way (see p.198). Discard the shells, but reserve the liquor. Melt the butter in a large saucepan and stir in the flour. Cook gently for a few minutes, then stir in the milk and stock gradually to make a smooth sauce. Season with the anchovy essence and cayenne pepper. Add the cream and simmer gently for about 15 minutes. Just before serving, add the oysters and their liquor and gently heat through, making sure that you do not overcook them. Season to taste with salt, freshly milled black pepper and a little lemon juice. Serve immediately garnished with chopped parsley and with brown bread and butter.

Norfolk Razor-Shell Clams

Beds of these delicious little shellfish live in abundance off the North Norfolk coast, just below the hard wet sand at the edge of the sea at the lowest point of the spring tides. Long and narrow, shaped like an old-fashioned cut-throat razor, they are able to burrow out of harm's way at an astonishing speed with their fleshy and powerful 'foot', also used for swimming. This ability makes them rather difficult to collect despite numerous local tips on how to trick them out of the sand! A pair of small holes and a pattern of splash marks are the signs to look for and once you have been shown these, all you need is a small trowel and a bucket. If possible, hold the razor clam firmly against the side of its hole, then carefully dig around and below it to ease it out. Drop it immediately into your bucket, or it will disappear again into the sand. Try not to crush the thin brittle shell of the clam when you are digging it out.

On reaching home, soak the razor clams in seawater for a few hours, or overnight, and then wash them well in clean water. They can be eaten raw like oysters and are deliciously sweet and clean-tasting. To open them, soak for a few moments in warm water, which makes it much easier to push a knife through the hinges of the shells. Remove the tip of the siphon, the feeding tube, which always has a few grains of sand sticking to it and the rest of the clam meat can be eaten with lemon juice, a dash of cayenne pepper or Tabasco sauce and wholemeal or rye bread and butter. To cook razor clams, steam them in a large covered pan with a little water over moderate heat until the shells open. Serve simply, with lemon juice, melted butter or Tabasco sauce. The whole fish can be used in most traditional clam, oyster or mussel recipes, especially soups and stews, while the sweet white foot makes a good substitute for scallops.

Razor Clams in Saffron Sauce with Samphire

Any other variety of clams, mussels or oysters can be used instead of razor clams in this recipe. Saffron crocuses were once commonly grown around Saffron Walden in Essex. The spice comes from the stamens and is highly prized for its delicate flavour and golden colour.

4 handfuls of samphire tips	Pinch of saffron steeped in a little boiling water
32 razor clams, soaked overnight	
$\frac{1}{4}$pt (150ml) dry white wine	$\frac{1}{4}$pt (150ml) double cream
2 small shallots, chopped	$\frac{1}{4}$pt (150ml) sour cream
1 medium carrot, chopped	A little cayenne pepper

Wash the samphire well and cook it in a little boiling water for a few minutes. Drain well and keep warm. Scrub the clams. Place the wine, chopped shallots, and carrot into a large pan and bring to the boil. Add the clams, cover with a lid and steam over a moderate heat for a few minutes until the shells open. Remove the clams and discard the shells reserving their liquor. Add this to the wine and vegetables and strain the liquid into another wide shallow pan. Add the steeped saffron and its liquor and boil the sauce to reduce by half. Stir in the double and sour cream and heat gently without boiling. Remove the sauce from the heat and stir in the clams. Season with pepper.

Spoon the clams with their sauce over the cooked samphire and serve immediately.

Poor Man's Asparagus

This is the old name for marsh samphire or glasswort, also evocatively called saltwort, pickle plant and crab-grass, which covers the lower levels of the salt marshes and mud flats of North Norfolk, from Brancaster to Cley and Salthouse. Years ago, it was known locally as 'sheep's samphire' from the sheep that once fed on the marshes. The plant is one of the first colonisers of a mudbank and sprouts from the bare mud like a forest of miniature trees trapping yet more silt, especially in the autumn, and building up mud at a rate of as much as $1\frac{1}{2}$ inches a year. The fleshy stems and branches, which are well adapted to retain the plant's moisture, are smoothly curved to offer the least resistance to the currents which will try to shift the seedlings from their shallow-rooted anchorages. In some creeks, the plants are pushed tight together and come up with just one straight stem, but the best to eat are the bushy plants.

Samphire has always been and still is, harvested for food from June to September along this coast. It is rich in iron and in summer you can gather it yourself or buy it by the pound from stalls outside farmhouses, particularly in Blakeney, and from local fishmongers and markets.

If you want to pick samphire yourself, wait for low tide and then walk out to the mud flats with a sharp pair of scissors or a knife and a vegetable net. Cut the plants just above the base or pull up by the roots remembering that the bushy bits are the best. Pack the samphire into your net and give it a good wash in one of the creeks. Take home plenty because it freezes very well. When you reach home, wash again very well and pick it over, removing any roots and the tough stems.

To Cook Samphire

In June and July, when the samphire is young and tender, the tips can be eaten raw as a salad, or the whole plant can be steamed or boiled briskly in unsalted water for 5 minutes, then drained and eaten with melted butter and black pepper like asparagus, using your fingers and drawing the stems between your teeth. Later on in the year, in August and September, the trimmed samphire can be dropped into unsalted boiling water and cooked for about 10 minutes, then drained and eaten as a vegetable with melted butter and black pepper. Traditionally it is served hot with mutton or lamb, but it is excellent with locally caught fish and shellfish. Samphire has an aromatic and salty taste.

Pickled Samphire

This is the traditional way of preserving samphire and there are several methods. Pickled samphire or samphire cooked and served, either hot or cold, in a dish of vinegar is a popular way of eating the plant in North Norfolk. The old way of pickling was to pack the samphire into jars with vinegar and store them in bread ovens which were cooling down on Friday night after the baking was finished. The jars were left until Monday morning. In the 19th century, barrels of pickled samphire were sent from Norfolk to London.

To pickle samphire, clean it well and dry with a cloth. Place it in a large bowl and cover with boiling vinegar. Leave overnight, then drain and reboil the vinegar. Pour it over the samphire again when it reaches boiling point. After a few minutes, pack the samphire into clean jars with a sprig of fresh tarragon or thyme. Cover with the boiled vinegar and seal securely.

An alternative way is to pack the uncooked samphire into jars and cover with cold vinegar.

Aldeburgh Sprats

Aldeburgh in Suffolk was a prosperous port in the 16th century, but is now widely known for its music festival started in 1948 by Benjamin Britten and held annually in June. Aldeburgh and Southwold sprats have been famous for centuries. The first catch of the season used to be smoked and sent to London for the Lord Mayor's Banquet. Their season is October to March and they are some of the best fish in East Anglia.

Sprats are small, silver fish, members of the herring family, but very cheap and highly nutritious. They are best bought on the beach straight from the fishermen's boats at Aldeburgh, Southwold or Dunwich. Jack Docwra, the National Trust's recently retired coastal warden for this part of the Suffolk coast, tells me that sprats usually appear at Dunwich in December and are used mainly as bait, because the Lowestoft fish market does not appear to be able to cope with large amounts.

To Cook Sprats

The best local way of cooking sprats is to put them in a very hot frying-pan with no fat, but just a sprinkling of salt, which draws out the oil from the fish. Fry them quickly, 2 or 3 minute each side. Local fishermen don't cut the heads or tails off the sprats so that they can eat them in their fingers. There is also no need to gut them as they are such a small fish, but if you want to, clean them through their gills so that the body of the fish is not damaged.

Another traditional way of cooking sprats is to grill or barbecue them whole for a few minutes on each side.

As with whitebait, their flavour is improved by a little lemon juice and cayenne pepper or mustard. For a starter you need to allow about 5 sprats per person.

Coupled Sprats   (serves 1)

This is another traditional East Anglian way of serving fresh sprats and makes an excellent first course for a dinner party, 2 or 3 pairs of fish being enough for each person. They may be shallow-fried instead if you prefer.

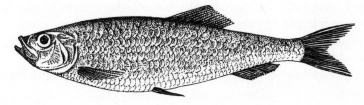

Sprat

4–6 fresh sprats	Beaten egg
Fresh parsley, finely chopped	Seasoned flour
Fresh chives, finely chopped	Groundnut oil for deep frying
A pinch of salt	Wedges of lemon to garnish
A little cayenne pepper	

To prepare the sprats, cut off their heads and tails, split them down one side of the backbone and open them out flat like miniature kippers. Remove the backbone by holding the flesh down with the first and second fingers of your left hand and pulling the bone up between them starting from the head end. Mix a little chopped parsley and chives with the salt and cayenne pepper. Sprinkle this mixture generously over the flesh side of the split sprats. Make the fish into pairs by putting them face to face, dip in beaten egg and then in seasoned flour. Deep-fry the fish for a few minutes until they are golden brown. Garnish with lemon wedges and serve with thin brown bread and butter and a glass of dry white wine, or the local Adnams brew.

Smoked Sprats

Aldeburgh and Southwold are the places in East Anglia to look for top quality smoked sprats. They are quite easy to cure and many local fishermen still smoke part of their catch. Sprats are cured like bloaters with a short soaking in brine and then lightly smoked. They are very cheap and excellent served as a starter on their own or as part of a mixed hors d'oeuvre. Eat with plenty of lemon juice, a little cayenne pepper and thin brown bread and butter.

Do make sure the smoked sprats you buy are not dry, they must be very moist inside or they are not worth eating.

Wells Whelks

Wells whelks are almost as famous as Cromer crabs; in fact, about 80 per cent of the whelks eaten in this country are caught in the waters off Wells-next-the-Sea, and to a lesser extent from nearby Brancaster. They are sold from stalls alongside cockles and winkles at most seaside resorts and are rich in protein and iron. In the past, whelks were much used in fish cookery as a garnish for larger fish or in stews, soups or salads. At the enthronement of the Archbishop of Canterbury in 1504, 4,000 whelks were offered to the more distinguished of the guests as a garnish for salted sturgeon.

To Cook Whelks

If you have the chance to cook your own whelks, steep them in cold fresh water for at least 12 hours in a large pail *with a lid*, or you will find them all over the kitchen in no time. Drain them, and put in a pan of boiling salted water or court bouillon (see p.208) and boil for about 10 minutes, or they may be steamed. Remove the edible flesh from the shells with a long pin or small fork. Serve sprinkled with lemon juice or vinegar, black pepper and melted butter. Whelks are also excellent served chilled as part of a seafood platter, with lemon or garlic mayonnaise and thin brown bread and butter.

Whelks in Sauce

Cook the whelks as above and slice up any large ones. Make ½pt (300ml) sauce using half milk and half cooking liquor from the whelks. Add the whelks and season with black pepper and lemon juice. Serve with or on hot buttered toast.

Deep-fried Norfolk Whitebait   (serves 6–8)

These tiny silvery fish are not a separate species, but the small fry of sprats, herrings and some twenty other near relations, all tasting the same at the table. In The Wash, enormous shoals of whitebait are caught by seine netting from June to October, and off the coast at Southend in Essex from Christmas to August.

At Southend, the 'Blessing of the Catch' still survives during the annual Whitebait Festival in September, although ironically the whitebait for blessing comes from the deep-freeze as the season finishes in August! The fish were traditionally a rich man's pleasure: in the 19th century, whitebait parties were held for Members of Parliament at the end of the parliamentary session at Greenwich, where they used to be caught. Whitebait are difficult to obtain fresh nowadays, but they do freeze very well, unlike prawns and shrimps.

Excellent whitebait, both fresh and frozen, is obtainable from Major Athill, an oyster farmer, who lives at Morston, between Wells-next-the-

Sea and Blakeney. The fish should be eaten whole, heads, bones, insides and all. The most nutritious parts are the bits which are removed in larger fish! Allow about 4oz (125g) per person. If using frozen whitebait, thaw before frying.

2lb (900g) whitebait

Approx. 5oz (150g) seasoned flour

A little milk

Groundnut oil for deep frying

Sea salt

Sprigs of fresh parsley

Wedges of lemon

Spread out the fish and pick them over, discarding any that are broken, but do not wash – little wisps of seaweed will add to the taste! Put the seasoned flour into a plastic bag, dip the whitebait in milk and toss them lightly in the flour. Heat the oil in a deep fryer and fry the whitebait in batches for 2–3 minutes until golden brown. Lift out and drain. Reheat the oil to smoking hot and fry all the whitebait in one go for another minute until crisp. Drain them well and serve in a white linen napkin, sprinked with sea salt and garnished with sprigs of deep-fried parsley and wedges of lemon. Accompany with thin slices of wholemeal bread and butter.

Variation:

Deep fry the fish as before, but sprinkle with cayenne pepper before serving.

SAUCES, STOCKS AND BUTTERS

Bearnaise Sauce

(makes approx. ½pt [300ml])

1 tablespoon (15ml) fresh tarragon, chopped

1 tablespoon (15ml) fresh parsley, chopped

1 tablespoon (15ml) onion, chopped

6 black peppercorns, crushed

2 tablespoons (2 × 15ml) white wine vinegar

¼pt (150ml) dry white wine

3 egg yolks

1 teaspoon (5ml) mustard powder

1 tablespoon (15ml) water

1oz (25g) softened butter

6oz (175g) melted butter

Salt

Boil the herbs, onion, peppercorns, wine vinegar and white wine in a small saucepan until reduced to about 3 tablespoons (3 × 15ml). Whisk the egg yolks and mustard together in the top of a double saucepan or in a basin standing over hot water. Strain the vinegar mixture through a fine sieve onto the egg yolks, add a tablespoon (15ml) of water and beat over hot water. Beat in the softened butter, about ½oz (12g) at a time, whisking until smooth after each addition. Gradually add the melted butter, a little at a time, still whisking, until the sauce has thickened. Season to taste and keep warm over the hot water until needed.

Beurre Manié

This is kneaded butter used for thickening sauces, soups and stews. Work twice as much butter as flour into a paste on a plate with a fork and add in small pieces to the sauce, soup or stew to be thickened. Reheat and if still not thick enough, add more kneaded butter.

Old Fashioned Melted Butter Sauce

(makes approx. ¼pt [150ml])

This is a basic sauce for fish. Shrimps, crabs, oysters, anchovies, lobster or hard-boiled eggs can be added.

2 teaspoons (2 × 5ml) flour

¼pt (150ml) water

Pinch of sea salt

3oz (75g) butter

A few drops of lemon juice

Mix the flour, water and salt together in a small saucepan. Stir over a gentle heat without allowing the sauce to boil. When it is hot, add the butter cut into small pieces. Stir well until smooth. Season with lemon juice.

Do not reheat or allow the sauce to boil.

White Wine Butter Sauce

(makes approx. $\frac{1}{4}$pt [150ml])

3 tablespoons (3 × 15ml) white wine

3 tablespoons (3 × 15ml) white wine vinegar

1 tablespoon (15ml) shallots, finely chopped

Pinch of freshly milled white pepper

6oz (175g) butter

Boil the white wine, vinegar, shallots and pepper in a saucepan until reduced to about $\frac{1}{2}$ tablespoon (7.5ml). Beat in the butter in small pieces, keeping the sauce warm enough to absorb the butter. Keep warm until needed.

Court Bouillon

(makes approx. 2pts [1.2 litres])

This is the most basic stock which can be used for poaching fish and shellfish. After the cooked fish has been removed, the court bouillon can be reduced to a half or one-third of the original quantity by boiling down hard. This concentrates the flavour and thickens the stock.

2pts (1.2 litres) water

2 medium onions, sliced

1 bouquet garni

$\frac{1}{2}$pt (300ml) white wine

8oz (225g) carrots, chopped

1–2 celery sticks

Pinch of sea salt

6 black peppercorns, crushed

Simmer all the ingredients except the peppercorns in a large saucepan for 40 minutes. Add the peppercorns for the last 15 minutes. Strain well and allow to cool until required.

Curry Sauce

(makes approx. $\frac{1}{2}$pt [300ml])

1oz (25g) butter

1 small onion, finely chopped

1 teaspoon (5ml) mild curry powder

1oz (25g) flour

$\frac{1}{2}$pt (300ml) milk

2 tablespoons (2 × 15ml) double cream

Sea salt and freshly milled pepper

Melt the butter in a small saucepan and cook the onion until tender but not brown. Add the curry powder and flour and cook for 1 minute, then gradually add the milk a little at a time until the sauce is thick and smooth. Stir in the cream and season to taste, but do not allow to boil. Serve with huss, members of the cod family and scallops.

Fish Stock *(makes approx. 1½pts [900ml])*

2lbs (900g) fish bones	1 clove garlic, unpeeled
3oz (75g) carrots, sliced	Sprig of fresh thyme
3oz (75g) onion, sliced	Few parsley stalks
Half a leek, chopped	6 black peppercorns
1 celery stick	½pt (300ml) white wine
1 bayleaf	1½pts (900ml) water

Remove any specks of blood or skin from the fish bones and put them in a large saucepan with the vegetables, herbs and peppercorns. Pour over the wine and water. Bring to the boil and simmer gently for 30 minutes. Strain and use as required.

Hollandaise Sauce *(makes approx. ½pt [300ml])*

3 tablespoons (3 × 15ml) white wine vinegar	3 large egg yolks
2 tablespoons (2 × 15ml) water	6oz (175g) unsalted butter, cut into 12 pieces
10 white peppercorns	Sea salt and lemon juice to taste

Put the vinegar, water and peppercorns into a small pan and boil down to about 1 tablespoon (15ml) of liquid. Leave to cool. Beat the egg yolks in a basin and add the reduced vinegar mixture. Pour the egg yolks and vinegar mixture into the top of a double saucepan or set the basin over a pan of barely simmering water on a low heat. Cook slowly without letting the water boil, or the sauce will get too hot and curdle. Add the butter, knob by knob, stirring all the time. The sauce is finished when it coats the back of the spoon and looks thick. Season to taste with salt and lemon juice. Keep warm on a very low heat until ready to serve.

Variations:

Cucumber Hollandaise

Basic hollandaise sauce	1 teaspoon (5ml) fresh fennel, chopped
Half a cucumber	
Sea salt	A few drops of Tabasco sauce

Slice the cucumber thinly. Put it into a colander, sprinkle with salt, and leave to drain for at least an hour. Rinse if the slices are too salty, squeeze them dry in a clean tea towel, then chop them roughly. Add the chopped fennel to the cucumber, then add the Tabasco to the basic hollandaise sauce and fold in the cucumber just before serving. Adjust the seasoning if necessary.

Hollandaise Sauce with Herbs

Add ½ teaspoon (2.5ml) of French mustard and 1 tablespoon (15ml) of mixed finely chopped chives, fennel, parsley and thyme to the finished sauce.

Orange Hollandaise

Stir the grated rind of a small orange, preferably a blood orange, into the sauce and use some of the juice instead of lemon juice for the final seasoning. Serve with any firm white fish, salmon, sea trout and scallops.

Horseradish Sauce *(makes approx. ¼pt [150ml])*

2 tablespoons (2 × 15ml) grated horseradish	¼pt (150ml) double cream
	1 teaspoon (5ml) mild mustard
1 teaspoon (5ml) tarragon vinegar	Pinch of salt

Mix all the ingredients together and add more cream if the sauce is too strong. Serve with smoked fish.

Mayonnaise *(makes approx. ¾pt [450ml])*

3 large egg yolks	1½–2 tablespoons (22.5–30ml) wine vinegar or lemon juice
½ teaspoon (2.5ml) dry mustard	
½ teaspoon (2.5ml) sea salt	¾pt (450ml) olive oil
Large pinch cayenne pepper	

Before starting to make the mayonnaise, make sure all the ingredients are at room temperature. Warm your mixing bowl and dry it carefully. Beat the egg yolks in the bowl for 1–2 minutes until thick and sticky. Add the seasonings and all but a few drops of the wine vinegar or lemon juice and beat for a further 1–2 minutes. Add the oil in drops, whisking continuously. Continue adding the oil very slowly until the mayonnaise begins to thicken. Once the mayonnaise has thickened, the oil can be added a little faster. When the mayonnaise thickens too much to whisk, add a few drops of lemon juice or vinegar and then continue adding the oil until it has all been absorbed. Check the seasoning and adjust if necessary.

Variations:

Curry Mayonnaise

Add $1\frac{1}{2}$ teaspoons (7.5ml) of finely-grated onion and $1\frac{1}{2}$ teaspoons (7.5ml) of curry powder or paste to the 3 egg yolks of the basic mayonnaise. Continue in the usual way. Serve with white fish, shellfish and pickled herrings or mackerel.

Garlic Mayonnaise

Make a basic mayonnaise, but add 1–6 well crushed cloves of garlic to the egg yolks with 2 teaspoons (2 × 5ml) of fresh parsley, finely chopped. Serve with cold white fish and shellfish.

Green Mayonnaise

Make a basic mayonnaise. Blanch $\frac{1}{2}$oz (12g) each of parsley, tarragon, chives and chervil and 1oz (25g) of young spinach and watercress leaves in boiling water for 2 minutes. Pour into a sieve and cool under the cold tap. Press out all the moisture and pound to a paste. Mix the paste into the mayonnaise just before serving with salmon, sea trout, shellfish and cold white fish such as turbot.

Orange Mayonnaise

Grate the rind of an orange into the bowl. Add the egg yolks with 1 tablespoon (15ml) of lemon juice. Flavour the mayonnaise with the juice from the orange and a little more lemon juice instead of vinegar. Serve with cold white fish and shellfish.

Mushroom Sauce

(makes approx. ½pt [300ml])

1oz (25g) butter

4oz (125g) mushrooms, sliced

Small clove garlic, crushed

1oz (25g) flour

½pt (300ml) milk

2 tablespoons (2 × 15ml) double cream

Sea salt and freshly milled black pepper

A little lemon juice

Melt the butter in a small saucepan and add the mushrooms. Cook until tender with the crushed garlic. Take off the heat and stir in the flour. Return to the heat and gradually add the milk, stirring continuously, until thick and creamy. At the last minute add the cream and season to taste with salt, black pepper and lemon juice. Serve with any white fish or shellfish.

Saffron Sauce

(makes approx. ¼pt [150ml])

1 small onion, very finely chopped

¼pt (150ml) dry white wine

¼pt (150ml) double cream

Pinch of saffron

Simmer the onion and the dry white wine in a small saucepan until the liquid is reduced to 2 tablespoons (2 × 15ml). Stir in the double cream and saffron and warm through very gently. Serve with turbot, sole and brill.

Brown Shrimp Sauce

(makes approx. 1pt [600ml])

This recipe can also be used for pink shrimps.

1pt (600ml) brown shrimps

½pt (300ml) fish stock

¼pt (150ml) dry sherry

Pinch of cayenne pepper

2 teaspoons (2 × 5ml) tomato purée

¼pt (150ml) double cream

Simmer the shrimps, including their shells, in fish stock for 10 minutes. Liquidise and sieve. Reheat the sieved liquid adding the sherry, cayenne pepper and tomato purée. Stir in the double cream and mix to a smooth sauce.

Sorrel Sauce

(makes approx. ¾pt [450ml])

2 shallots, finely chopped

¼pt (150ml) fish stock

3 tablespoons (3 × 15ml) dry vermouth

5 tablespoons (5 × 15ml) dry white wine

½pt (300ml) cream

4oz (125g) sorrel leaves, ribs removed and finely chopped

2oz (50g) spinach or watercress leaves, ribs removed and finely chopped

1oz (25g) butter

A squeeze of lemon juice

Fresh ground black pepper

Put the shallots in a pan with the stock, vermouth and wine. Cook over a high heat until the liquid reduces to a syrupy glaze. Stir in the cream and cook at just under boiling point, stirring all the time, until the sauce has slightly thickened. Now add the chopped leaves and cook for a further 30 seconds, adding scraps of butter and the lemon juice in the final stage. Season to taste and serve. Serve with salmon, trout and any white fish.

Tartare Sauce

(makes approx. ¾pt [450ml])

2 hard-boiled egg yolks

2 raw egg yolks

12fl oz (350ml) olive oil

1–2 tablespoons (1–2 × 15ml) vinegar

Salt and freshly milled pepper

1 teaspoon (5ml) capers, chopped

1 teaspoon (5ml) gherkins, chopped

2 teaspoons (2 × 5ml) chives or spring onions, chopped

2 hard-boiled egg whites, chopped

Make as for mayonnaise, mixing the mashed hard-boiled egg yolks with the raw egg yolks. Add the capers, gherkins, chives or spring onions and egg whites to finish the sauce.

Tomato Sauce

(makes approx. ¾pt [450ml])

1 tablespoon (15ml) olive oil

1 small onion, finely chopped

1 clove garlic, crushed

1lb (450g) ripe tomatoes, skinned and chopped

1 teaspoon (5ml) tomato purée

2 teaspoons (2 × 5ml) fresh basil

Sea salt and freshly milled black pepper

Heat the oil in a saucepan, and soften the onion and garlic in it for 5 minutes without letting them brown. Then add the tomatoes, tomato purée, basil and a seasoning of salt and pepper. Give everything a good stir, cover the pan and simmer slowly for 15 minutes. Cook uncovered for a further 10–15 minutes for the sauce to reduce slightly.

Fish Velouté   (makes approx. ½pt [300ml])

This is made in the same way as a basic white sauce (see below) but fish stock and sometimes wine is substituted for all or half the milk. Many of the seasonings used to flavour white sauce, such as mustard or shellfish, can also be used with a velouté sauce. Serve with any fish.

1oz (25g) butter

1oz (25g) flour

½pt (300ml) fish stock (see p.209)

1oz (25g) mushroom stalks, chopped

Sea salt and freshly milled black pepper

Melt the butter, stir in the flour and cook for a minute. Gradually add the heated stock and continue cooking to make a smooth sauce. Add the chopped mushrooms and cook until creamy. Season to taste.

Basic White Sauce   (makes ½pt [300ml])

½pt (300ml) milk

1 bayleaf

1 blade mace

1 shallot, chopped

1oz (25g) butter

1oz (25g) plain flour

Sea salt and freshly milled pepper

Place the milk, bayleaf, blade of mace and chopped shallot into a small saucepan and bring to the boil very gently. Remove from the heat and allow to infuse for 20 minutes. Then strain the milk into a jug. Melt the butter in a small saucepan very slowly. Take it off the heat as soon as the butter has melted and stir in the flour. Stir to a smooth paste, then return the saucepan to a medium heat and add the milk a little at a time, making sure all the milk is incorporated before adding any more. When all the milk has been incorporated, turn the heat very low and let the sauce cook for about 5 minutes. Season to taste with sea salt and freshly milled pepper.

Variations:

Anchovy Sauce   (makes approx. ½pt [300ml])

Add 3–4 pounded anchovy fillets or a few drops of anchovy essence to the finished sauce. Serve with whiting, cod, pollock, turbot, brill and sole.

Caper Sauce *(makes approx. $\frac{1}{2}$pt [300ml])*

Add 1 tablespoon (15ml) of capers and a little chopped parsley to the finished sauce. Serve with skate, halibut, turbot, cod, whiting and pollock.

Cheese Sauce *(makes approx. $\frac{1}{2}$pt [300ml])*

Add 2–3oz (50–75g) of grated Cheddar cheese and 1oz (25g) of grated Parmesan cheese with 1 teaspoon (5ml) of English mustard to the prepared sauce and serve with any white fish or shellfish.

Crab Sauce *(makes approx. $\frac{3}{4}$pt [450ml])*

Add 4oz (125g) of crab meat to the milk for the white sauce. Liquidise in a blender and add to the roux in the normal way. Serve with brill, turbot, sole and plaice.

Crab and Brandy Sauce *(makes approx. $\frac{3}{4}$pt [450ml])*

Proceed as above, but add 2 tablespoons (2 × 15ml) of brandy to the blender.

Cream Sauce *(makes approx. $\frac{3}{4}$pt [450ml])*

Add $\frac{1}{4}$pt (150ml) of double cream to the white sauce. Stir until thick and smooth.

Herb Sauce *(makes approx. $\frac{1}{2}$pt [300ml])*

Add 2 tablespoons (2 × 15ml) of fresh herbs, finely chopped (dill, tarragon, fennel leaves, chervil or coriander) to the finished sauce. Serve with bass or salmon.

Fennel Sauce *(makes approx. $\frac{1}{2}$pt [300ml])*

Add 2 tablespoons (2 × 15ml) of finely-chopped fresh green fennel to the white sauce.

English Lobster Sauce *(makes approx. $\frac{1}{2}$pt [300ml])*

Stir 2 tablespoons (2 × 15ml) of chopped lobster meat, including the coral, into the white sauce. Season with a little anchovy essence and cayenne pepper. Serve with sole, turbot and brill.

Mussel Sauce *(makes approx. $\frac{3}{4}$pt [450 ml])*

Open 12 fresh mussels and liquidise in a blender with their liquor and the milk for the white sauce. Add to the roux in the usual way with a little chopped parsley. Delicious with sole, brill, plaice and turbot.

215

Mustard Sauce   *(makes approx. $\frac{1}{2}$pt [300ml])*

Whisk 1–3 teaspoons (5–15ml) of prepared English or French mustard into the sauce at the last minute with a generous squeeze of lemon juice before serving with herrings, cod, mackerel, coley or sea bream.

Parsley Sauce   *(makes approx. $\frac{1}{2}$pt [300ml])*

Add 1oz (25g) of chopped fresh parsley to the basic white sauce. Season with lemon juice and add a little melted butter. Serve with any white or smoked fish, salmon and sea trout.

Prawn or Shrimp Sauce   *(makes approx. $\frac{3}{4}$pt [450ml])*

Add 4–6oz (125–175g) of peeled and chopped prawns or shrimps, a squeeze of lemon juice and 2 tablespoons (2 × 15ml) of prawn or shrimp stock if available. Serve with turbot, bill, sole and plaice.

Anchovy Butter   *(makes approx 4oz [125g])*

Pound 6–8 anchovy fillets and add to 4oz (125g) of softened butter. Serve with any white fish.

Garlic Butter   *(makes approx. 4oz [125g])*

Pound 4 cloves of garlic with 4oz (125g) of softened butter and 1 teaspoon (5ml) of finely chopped parsley.

Lime, Lemon or Orange Butter   *(makes approx. 4oz [125g])*

Add 4 teaspoons (4 × 5ml) of lime, lemon or orange juice, 4 teaspoons (4 × 5ml) of appropriate grated rind and freshly milled black pepper to 4oz (125g) of softened butter. Serve with any white fish, salmon, sea trout, river trout and shellfish.

Mustard Butter   *(makes approx. 4oz [125g])*

Cream 4oz (125g) of softened butter with 1 tablespoon (15ml) of French mustard. Season with sea salt and black pepper and serve with herring and mackerel.

Herb Butter, or Maître D'Hôtel Butter

(makes approx. 4oz [125g])

This butter is excellent served with all fish, particularly grilled salmon, sole, cod and turbot.

Beat 4oz (125g) of softened butter with 2 large tablespoons (2 × 15ml) of chopped fresh parsley. Season with lemon juice. Form into a roll, wrap in foil and store in the fridge until needed. Cut neat round slices as necessary and serve on top of the fish.

Shrimp or Prawn Butter

(makes approx. 8oz [225g])

Pound 4oz (125g) of shrimps or prawns and mix with 4oz (125g) of softened butter. Serve with any grilled white fish.

Smoked Salmon Butter

(makes approx. 8oz [225g])

Pound 4oz (125g) of smoked salmon trimmings with 4oz (125g) of softened unsalted butter until well mixed. Serve with white fish.

BIBLIOGRAPHY

Myrtle Allen, *The Ballymaloe Cookbook*, Gill & Macmillan, 1984

T. C. Barker, J. C. McKenzie, J. Yudkin (eds.), *Our Changing Fare*, MacGibbon & Kee, 1966

John Burnett, *Plenty and Want*, Nelson, 1966

David Butcher, *Living from the Sea*, Tops'l Books, 1982

Richard Carew, *The Survey of Cornwall*, Augustus M. Kelly, New York, 1969

Margaret Costa, *Four Seasons Cookery Book*, Macmillan, 1984

Elizabeth David, *Spices, Aromatics etc in the English Kitchen*, Penguin

Alan Davidson, *North Atlantic Seafood*, Penguin, 1980

G. M. Dixon, *Traditional Norfolk Recipes*, Menuman Books, 1982

Patricia Donaghy, *Northumbrian and Cumbrian Recipes*, Oriel Press

J. C. Drummond & A. Wilbraham *The Englishman's Food* (ed. D. Hollingsworth), Cape, 1957

George Ellis & Sarah Foot, *A Cornish Camera*, Bossiney Books, 1982

George Ewart Evans, *The Days That We Have Seen*, Faber & Faber, 1975

Sally Festing, *Fishermen*, David & Charles, 1977

Theodora Fitzgibbon, *The Art of British Cooking*, Dent, 1965

Theodora Fitzgibbon, *A Taste of Ireland*, Dent, 1968

Theodora Fitzgibbon, *A Taste of the West Country*, Pan, 1975

Theodora Fitzgibbon, *Traditional West Country Cookery*, Fontana, 1982

Rena Gardiner, *A Journey of Discovery*, The National Trust, 1985

Winston Graham, *Poldark's Cornwall*, Webb & Bower, 1983

Jane Grigson, *English Food*, Penguin, 1974

A. K. Hamilton Jenkin, *Cornwall and its People*, Augustus M. Kelly, 1970

Dorothy Hartley, *Food in England*, Futura, 1985

Macdonald Hastings & Carole Walsh, *Wheeler's Fish Cookery Book*, Michael Joseph, 1974

Susan Hicks, *The Seafood Cookbook*, Hamlyn, 1986

Peggy Howey, *The Geordie Cookbook*, Frank Graham, 1982

Florence Irwin, *The Cookin' Woman: Irish country recipes*, Blackstaff Press, 1986

Mary Kinsella, *An Irish Farmhouse Cookbook*, The Appletree Press, 1985

Frederick C. Moffat, *Two Penn'orth of Herrin'*, 1982

Frederick C. Moffat, *Another Penn'orth of Herrin'*, 1985

Cyril Noall, *Tales of the Cornish Fishermen*, Tor Mark Press, 1970

Northern Counties College, *The Northern Counties Cookery Book*, Andrew Reide, 1962

Mary Norwak, *East Anglian Recipes*, East Anglian Magazine

Derek J. Oddy & Derek S. Miller, *The Making of the Modern British Diet*, Croom Helm, 1976

Ann Pascoe, *Cornish Recipes Old and New*, Tor Mark Press, 1970

Pamela Pascoe, *Cousin Jennie's Cornish Cook Book*, Lodenek Press, 1976

Mary Ann Pike, *Town & Country Fare & Fable*, David & Charles, 1968

Joan Poulson, *Old Anglian Recipes*, Hendon Pub. Co., 1976

Joan Poulson, *Yorkshire Cookery*, Batsford, 1979

Gerald Priestland, *Frying Tonight – The Saga of Fish & Chips*, Gentry Books, 1972

A. L. Rowse, *Tudor Cornwall*, Macmillan, 1969

Margaret Slack, *Northumbrian Fare*, Frank Graham, 1981

Tony Soper, *The National Trust Guide to the Coast*, Webb & Bower, 1984

Colin Spencer, *Fish Cookbook*, Pan, 1986

Reay Tannahill, *Food in History*, Eyre Methuen, 1973

R. A. Taylor, *The Economics of White Fish Distribution in Great Britain*, Duckworth, 1960

Michael Watkins, *A Taste of East Anglia*, East Anglian Magazine, 1977

Florence White, *Good Things in England*, Futura, 1974

Douglas Williams, *Mount's Bay*, Bossiney Books, 1984

Rev. James Woodforde, *The Diary of a Country Parson* (Vol. III), Oxford University Press, 1927

Mary Wright, *Cornish Treats*, Alison Hodge, 1986

J. Yudkin & J. C. McKenzie, *Changing Food Habits*, MacGibbon & Kee, 1964

INDEX